Early Victorian Railway Excursions

'The Million Go Forth'

Early Victorian Railway Excursions

'The Million Go Forth'

Susan Major

PEN & SWORD
TRANSPORT

First published in Great Britain in 2015 by
Pen & Sword Transport
an imprint of
Pen & Sword Books Ltd
47 Church Street
Barnsley
South Yorkshire
S70 2AS
Copyright © Susan Major 2015

ISBN 978 1 47383 528 3

Typeset in Perpetua by
Mac Style Ltd, Bridlington, East Yorkshire
Printed and bound by Replika Press Pvt. Ltd.

Pen & Sword Books Ltd incorporates the imprints of Pen & Sword Archaeology, Atlas,
Aviation, Battleground, Discovery, Family History, History, Maritime, Military, Naval,
Politics, Railways, Select, Transport, True Crime, and Fiction, Frontline Books, Leo
Cooper, Praetorian Press, Seaforth Publishing and Wharncliffe.

For a complete list of Pen & Sword titles please contact
PEN & SWORD BOOKS LIMITED
47 Church Street, Barnsley, South Yorkshire S70 2AS, England
E-mail: enquiries@pen-and-sword.co.uk
Website: www.pen-and-sword.co.uk

Contents

List of Illustrations

Acknowledgements

This book is based on my doctoral research at the University of York/National Railway Museum Institute of Railway Studies. I would have been unable to extend this over a wide geographical area without the *British Library 19th Century Newspapers Online*, a wonderful resource which luckily for me started to develop soon after I embarked upon this study.

I would particularly like to thank my supervisor, Dr Barbara Schmucki, for her unfailing support throughout six years of research on this topic. Advice and comments from Professor Colin Divall (University of York) and John Walton (Ikerbasque Research Professor) were also especially helpful. Other comments and ideas were contributed by Dr Mark Roodhouse (University of York) and Dr Hiroki Shin (now Manchester University). The staff at the National Railway Museum Search Engine Archive allowed me to access their rare collection of excursion handbills and other items, which proved most useful. Andrea Knowles, Maurice Handley and Dr Janette Martin have all helped with supporting material, for which I am very grateful. I would also like to thank my copy-editor at Pen & Sword, Barnaby Blacker, for his valuable suggestions. For their financial support during my doctoral studies I am extremely grateful to the Historic Model Railway Society.

Lastly, but by no means least, I would like to thank my husband Ralph, for doing all the things that needed to be done while I was busy exploring railway excursions.

Foreword

It is hard to imagine the thrill that must have been felt in the 1830s when posters went up advertising the first ever excursion train from the local station. Perhaps the build-up to the trip was like the excitement felt by (some) people today as they queue for the latest smart phone or tablet: you know roughly what you are going to get – access to a wider world – but you don't really have a sense of what that will mean until you've tried it. Folk in the eighteenth and early nineteenth centuries had sometimes covered fair distances on foot, cart or boat to collectively enjoy themselves (going to the races perhaps, or the seaside), but the excursion train made travel easier and, above all, affordable, and opened up many more places to day-trippers, in turn helping to expand the kind of activities on offer to all but the poorest workers and their families. So, while the railway helped to impose the discipline of factory time onto almost all facets of working-class life, creating for the first time a sharp distinction between 'work' and leisure', the excursion partly compensated by providing the means to escape, if only temporarily, substituting the rhythms of the rail for those of the loom. It must have been exciting, and perhaps more than a little nerve-wracking given the cut-and-try way in which those early trains were run.

None of this had been uppermost in the minds of railway promoters, investors, directors and managers as the mainline network grew from 1830. True, the excitement of the opening of the Liverpool & Manchester Railway had encouraged the directors to put on excursions, but they thought the real money lay with goods traffic. The explosion in passenger travel over the next three decades as the iron tentacles spread was both unexpected and, at least at first, largely restricted to the elite, who could afford it. Indeed several companies went out of their way to make travel by ordinary trains difficult for anyone who was not prepared to pay a premium fare. Even Gladstone's famous 'Parliamentary' trains, introduced in 1844, didn't make that much difference since penny-a-mile fares soon added up to more than most workers could afford. So the cheap excursion train, promoted for a wide variety of reasons by social reformers, entrepreneurs and, quite soon, even the railway companies themselves, was an unanticipated development that nevertheless quickly became an important part of the railways' business.

But just how important and just how quickly is not something that historians fully appreciated until Susan Major completed the doctoral thesis on which this book is based.

She brings to life the story of working-class excursions, giving us a real sense of what it was like to travel on those early trips and why people put up with all the discomforts. Enjoy the journey to come – I promise that you will never complain about a crowded train again!

Colin Divall
Professor of Railway Studies, University of York

Chapter One

Exploding Mobility

'I was at the York Railway Station, on Tuesday afternoon, when an excursion train was about to start for Newcastle. The train consisted of four first-class, two second-class, and three third-class open carriages or tubs, which are only a fit conveyance for pigs and sheep. Several of the passengers had tickets for covered carriages, but were forced into the open tubs by the officials, and were thus obliged to travel eighty-five miles on a wet night, exposed to all the inclemency of the weather.[1] *(York, 1856)'*

While it might be imagined that a typical railway excursion for ordinary people in the middle of the nineteenth century would feature a warm carriage full of excited travellers, it was not necessarily the case. Conditions such as those experienced above, riding in an open wagon on a wet night for three or four hours are unimaginable today, but these failed to deter the working classes from seizing this new opportunity. The sudden explosion of railway excursions in Britain was offering new incentives of price and speed to venture long distances away from home and this meant that all classes were becoming much more mobile. While steamer companies had offered mass excursions accommodating up to 700 people or so since the early part of the century, their activity was limited to coastal areas and rivers.[2] Many more people could now use the new railway lines, which extended through heavily populated parts of the country.

Some thought that this tremendous demand among the working classes for the new railway excursions in the 1840s arose from a desire to imitate middle-class leisure habits. But in Lancashire, for example, ordinary people had traditionally flocked to the Blackpool seaside in great numbers on foot or in heavily laden carts before the railways arrived.[3] Communities had distinct holiday habits. Preston, in Lancashire, was described by the commentator Granville in 1841 as a rising manufacturing town with narrow, crooked and dirty streets, 'which had not made any advances in civilisation, cleanliness and amelioration of the material part of the city.' He noted that even before the railway, Preston people liked to visit Blackpool ('manufacturing people') whereas Manchester people liked Southport.[4] While, in some northern areas, crowds of people had traditionally visited local fairs and taken part in wakes week celebrations, the new excursions generated a distinctive kind of mobile crowd phenomenon, transforming the leisure experience for many ordinary working people. It was common of course for people at this time to make permanent residential moves from working in the fields to living in the towns, where they could be employed in the new factories. But the ability to use a cheap railway excursion to travel away and return home meant that now the working classes could take part in tourism and leisure activities for the first time in great numbers. This was generally viewed at the time as a public good, and supported by the press. A correspondent for *The Era* was moved to comment at Whitsun 1853, likening the revolutionary effects of the new excursions to a champagne cork:

> 'The holy days of old have in modern times been changed into holidays; and, when the times are good (which means prosperous), as they are at present, these holidays inevitably become jolly days. You cannot hold back the life and spirit of the human heart; up these will spring at every opportunity, like a champagne cork when the wire is cut; and the Million go forth, a thousand strong at a time, on an excursion trip, with blithe faces and liberal hands, so long as daylight and their money last.' (Whitsun, 1853)[5]

Commentators were keen to demonstrate how working-class habits might be shaped by the new excursions. When the railway opened from Preston through to Blackburn in June 1846, it was suggested somewhat patronisingly that the new trips would encourage a different kind of behaviour amongst the poor:

> 'these iron roads had a tendency to refinement. A family had spoken of having a trip, when one said "We must save a little money first." Here forethought was inculcated. "Mary, too, must have a new gown." Here, was advancement in refinement. So would the poor be benefited. They could now have long journeys without the intemperance that formerly disgraced the long trips of the lower classes. Many barriers to travelling were removed. Distant inhabitants were brought together as brothers.'[6]

These comments reflected the idea of 'rational recreation', a form of social control inflicted by powerful groups on the working classes, heavily promoted and debated in the 1830s and 1840s. It suggested that there were particular ways in which the working classes should be spending their leisure time that were acceptable, and others that were not. The concept was not new however. As early as 1775, in a House of Lords debate on the Manchester Playhouse Bill, a speaker suggested:

> 'I see no ill consequences that can flow from the poor workman alleviating the severity of his labour, by a rational recreation, by an amusement which will tend to

soften his mind, to mend his morals, and to teach him in an agreeable manner the lessons of humanity.'[7]

The rational recreationalists in the mid-nineteenth century were primarily middle class, especially Sabbatarians, keen to defend the observance of Sunday as a day of rest. They were reformers involved in voluntary societies, churchmen and editors of provincial newspapers. The rational recreation debate featured prominently in the press, and this could be seen to give these powerful groups 'approval' for their campaigns. They were keen to persuade the working classes to avoid what were seen as immoral pursuits, such as the public house, cruel sports, gambling and street games, and preferred to offer libraries, museums and baths, and the new excursions.[8] At the same time however the 1840s was a decade of political agitation, featuring plug-plot riots and the Chartist general strike in 1842 in the North.[9] The varying level of crowd activity generated by Chartism and Radicalism in the 1840s meant that large and sometimes angry crowds might be a regular phenomenon in many towns, giving rise to concerns about the mob. As a result this suggested the potential to raise concerns about the new excursion crowds and how they were viewed by observers.

Industrialisation had changed living and working conditions for the working masses by the mid-nineteenth century. For most ordinary people the working week extended from Monday to Saturday, leaving only Sunday free. Otherwise the main opportunities for holiday and leisure activities were at Christmas, Easter and Whitsuntide, together with any traditional fairs and wakes still being celebrated. Whitsuntide was the main holiday period, especially in Manchester, which had no wakes. Whit week there attracted huge crowds in the 1850s, including 'gaping Saturday', when people came to look in the shop windows.[10] Otherwise the focus of everyday leisure for the working class in Manchester was the public house, where there was one liquor establishment for every 154 inhabitants in 1843, with activities such as music and friendly society meetings based there, as well as drinking.[11]

The effects of industrialisation had led to a major increase in scale for most social groupings, and as industrial cities grew, the industrial 'masses', the semi-skilled factory workers, were segregated into certain central areas, often ignored and living in very crowded conditions. Changes in towns and cities had resulted in overcrowded narrow streets, restricting the open air space available to these workers. In 1841 Leeds was said to be filthy with foul air: 'at Leeds factories and tall chimneys are interspersed with private houses' and at Manchester, 'private houses are interspersed with factories and tall chimneys'.[12] Now the new excursions gave workers access to a significant amount of new space, much more than their traditional activities at markets, fairs and race meetings and during wakes celebrations.[13] Using manual labour to represent the working class, around 75–80 per cent of the population were in this group in Britain in the middle of the nineteenth century, a total of 16–18 million people between 1851 and 1861.[14] Thus the explosion of railway excursions at this time offered a significant response to the aspirations of large numbers of ordinary people to move around the country for leisure.

In the early days of railway excursions the sight of a 'monster excursion' train arriving was viewed as a huge spectacle. In August 1840 a huge train, 'the longest perhaps ever known', had travelled on the Midland Counties Railway from Nottingham to Leicester with four engines, sixty seven carriages and nearly 3,000 passengers. This had been organised as a return visit for the committee and friends of the Nottingham Mechanics Exhibition to the Leicester Mechanics Exhibition, and the *Yorkshireman* described it as 'like a moving street, the houses of which were filled with human beings.'[15] A press report on a Sheffield excursion to Leeds, in October 1840, described five engines and sixty-one carriages full of Sheffield mechanics, 'the most extraordinary cargo that ever left the smoky region of Hallamshire.' It attracted a large audience with 'exclamations of wonder and delight' as it passed the assembled thousands.' The scene was remarkable: 'on each side the line as far as Brightside, the fields were lined with spectators, who in spite of rain and mud, patiently awaited the magnificent sight.'[16] This particular trip suffered a common failing, when the large number of passengers and carriages caused traction problems and the weary passengers failed to return until one o'clock the following morning.

Sometimes the new phenomenon caught people by surprise. In 1841 a railway excursion crowd involving several hundred mechanics and their families was observed to emerge at the London terminus of the London & Birmingham Railway, two hours before the arrival of the normal first train, generating much astonishment and attention around the station. This gave rise to a typically pompous comment in *The Times:* 'Thus, are railways not only become conducive to commerce, but to the intellectual gratification of numerous persons whose avocations would not have afforded them such advantages by the old mode of travelling.'[17]

When 180 boys from Herriot's Hospital in Edinburgh went on a trip to Berwick in July 1846 on the North British Railway, 'the visitors excited a great sensation among the inhabitants, and were everywhere followed by a large and admiring crowd.' As they marched around Tweedmouth, 'great crowds followed and cheered the interesting procession.'[18] A report of an 1849 excursion to Whitby noted that 'a "monster train" from Hull, and the East Riding, arrived at this interesting watering place on Monday last, when upwards of 1,000 persons were privileged to enjoy the scenery of the beautiful valley through which the railway passes.'[19] In August 1851 another 'monster train – one of the largest trains ever seen on the Scarbro' Railway arrived there from Derby, Nottingham, Leicester, and other places, bringing with it nearly 3,000 persons to the seaside, who have liberty to sojourn a week in Scarbro'.'[20] There were frequent references to the number of carriages and people in these reports. In June 1850 a Sunday school trip from Ripon to Scarborough attracted so much interest from local people that there were eventually 1,300 people from Ripon in 39 carriages 'densely filled', accompanied by the band of the Yorkshire Hussars with colours. It then took up further passengers at Wath, Thirsk and York and ended up at Scarborough with 49 carriages, two engines and about 1,600 visitors.[21] In July 1850, large numbers of people descended on local towns – a total of 6,600 passengers from Yorkshire and Lincolnshire visited Hull for a Grand Temperance Gala.[22]

During the very early period in particular these railway trips were notable for the importance of the journey itself in a new kind of technology, as well as the attractions of the destination. Indeed at times excursion crowds enjoyed the journey even more than the destination. In July 1835 the Whitby & Pickering Railway ran a carriage to take local people from Whitby to Ruswarp Fair and back (a journey of around 2 miles each way). Over 1,000 people were carried in sixteen two-way crowded trips in this fashion. However the local press reported that traders had complained, because the families spent all their money riding backwards and forwards rather than at the fair.[23]

The excursion was often reported as a type of 'performance' in the nineteenth-century press. In the early days in 1840 the report of the visit by artisans from Sheffield to Leeds dramatically describes a 'Leviathan train' watched by an audience, in a stage setting along on the line, with the cry of 'they're off'.[24] Later trips used brass bands not only to welcome excursionists at their destination but also to accompany them on the train, for example a large party from the West Yorkshire Mechanics Institutes visiting Castle Howard in June 1847 and 800 members of the Leeds Teetotal Society visiting Ripon in August 1849.[25] Thomas Cook's Whitsuntide Holiday-Trip to Scotland in 1850 promised the Shapcott Sax Horn Band to accompany the party, performing as the train crossed the bridges at Newcastle and Berwick and at the principal stations.[26] Where either children or members of a particular group were concerned they would often be reported as walking through the streets at their destination in procession, for example a Sunday school trip from Hull to Beverley in July 1849.[27]

There were of course other types of excursion transport operating in the 1840s, for example steamer trips, which had a long history. Steamer companies operated excursions themselves, demonstrating to the railway companies how it could be done and setting an example to influence railway company thinking. However their activity was limited to coastal areas and rivers, whereas railway line access was much more widespread.[28] Sometimes however railway companies were able to work with the steamer companies to enhance the popularity of the excursion, for example the new Preston & Wyre Railway, which opened in 1840, encouraged steamers to use Fleetwood to develop their service to Ardrossan in Scotland, with onward travel by railway to Glasgow.[29] By 1845 Joseph

Crisp and Thomas Cook both came forward with excursion trips combining rail and steamer. Cook's Scottish trip by rail and steamer in 1846 was the first to that country, as there was no continuous railway line at that time.[30] The impact of this new modernity affecting the steamer company was highlighted in a trip in 1835. This involved passengers setting off from Leeds in one of the new trains at 4.20am and travelling to Selby, where they picked up a steamer called *Railway*, which took them to Hull and the sea around Spurn, carrying '550 males and females of different ages, occupation and station in life', charging 6s second-class fare from Leeds to Spurn return, including fore cabin.[31] They eventually returned to Leeds just after midnight. This was a long and tiring trip of 208 miles in twenty hours, something which in modern days would be regarded as a journey to be endured rather than enjoyed as a pleasure trip, but this report allows us to imagine how the novelty of this activity might be weighed positively at the time against the disadvantages. Its importance might be measured by the fact that it was reported widely across the north of England.

The railway excursion may generally be defined as a return trip at reduced fares, either organised and promoted by a railway company or by a private organiser working in concert with the railway company, and restricted to a discrete group and/or offered to the general public.[32] There were overlaps with the use of 'special trains' at this time, which were passenger trains provided by railway companies for a particular purpose. For example in June 1846 the Nottingham Ancient Imperial United Order of Oddfellows, led by their Grand Master Lord Rancliffe, advertised a trip for their members to see their colleagues in Northampton as an 'Especial Train'. As the Grand Lodge had given a guarantee to the company for a 'large number' this was thrown open to the public. The organisers were forceful in their instructions, warning that 'the time of departure, each way, will be most *strictly* observed—as otherwise, a delay of TWO HOURS in the course of the journey, to or from, will be *unavoidable*.'[33]

In theory anyone with money could hire a train, and clubs and other organisations could do this with the aim of taking their members on a mass excursion. In some cases participants might be carried in carriages attached to an existing train under a special arrangement. At times the railway companies offered return tickets on normal trains for a single fare, usually at holiday times such as Whitsun. The latter may perhaps not necessarily be thought of as an excursion but it generated large crowds and from the participants' point of view it was considered to be a special trip at a greatly reduced price.

It has been suggested that some of the first organisers of excursion trains were in Scotland, examples being the Garnkirk & Glasgow Railway in 1834, and in Lancashire the Bolton & Kenyon Railway in 1836.[34] In 1835 a daily first-class 'railway pleasure trip' was offered from Glasgow to Gartsherrie, mainly to avoid crowds and stops, with only one hour at the destination.[35] Hull & Selby Railway was active in offering special fares in 1840 to people going to Hull market from Selby, which were very popular.[36] The Bodmin & Wadebridge Railway organised a trip in June 1836, from Wadebridge along the length of this small line to Bodmin, at 1s for the day, accompanied by a musical band. This was unusual in being in the south of England, whereas most early excursions were in the north.[37]

Up until this time traditional entertainment would have been home-based, including the spectacle of circuses, fairs, travelling showmen, the race track and public hangings, importantly including elements of vision and movement.[38] The railway excursion changed the holiday from a home-based celebration to an activity away from home, often at the seaside but not always. Inevitably there was a growing demand from the working classes for seaside holidays in the later nineteenth century.[39] The Lancashire coast led the way as a focus for demand, followed by the Yorkshire coast, with north-east England lagging behind. While the Lancashire cotton workers benefited from their new mobility on the train, rural labourers were, however, generally too poorly paid and tied to the routines of their work to benefit.

Early excursions were organised by Sunday schools, temperance groups and employers, as a supposedly better influence than the trips to fairgrounds and race meetings which had been popular. The seaside was believed to provide opportunities for 'health and educative recreations'.[40] Yorkshire, for example, had the natural advantage of a beautiful coastline as well as many attractive market towns, so local people benefited from their proximity to these, in comparison with excursionists from the Midlands. After the opening up of railway lines from other parts of the country to York, and before the Scarborough line opened in 1845, the stagecoach companies had aligned their summer services to Scarborough with the arrival of trains into York (outside fare 7s one way) and taking four hours.[41] Such journeys would have only been affordable however by the richer classes. In 1849 special arrangements were made for 'husbands' trains' by which gentlemen could buy tickets for Saturday evenings on the York to Scarborough railway, returning on Monday mornings, to enable them to visit their families on holiday there.[42] These were again, of course, for the wealthier middle classes and reflected similar arrangements on steamboats in the 1830s.[43]

Railway excursions could be day or staying trips, although the latter had implications for rarely available time off work and for accommodation costs. They were often referred to in publicity and reporting as 'cheap trips'. These excursions generated very large crowds, beforehand at the station, during the journey, in this new kind of travel space, and after the journey, at the destination. These crowds gave rise to considerable dangers and difficulties, but also inspired much reporting in the press.

A wide range of destinations featured in advertisements and reports about the new excursions, not just the seaside. Seaside resorts had attracted middle-class visitors until the new cheap trips arrived and in many cases changed the social tone of many of these. There were also spa towns; some such as Scarborough were also seaside resorts. London, the Metropolis, was a figurehead for the new trippers, made even more popular in 1851 by the Great Exhibition at the Crystal Palace. Other events attracted trips; in 1852 special excursions to London were organised by Grant & Co., with the Great Northern Railway, to witness the 'Great National Funeral' of the late Duke of Wellington.[44] An apprentice silk weaver from Coventry, William Andrews, notes in his diary that he went with his father on a similar excursion from Coventry, setting off on 17 November. On arrival they went to the West End to see the preparations and then left their lodgings at 7am the following morning to take up their position at the corner of Cockspur Street. It was a tremendous spectacle for them: 'The funeral took 2 hours to go past. Street frightfully crammed, 5,000 troops present.'[45]

Large towns and cities, such as Liverpool and Manchester, attracted both countryside dwellers and those living in neighbouring towns on trips, supported by the developing railway lines at an early stage. Historic cities and market towns such as York were also popular. In the countryside, large country estates such as Chatsworth, Wentworth Park and Castle Howard drew many working-class visitors in large groups, especially mechanics institutes and temperance societies. The nobility used these trips as a public relations exercise, to show that it was willing to extend a gracious welcome to its tenantry and others in the surrounding countryside and nearby towns. The aristocracy was at the time surprisingly hospitable; during an excursion by 4,000 people to Elvaston Gardens in Nottinghamshire in 1852, hosted by the Earl of Harrington, it was reported that a heavy rainstorm led to the Earl throwing open his mansion for shelter, a brave enterprise with such a crowd.[46]

Pleasure gardens and concert halls were popular, and some attraction owners took a proactive role in encouraging excursions. John Jennison, who established the Belle Vue pleasure gardens in Manchester, was keen on attracting excursion traffic during wakes weeks, especially from the north of England and the Midlands.[47] Again in Manchester an unusual strategy was employed in September 1845, when the proprietor of the Star Concert Room and Museum in Bolton hired a special train to take excursionists from Manchester to Bolton to spend the day at his attraction, for one shilling.[48]

Historic locations such as churches and castles proved very popular, as did natural features such as rivers, rocks and other landscape elements. Exhibitions held in towns and cities were a particular magnet for excursionists in the 1840s, particularly from mechanics institutes. The Leicester Exhibition included a surprising number of works of art by important artists as well as technological artefacts, creating a particular drawing power for people in neighbouring towns, made possible as a result of the opening of the railway a few months earlier.[49] The most significant destination though was the Great Exhibition of 1851, tremendously effective in mobilising companies to offer excursion options. The cheapness of the fares attracted a range of visitors, and some newspapers reported on the number of working-class excursionists attending in their smock frocks and corduroys.[50] Six years later in 1857 the Manchester Art Treasures Exhibition was also a great attraction.[51]

A wide range of other events generated trips, some with unruly crowds, such as race meetings and prize fights. There were many excursions to hangings; in 1859 the Lancashire & Yorkshire Railway laid on an excursion from Accrington, in Lancashire, to York, for the execution of murderer John Riley, swelling the crowd to many thousands. The next day, the press published an account of the hanging, with a description of the crowd, the moral lessons and the man's death struggles.[52] Other events, such as temperance galas and 'demonstrations', presented a more well-conducted presence. Cheap excursion trains ran in 1849 to Stowmarket for people to watch a balloon ascent, by Mr C. Green, aeronaut to the Royal Garden at Vauxhall.[53] Spectacle sometimes featured as a destination; surprisingly there was a special train in March 1852 with 200 passengers from York to Holmfirth to 'the scene of the recent awful calamity' caused by flooding there. Reporters emphasised the security of their transport mode. 'The day was beautifully fine. After viewing the dreadful wreck and destruction of property, the travellers returned in the evening to York, where they arrived in perfect safety at half-past eight o'clock.'[54] The same year, a trip was organised to an illuminated salt-mine in Cheshire.[55] Some host cities and towns included tours of manufacturing processes in the trips. Military musters and encampments were a surprising destination, for example a camp near Winchester in 1860 was served by London & South Western excursion trains, a profitable exercise in the late autumn 'shoulder season'.[56] At times the military used holiday crowds to recruit volunteers, such as at Sheffield in June 1854, when military bands paraded the streets at holiday time.[57]

At this time industrial developments which were striking and innovative attracted visitors, symbolising a new modernity, thus the Britannia Tubular Bridge in North Wales was a very popular destination, together with important new boats.[58] As many as fifteen excursion trains a day took passengers from Chester and other large towns to see Brunel's steamship *Great Eastern* at Holyhead in October 1859.[59] Other types of spectacle featuring in excursions involved feats of railway engineering, such as a trip to Burdale Tunnel from Malton in 1851 (just over a mile in length, constructed in 1847–53 and referred to by Pevsner, as 'a remarkable piece of Victorian civil engineering'). Crimple Viaduct (built in 1847) was offered as an add-on to a trip to Knaresborough in 1849.[60]

Eventually there were excursions to the Continent, for example Henry Marcus organised trips on behalf of the South Eastern & Dover Railway from London to 'aris in

1850.[61] Some trips were promoted (and/or organised) to and/or by the working classes, for example a Working Men's Excursion to Paris, promoted in 1860.[62]

There was a tremendous variety of destinations, most of which had not been visited by the masses in great numbers until the advent of excursions. These featured in advertisements, reports and commentary in many newspapers. These accounts and reports were almost always seen through the eyes of middle-class observers, and edited according to the views and political stance of the newspaper proprietor. This could often be patronising and critical, for example:

> 'It is interesting to walk among the knots of persons—mostly of the working classes—thus brought from inland, and to hear their observations on the various objects which meet their eye for the first time. Some of them are exceedingly naïve.'[63] (Press report from Scarborough 1846)

However there are occasional first-hand accounts by working-class excursionists, and newspapers provide much information about the scale, characteristics and diversity of this new phenomenon.

During the 1840s, railway excursions were an exciting innovation, and as a result this shaped the way that activity was reported, in great detail, often theatrically in the early days, as in the case of the Nottingham to Leicester trip in 1840. By 1860 however, the *Nottinghamshire Guardian* was describing a wide range of trips in every direction from Nottingham at Whitsun, involving thousands of excursionists.[64] A similar development can be traced in reporting from Manchester. In 1840 a brief paragraph described short 'excursions' from Manchester at Whitsun, which were available along the numerous railways that had recently opened, as well as on rivers and canals. These were, however, opportunities for pleasure trips on normal services, thus not designed to suit the pockets or time available of the working classes.[65] By comparison, in 1860, the paper was describing the abundance of cheap trips and special trains at Whitsun, accommodating hundreds of thousands of people, setting off in many directions from Manchester.[66]

Stereotypical language in the press coverage of excursions in this period pointed to those aspects of reporting which were important to a newspaper. These featured, for example, a positive view of a crowd of ordinary people (attempts to move away from the idea of presenting crowds as potential rioters), a universal admiration for all that the excursionists saw (a somewhat patronising view of the working classes), the lack of damage at the host destination (important to the local economy), the absence of any injury and a safe return home (supporting the railway company). Excursion advertising was often supported by accompanying 'puffs' in the reporting columns. Such items would start in a normal way by commenting on the joys of excursions and then slip in a reference to an excursion advertisement which was carried either on the front page or another page. The advertisement in Figure 1, for an 1857 trip from Chester, Wrexham and Shrewsbury to the Wrekin, Wolverhampton and Birmingham, was accompanied by a lengthy editorial paragraph, extolling the social changes brought about by the new excursions, enabling the 'toiling mechanic' to ride by rail or steamboat, 'gazing on the beauties of nature'.[67] It then draws the reader's attention to the advertisement for a cheap excursion, hoping that 'the public will avail themselves of it.' This was a trip for rural people to visit industrial towns, with an opportunity to see 'where so many of our "precious metals" are produced.' Such editorial provides valuable insight into both the media view of the excursion and the market for such trips, with descriptions of potential customers, using words such as 'old people', 'workmen' and 'rustic youth', although it is possible that the perspective of the newspaper on the potential market may not have coincided with reality. Again the advertisement at Figure 2, for trips from Normanton, near Wakefield, in 1850 to Derby, Birmingham, Bristol, Hull and Bridlington, was accompanied by a piece praising the new excursions and emphasising the 'careful' arrangements of excursion agents Messrs Cuttle and Calverley of Wakefield.[68] The amount of 'advertorial' gained appeared to bear no relationship to the size of the paid-for space. It is unclear whether the payment for the advertising space carried a promise of editorial support as a 'sweetener'. In both examples, these were the only trips advertised in the issue, and it may be that the newspapers were attempting to attract more excursion advertisers by offering extra space. The 'puffs' certainly added to the marketing of a trip, by emphasising the way that the cheap railway excursion had revolutionised leisure mobility for ordinary people.

In 1850 there was an unusual example of copywriting language by a railway company – the Midland – in promoting a trip to Matlock, which might be seen to incorporate its own

Figure 1. Advertisement in *Wrexham and Denbighshire Weekly Advertiser*, 18 July 1857. *(British Library)*

CHEAP TRIPS ARRANGED FOR AUGUST, 1850.

TO DERBY, BIRMINGHAM, AND BRISTOL.

ON TUESDAY, 13th August, 1850.—To leave NORMANTON STATION at Half-past Nine in the Morning, for the above three important places.

FARES FROM NORMANTON.

	First Class.	Second Class.	Third Class.
To Derby and Back	9s. 0d.	7s. 0d.	5s. 0d.
To Birmingham and Back	12s. 6d.	9s. 6d.	7s. 6d.
To Bristol and Back.........	17s. 6d.	13s. 0d.	10s. 0d.

Children under Twelve Years of age Half-price.

The Train will return on Monday, 19th August, leaving Bristol at 6 30 a.m., Birmingham at 12 noon, and Derby at 2 30 p.m.

TO HULL AND BURLINGTON.

On WEDNESDAY, 21st August, 1850.—To leave NORMANTON STATION at Half-past Nine o'clock in the Morning, for the above last named two places.

FARES FROM NORMANTON.

	First Class.	Second Class.	Third Class.
To Hull and Back.............	4s. 6d.	3s. 6d.	2s. 6d.
To Burlington and Back ...	6s. 0d.	5s. 0d.	4s. 0d.

Children under Twelve Years of age Half-price.

RETURNING FROM

Hull the same evening, or Thursday, 22nd, at ...... 6 p.m.
Burlington on Friday or Saturday, 23rd and 24th, at 4 p.m.

N.B.—The RETURN on Saturday the 24th being only extended to First and Second Class passengers from Burlington.

Parties can join the above two Trips at Normantom by Train leaving MANCHESTER at 6 a.m., calling at

Sowerby Bridge, at,.................................	7 38 a.m.
Halifax, at	7 35 ,,
Elland, at	7 50 ,,
Brighouse, at	7 58 ,,
Huddersfield, ...	8 3 ,,
Mirfield, at	8 13 ,,
Dewsbury (Thornhill Lees), at..................	8 26 ,,
Horbury, at	8 35 ,,
Barnsley, *via* }	8 20 ,,
Wakefield, at }	8 45 ,,

Tickets may be bought at the Huddersfield and principal Stations, or will be sent by return of post on receipt of a post-office order. Letters prepaid, and enclosing postage stamp for reply, addressed to Mr. JOHN CUTTLE, ACCOUNTANT, WAKEFIELD.

Figure 2. Advertisement in *Huddersfield Chronicle and West Yorkshire Advertiser*, 10 August 1850. *(British Library)*

advertising 'puff', whereas by contrast most railway excursion advertisements were plainly factual.[69] In this case the advertisement uses 'the greatest Railway Treat of the Season' to draw in potential customers (Figure 3). Such advertisements formed only one element of the marketing of excursions at this time, as a press report from Nottingham in 1860 describes a range of advertising material, aimed squarely at the working-class masses. These included 'huge "posters", moderate-sized placards, and the diminutive "handbills"…on every hand', announcing cheap trips.[70] Posters and handbills were particularly useful for the excursion organiser, as they were free of tax duty, not subject to the limitations of costly space for which newspapers charged, and were fast to produce and distribute or post on walls, with cheap labour for this.[71] This Stockton & Darlington Railway excursion handbill from 1859 shows a typical economy of detail, with no attempt to promote the attractions of a trip to Redcar in June (Plate 1).

Other advertisers were also excited by the new excursions, adopting them as an emblem of modernity. Some traders used 'cheap excursion' as a header for their advertisements, inviting people to enter their emporia.[72] Tailor and outfitter S. Hyam of Briggate in Leeds frequently used poetry in its advertisements and these regularly appeared on the same page as the railway advertisements. (Figure 4) They extolled the pleasures of cheap trips, using 'cheap trip to London and France, at prices extremely low!!!' as a heading to promote clothing.[73] Other businesses took the opportunity to link clothing to this new activity, for example a Manchester clothier advertised 'wide awakes' in 1849 for pleasure trips, at 2s 6d each (these were a kind of countryman's hat, a broad brimmed felt hat with a low crown).[74] Another advertising campaign caused an unexpected problem. The Midland Railway complained to Sheffield Magistrates in 1855 about tailor and clothier Moses and Son, with branches in the north of England. Moses had distributed advertising material in the form of realistic looking Midland Railway excursion tickets, which some members of the public had managed to use successfully for trips between Sheffield and Rotherham.[75] Clothing was, however, a precious

MIDLAND RAILWAY.—The greatest Railway Treat of the Season! EXCURSION to MAT-LOCK.—On Monday, June the 10th, 1850, a SPECIAL TRAIN will leave LINCOLN at 7.0 a.m.; NEWARK at 7.30 a.m.; and NOTTINGHAM at 8.30 a.m., for MATLOCK.

Passengers by this Train will be admitted FREE to that extraordinary and stupendous Work of Nature, the Royal Rutland Cavern, through which visitors will pass direct to the summit of the Heights of Abraham and Victoria Prospect Tower, commanding one of the most extensive and interesting views in the County of Derby. From this lofty eminence, the High Tor, a broad mass of perpendicular Rock rising to the height of 400 feet from the River, is seen to advantage; also Middleton and Wirksworth Moors, Cromford Moor, Crich Chase and Cliff, Riber Hill; and between these bold objects, the lovely Vale of the Derwent, rich in meadow, wood, and water.

Visitors will also have FREE admission to the Romantic Lovers' Walks and far-famed Cliffs of Matlock, without any charge for the Ferry across the River Derwent.

The celebrated Petrifying Well will also be shown to visiters.

Fares there and back :

	First Class.		Second Class.	
	s.	d.	s.	d.
From Lincoln,........	7	0	5	0
Newark, ...	6	3	4	6
Nottingham, ...	5	6	4	0

The Train will leave Matlock in returning at 6.0 p.m.

An early application for Tickets is requested, as only a limited number can be issued.—Tickets to be had at the Railway Station, only.

(By order)   JOSEPH SANDERS,
June 1st, 1850.   General-Manager.

Figure 3. Advertisement in *Nottinghamshire Guardian*, 6 June 1850. (*British Library*)

JOYOUS THOUGHTS OF WHITSUNTIDE!

We hear with delight,
At this season so bright,
    Arrangements are making tremendous :
We own it is just,
And we only do trust,
    That each province some thousands will send us.
A welcome to all
Will we give when they call,
    With pleasure fulfil each commission :
For HYAM, 'tis known,
Is the star of the town,
    And his shop is a CLOTHES EXHIBITION !
If Garments you would
Have both useful and good,
    Then honest advice would we tender ;
We would have you excel,
Save money—do well—
    His clothes boast of cheapness and splendour.
His popular name
Throughout England's the same,
    Whilst his Garments enhance this assertion ;
And he will not slip,
For the Whitsuntide trips,
    Cheap Clothes for your Summer Excursion !!

Now to attempt to give any definite idea of the gigantic
    Assortment of
READY MADE CLOTHING
KEPT AT
The PANTECHNETHECA, 9, Briggate, Leeds,
Would be perfectly impossible; suffice it to say, that
Firstly—Hyam's Clothing is the best and cheapest in the
    Kingdom !
Secondly—Hyam's Stock is the largest in England !
Thirdly—Hyam's Prices are such that they enable every Pur-
    chaser to pay Railway Fares—and thus enjoy a
RAILWAY TRIP FOR NOTHING !!

S. HYAM'S
TAILORING, WOOLLEN DRAPERY, & OUTFITTING ESTABLISHMENT,
9, BRIGATE, LEEDS.

Figure 4. Advertisement in *Leeds Mercury*, 30 May 1846. (*British Library*)

commodity in Victorian Britain and disasters could happen. At Whitsun 1849 a report tells of a young man on an excursion from Preston to Liverpool who equipped himself 'from "top to toe" with a splendid suit of clothes,' which were stolen from him during the trip and as a result he travelled home (20 to 30 miles) 'almost, if not entirely, in a state of nudity', arriving there around 3am.[76]

This book explores how the railway excursions developed in Britain in the 1840s and 1850s, the experiences of the excursionists at this time, the extreme levels of discomfort and risk in which they travelled, and how their behaviour was reported. At times these accounts of behaviour at their destination might be distorted by campaigners against Sunday leisure. While traditional railway histories focus on Thomas Cook when describing early excursions, in fact he only played a very minor role in helping the masses to break out for pleasure. Many other people and groups were much more important at the time, some surprisingly so. The first of these were the railway companies.

Chapter Two

The Railway Companies

'The policy of giving cheap pleasure-trips to encourage a desire for travelling amongst the humbler classes has at length penetrated the heads of most of our railway directors, and it is to be hoped that, in this neighbourhood at least there will be no further necessity for a legislature to step in and teach them their own interests by a compulsory reduction of fares, as was the case in the penny-a-mile provision of the late act.[1] (Manchester, July 1845)'

It was the railway companies, powerful institutions, which played the most important part in the explosion of railway excursions for the masses in the mid-nineteenth century. The above comment from the *Manchester Times* in 1845 demonstrates the groundswell of public opinion in favour of such trips. The rapid construction of railway lines throughout England during the 1840s offered great potential for railway companies to meet the demands of ordinary working people for travel for leisure. This is illustrated by the maps on Plates 2 and 3, which show the remarkable spread of these lines between 1841 and 1863 (although lines through Scotland and Wales were much rarer).

It was not straightforward. The relative newness of passenger operations in the 1840s meant that decisions by railway companies were not generally based on years of habitual practice, but more often determined in a very makeshift way. Those taking decisions found it hard to move away from the kind of thinking about moving freight before the railways developed, and the main aim of the companies was to improve transport for existing operations.[2] The larger trunk line railways initially specialised in expensive passenger business, but Gladstone's 1844 Railway Regulation Act led to a growth in cheap travelling, and traffic managers had to move towards a larger volume business with lower margins. Between 1845 and 1870 there was a gradual changeover in the passenger profile: while in 1845–6 third-class passengers numbered almost half the total traffic and a fifth of total revenue, by 1870, 65 per cent of the passengers travelled third class, providing 44 per cent of the revenue.

Some entrepreneurial chairmen recognised the potential for speculative strategies for excursion outings at an early stage in the early 1840s. Their companies organised special trips, usually at half fare, with a free return journey to minimise passenger duty, often during the Easter or Whitsun holidays.[3] The handbill on Plate 4 promoted one of these early excursions at Easter 1841, from York to Leeds and Hull, presumably offered by the York & North Midland Railway, although their name is not used.

Lines in the north east of England had recognised the potential of trips at an early stage; the Whitby & Pickering line offered a trip to Grosmont in 1839.[4] Very early ventures were often devised by railway companies in response to the demands of large groups, each guaranteeing a number of passengers and therefore at no risk to the railway company. For example, in May 1840, mechanics institute members from Carlisle visited a Polytechnic Exhibition in Newcastle at reduced fares on nominated trains on the Newcastle & Carlisle Railway. The following month members of the Leeds Mechanics Institution went on a Monday trip to York on the Leeds & Selby and York & North Midland Railway, again paying a reduced price. A works outing from R. & W. Hawthorn in June 1840 from Newcastle to Carlisle carried 320 passengers at half price. In August 1840 a trip from Leeds to Hull carried around 1,250 textile operatives in forty carriages, apparently a record for the time. Both works outings took place on Sundays, despite Sabbatarian pressures at this time. Railway companies were at times proactive in running temperance day trips. Excursion trains brought thousands of people to a big Temperance meeting in Derby in August 1841 from a range of towns in the Midlands and north of England.[5] Unusually there is at least one early example of a private individual running trips using his own locomotives – John Hargreaves Jr of Bolton, a local carrier, who organised excursion trips from Bolton to Liverpool, London and Manchester from 1841 until 1845, when the Grand Junction Railway took over.[6]

The London & South Western Railway started excursion activity as early as 1841-2, and was offering cheap weekend tickets from 1842.[7] Many of the other southern railway companies embarked upon excursion business from Easter 1844, for example the London & Brighton, Eastern Counties and South Eastern Railways, with the press heralding 'a new era of holiday travelling'.[8] But there were complaints about the South Eastern Railway in 1847, when it displayed placards promoting 'Holiday Trains' from London to Ramsgate, Margate and Dover. It was assumed that these were cheap trips, but in fact they were charging the normal fares.[9] The press suggested that the new excursions arose from the directors of the railway companies following the lead of steamer companies in offering cheap holiday trips. They predicted that once the lines to Dover, Brighton and Southampton were open in the early 1840s, it was a natural progression to offer cheap railway trips to those seaside places. They also attributed this innovation to a desire by railway companies to reduce fares, and published evidence which indicated that low fares for excursions did not detract from regular traffic.

In April 1840 an excursion ran from Wadebridge in Cornwall, with three trains carrying 1,100 people, to see the public execution of the Lightfoot brothers at Bodmin Gaol, convicted of murder.[10] The first excursion from London to Bath, Bristol and Exeter on the Great Western Railway ran in September 1844, although the company had run its first trip in the opposite direction as early as 1842 (a cheap two-day trip from Bath and Bristol to London for the Michaelmas holiday in September, with around 800 excursionists).[11] Break of gauge problems added lengthy delays to excursion trains between the North East, Birmingham and the South West in the 1840s, where passengers had to change carriages. This was in addition to occasions when carriages had to be lifted one at a time on to different rails, at Birmingham in 1849 for example.[12]

The press played their part in presenting these excursions as a large favour to the public, disregarding the profit-generating motives which would have been behind them. Reports referred to the 'kindness of the directors' and 'liberality of companies'.[13] Emphasis was placed on the arduous efforts of the companies involved to arrange trips. The promoters of an Edinburgh excursion from York in September 1847 were reported as being 'happy to state they have, after much labour, succeeded in arranging for the above unprecedented treat.'[14] By 1856 however the railway companies had recognised the profitable opportunities to meet the demand for excursions and a correspondent in the *Manchester Guardian* was pointing out the number of cheap trips available from London, at third-class fares:[15]

South Western Railway
Sunday trips: Isle of Wight 5s, Portsmouth, Salisbury, Winchester, Southampton and Farnborough (for Aldershot Camp) 3s 6d
Weekday trips: Windsor 2s 6d, Richmond 1s, Hampton Court 1s 3d

London, Brighton & South Coast Railway
Sunday trips: Brighton 3s 6d

South Eastern Railway
Sunday trips: Hastings, Margate, Ramsgate, Sandwich, Dover, Deal, Folkestone 5s, Tunbridge Wells 3s, Aldershot Camp 3s, Strood for Chatham and Rochester 2s, Gravesend 1s 6d

Great Northern Railway
No Sunday trips at this time
Weekday trips: Boston 6s, Lincolnshire, Nottingham, Sheffield and Doncaster 7s 6d, Wakefield, Leeds, Bradford and Halifax, 8s 6d, York 11s

Great Western Railway
Sunday trips: Bath 5s, Bristol 6s (prevented from running Sunday trips to Oxford by opposition of Oxford dons)

Weekday trips: (Sat to Wed) Weston-super-Mare 13s, Exeter 16s, Torquay or Totnes 18s, Plymouth 20s, (Sat for fortnight) Birmingham 9s 6d, Chester 15s, Birkenhead and Liverpool 17s

The Brighton excursions were illustrated in Charles Rossiter's painting *To Brighton and Back for Three and Sixpence* (see Plate 5), which shows a very cramped carriage full of families. In this case the carriage had a roof but open sides. Some companies however, such as the Eastern Counties, ran very few excursions.

Railway companies rarely reflected the advertising approaches of the steamboat companies, who emphasised speed and power in promoting their trips. They kept to the minimum of factual information, presumably because they provided the only means of making a particular land journey within the time-scale available, as illustrated by the following joint advertisement (Figure 5). Where the railway excursion was competing directly with the steamer excursion, then it is noticeable that the steamer company used descriptive phrases, such as 'favourite and fast-sailing' and 'having undergone a complete overhaul in every department' in relation to the steamboat (Figures 6 and 7). It may well be that railway companies could not predict which of their stock would be used for a trip, possibly it might be old and unsuitable, whereas the steamer companies could be clearer about their planning, with state-of-the-art steamers.

The Great Exhibition of 1851 was a turning point, with a market clearly demonstrated by the formation of exhibition clubs, and hundreds of thousands of people taking advantage of cheap trips to London.[16] Railway companies such as the Great Northern, the Midland and the London & North Western offered trips from West Yorkshire to London, and the Great Western Railway ran similar excursions.[17] This was tremendously successful for a number of reasons. There was by now an extensive infrastructure of railway connections, there was a reasonable level of working-class prosperity, and, importantly too, a good supply of affordable lodgings in London.[18] The London & North Western was even able to harness a new technology to competitive advantage, using the new electric telegraph, which allowed staff to

Figure 5. Advertisement in *Leeds Mercury*, 7 September 1844. (*British Library*)

GLASGOW AND AYRSHIRE RAILWAY.

FAIR HOLIDAYS.

GRAND PLEASURE EXCURSION to KILMARNOCK and AYR, on FRIDAY and SATURDAY the 18th and 19th July. TWO SPECIAL TRAINS, Of FIRST, SECOND, and THIRD CLASS CARRIAGES, for KILMARNOCK and AYR, will, on each of the above HOLIDAYS, Start at the undernoted Hours:—

† AT HALF-PAST EIGHT o'CLOCK MORNING, AND HALF-PAST NINE o'CLOCK MORNING,

When the following REDUCED FARES will be Charged by these Trains only:

	1st Class.	2d Class.	3d Class.
To KILMARNOCK AND BACK,	4s.	3s.	2s.
To AYR AND BACK,	5s.	4s.	3s.

Passengers purchasing a KILMARNOCK Ticket, will be allowed to travel to and from LOCHWINNOCH, BEITH, KILBIRNIE, DALRY, or STEWARTON; and Parties having an AYR Ticket, will have the privilege of coming out at any Station on the Line, and return to GLASGOW.

The RETURN TRAIN will leave AYR at 6 o'clock Evening, and KILMARNOCK at 20 minutes past 6 o'clock Evening.

Parties will thus have an opportunity of spending SEVEN or EIGHT HOURS in Viewing the Beautiful and Romantic Scenery of the

LAND OF BURNS.

Figure 6. Advertisement in *Glasgow Herald*, 14 July 1845. (*British Library*)

CHEAP PLEASURE SAILING.

THE Favourite and Fast-sailing STEAMER ENGINEER, having undergone a complete overhaul in every department, before resuming her regular Station, will make a

PLEASURE EXCURSION TO CAMPBELTON, ON THURSDAY THE 17TH JULY,

Leaving GLASGOW BRIDGE at Six o'Clock Morning, calling at GREENOCK, GOUROCK, DUNOON, and ROTHESAY. The Steamer will then proceed to CAMPBELTON, allowing Passengers sufficient time to view the beauties of the Town and surrounding Country, calling at all the above Ports on her return in the Evening.

The following Low Fares will be taken for the Whole Day's Sailing:—

From Glasgow—Cabin, 4s.; Steerage, 2s.

The Public are respectfully informed that the ENGINEER will shortly commence to Ply between GLASGOW and CAMPBELTON, *Via* AYR, in connexion with the GLASGOW and AYR RAILWAY. The Passage will then be accomplished betwixt Glasgow and Campbelton in 5 Hours, instead of 9 Hours, as taken by the Steamers from the Broomielaw. The time of Sailing, and other arrangements, will be announced in future advertisements.

Glasgow, 11th July, 1845.

Figure 7. Advertisement in *Glasgow Herald*, 14 July 1845. (*British Library*)

communicate with London over the levels of traffic expected.[19] But a price war between the Great Northern, the Midland and the London & North Western caused considerable problems for the companies. The Midland complained that half of their ordinary passenger traffic was destroyed by the Exhibition, because of low fares and the short distance over their lines, and the diversion of profitable traffic from other parts.[20] The competitiveness of the railway companies astonished the press; a report in July 1851 reflects in rather ungainly language that while 'the public were led to suppose that very gracious condescensions would be made by railway companies for the accommodation of the unwieldy mass denominated by that noun of multitude … none would suppose the companies would have so far endeavoured to outvie each other as to make the announcements that have, within the last seven days, startled the usual quiet of our fellow-citizens.'[21] Eventually a Great Northern excursion agent offered to undercut the extremely low price of 5s return to London from Leeds by sixpence, but the Great Northern eventually had to withdraw, as the toll they were paying to the Manchester, Sheffield & Lincolnshire Railway cancelled out their profits.[22]

It is very difficult to find any clear evidence about the number of excursion passengers and receipts in this period. There are occasional reports in the press of half-yearly meetings.[23] The London, Brighton & South Coast Railway reported a substantial increase in excursion passengers for the second half year 1849, with 26,329 of these, generating £1,981, compared to 2,373 the previous year, which had only generated £481, and that there had been no decrease in regular traffic.[24] By 1851, their excursion traffic was generating £17,715 for the year, an increase of £15,695 over 1850, but they admitted to a decrease in local and London traffic.[25] A report in *The Builder* in 1850 tried to estimate the profit from excursion traffic, with working expenses and estimated income. They calculated the estimated income from a trip from Oxford to London with 3,200 passengers at £650, less working expenses of £30. Editor George Godwin was keen to support such profitability at this time, arguing that cheapening the cost of leisure travel might be seen as a universal benefit, different to 'cheapening and screwing in trade'. He suggested that it 'promotes nothing like the overreaching, sweating, and other evils and mischiefs resulting from ruinous competition.'[26] He did however change his mind later because of the way that railway companies conducted disorderly excursions.[27] Simplistic calculations on the cost of running excursions were later criticised by financial analysts, who explained the need to add a contribution to general expenses to the traffic expenses (which were usually merely labour and coal), and also to take special costs into account, such as the demand for extra trains and delays to other traffic.[28]

The Great Western Railway was prominent in running excursions in 1850, especially on Sundays, which were reported to have increased its weekly receipts by £2,000.[29] Its chairman claimed in 1851 that their excursion trains were cheaper to run than other lines as they were heavier and only needed one engine.[30] In the first half of 1851 the company was reporting that it received £5,000 more from excursions than in 1850 (out of a total passenger receipt increase of £37,115).[31] By the second half of that year it benefited from a 'remarkable' increase in Exhibition excursion traffic, with half year passengers rising by 487,549 of which 266,645 were in excursion trains, and receipts increasing by £122,427, of which £43,329 was from excursion trains.[32] By contrast there were complaints that the Great Northern Railway was running no excursions at Whitsun in 1852.[33]

Some strategically placed stations were considerably overwhelmed with excursion traffic. In 1857 up to a third of a million excursion passengers were reported to come through Chester Station during the second half-year, around 12,000 a week, in addition to ordinary traffic, which generated 110 trains a day and 50,000 passengers a week. Half travelled on the Great Western Railway through North Wales, and the rest from Birkenhead to Manchester and London. The Chester & Holyhead Railway was pleased to report somewhat optimistically however that 'it involved no additional outlay, but much cheerful labour to the railway employees.' These excursions were 'conducted' by Mr Jones and Mr Mills at Chester, Mr Kelly at Shrewsbury and Mr McKee at Birkenhead, presumably all excursion agents.[34] While these figures might seem impossibly excessive, it was reported in 1858 that over 52,000 excursionists visited Chester by rail in Whit Week.[35]

There were many ways in which the organisation and policies of the railway companies shaped excursions and their crowds in the mid-nineteenth century. Their decisions about fares, timing, seasonality and frequency of services encouraged or discouraged working-class travellers from taking part. Furthermore, companies made decisions about facilities offered – a comfortable carriage or an open wagon – which might encourage or discourage excursionists. Companies could also take advantage of existing connections to attractive geographical features such as a coastline, lakes, towns and cities.

Companies were supported and encouraged in their initiatives by commentaries in the press about the economic benefits. These attempted to assess the spending power generated by excursion passengers, recognising the beneficial effect on the local economy. In 1852 it was estimated that spending by excursion crowds in Sheffield at an August temperance demonstration amounted to £1,500, including railway fares, gardens admittance and other costs.[36] In 1857 a report from Blackburn on the Art Treasures Exhibition described Manchester as 'the cheap trip district' of Great Britain, and predicted that the Exhibition, in drawing crowds from other parts of the country, would stimulate the staple trades of Lancashire, Yorkshire and Cheshire.[37] At the same time it was common in editorial features to use railway excursion business as a proxy for prosperity levels for the masses, and this may have served to allay the conscience of the more sensitive of the middle classes about social and economic conditions among the 'deserving' poor.[38] In 1850 it was suggested that the evidence of thousands of travellers on cheap trains arriving in Liverpool from Whitsun to the summer meant that times were prosperous, especially as they all looked well-clothed and well-fed people 'who are earning not only enough to supply them with necessaries, but a little more to make life pleasant.'[39] Thus the middle classes felt reassured of the 'respectable' values presented by the appearance of these working-class excursionists. Again, the *Liverpool Standard* noted in 1851 that the East Lancashire Railway helpfully produced a tabular printed listing of excursion events, with origin and destination, number of passengers carried and type of organising body, and that this was 'a tolerably good criterion of the moral and industrial condition of the manufacturing districts.'[40]

There was little technological development to meet the needs of excursionists in the mid-nineteenth century. Companies continued to use a mixture of existing and old carriages, both open and closed, with no lighting or heating. Sometimes freight wagons were used, and there were problems with crowding at stations, ill-equipped to deal with thousands of excursionists massing at a single time. By 1852 it was reported that the general opinion of some railway boards was that 'extra-ordinary income' from excursion traffic should be retained rather than issued as a dividend, as it incurred much wear and tear on the system – rails, engines, carriages – and that stations and sidings should be improved.[41] It seems that railway companies were unable to decide if excursions were a profitable opportunity and therefore to be encouraged, although eventually, later on in the century, stations gradually adapted to solve the problems of large and unpredictable passenger loads. Special excursion platforms started to appear from the 1850s to cope with the crowds. On the Bristol & Exeter Railway, they were introduced in Weston-super-Mare and Bristol in 1854. On the North Eastern Railway at York, an excursion platform was in use at Holgate Bridge in 1864, at Redcar in 1865, Scarborough in 1869 and Middlesbrough in 1870, later extended in 1873. On the London & North Western Railway, in Birmingham New Street, one was in use in 1866, and on the Preston & Wyre Railway, in Blackpool in 1871.[42]

A new organisation was to play a part. The Railway Clearing House (RCH) was established in 1842 by nine railway companies, with the aim of coordinating their operations, including, importantly, facilitating the through-booking of passengers.[43] Thus it carried out a crucial role in enhancing the ability of companies to organise excursions which extended across several different lines, something which was desirable in response to market needs and to stimulate traffic. The RCH had support from powerful players such as George Carr Glyn, chairman of the London & Birmingham Railway, George Hudson of the York & North Midland Railway and Captain Laws of the Manchester & Leeds Railway among others, covering lines from London to Darlington, and Liverpool and Manchester to Hull (Figure 8).[44] Glyn was the prime mover, particularly keen to standardise practices across the railway companies. However, although through-booking was important for excursions, the RCH was not particularly interested in third-class passengers until the 1851 Great Exhibition, when regular meetings of general managers started, which continued until 1947. Indeed there was a lack of interest generally by the RCH in the third-class passenger until 1872.

In 1851 managers were keen to meet under the auspices of the RCH to discuss their strategy on excursion fares and length of trips to what was predicted to be an important event – the Great Exhibition – likely to attract hundreds of thousands of visitors travelling long distances.[45] They decided that there should be no excursion trains to the Great Exhibition until 1 July, but Joseph Paxton, the Crystal Palace designer, had greater power and influence, persuading them to allow these from 2 June.[46] He was able to do this at a Clearing House meeting as a director of the Midland Railway and an important member of the sponsoring commission. Paxton was a populist, in favour of encouraging the working classes to extend their horizons, but also presumably keen to ensure the Midland took a share of the traffic as soon as possible.[47] A further argument seems to have been over the division of the traffic which the Whitsun holidays generated, in the north of England especially.[48] Because of competition from the Leith to London steamships, companies had to agree to reduce their fares, and also agreed to give members of working-class exhibition clubs reduced rates, together with their families, recognising the value of these committees in generating high levels of excursion traffic. Trade was so extensive that excursionists were sometimes carried home on ordinary trains as well as special trains.

Figure 8. Railway Clearing House lines, 1842.

There were, however, underlying concerns about the effects of rivalry between companies in pricing them out of the market or causing business failure. The strategy of reducing fares to encourage excursion business was not universally popular. Some shareholders complained of a loss of profit, due to the drastic reduction in fares in 1851, especially as omnibus proprietors were apparently taking a different approach that year, raising their fares by 25 per cent on short haul journeys with possibly limited competition.[49] For the 1853 season the RCH turned their attention to excursion agents, keen to maintain a standard commission paid to these, 'with the view of preventing the present ruinous competition.' A group was set up by Hargreaves of the Manchester, Sheffield & Lincolnshire Railway. Statements were produced of amounts produced by excursion trains in the previous three seasons, together with commission paid, and the printing costs of publicity for those trips promoted by the company. These covered excursion fares and rates of commission to agents, which apparently varied from 5 to 20 per cent. A set of recommendations was agreed for circulation to companies and recommended for adoption.[50] The committee recommended a maximum rate of 7½ per cent commission for provincial towns where necessary, although they proposed that agents should be avoided where possible. Finally they suggested that excursionists should not be allowed to travel by ordinary trains as this 'seriously obstructs and injures the regular traffic.' Although the RCH companies were major players in the market, they were worried about competition and keen to use cooperation as a tool to defend themselves against this. It is frustratingly unclear what happened after this discussion. The recommendations are very sweeping, therefore it may be that they were not carried by the boards of the full RCH membership.

In April 1857, with the Manchester Art Treasures Exhibition of that year on the horizon, the passenger superintendents met again to discuss excursion arrangements for the coming season. Their recommendations included minimum fares in Whit week for scholars and friends, with no commission to 'the Proposer or Conductor' of school trips, that third-class excursion trips from Manchester to Liverpool should be day trips only, apart from Saturday to Monday, and that excursion passengers should be restricted as far as possible to special excursion trains.[51] This indicates that companies recognised the need to plan ahead for critical events likely to generate lucrative mass excursion business and to coordinate their arrangements, adopting protective measures against others who might seek to undercut their rates.

In creating mechanisms for through-booking the RCH was an essential element to the success of excursions across the country, although in 1845 only 55 per cent of railway mileage was owned by RCH companies.[52] But there is little evidence that it employed a strategic outlook in shaping excursions during this period. It could have chosen to standardise elements such as pricing, timing, seasonality and commission arrangements, or even to declare that excursions would no longer run. However, in the face of competition, companies appeared to prefer to keep their commercial approaches to the use of agents secret, and their dealings appeared to be reactive rather than proactive, for example in agreeing positions about traffic to large-scale events. The companies chose to hang on to their individual power rather than dilute this through the RCH, which carried out only limited decision-making to shape the timing and fares for excursions.

The business strategies adopted by railway companies in relation to excursion trains were influenced by the attitudes of decision-makers such as chairmen and directors. These could be based not only on profit but on underlying beliefs, which might be opposed to certain kinds of profit. As a result the availability, pricing and timing of excursion trips were affected. Some directors could see the benefits. They recognised that in being viewed as acting for the public good, this might improve their reputation and assist them in gaining support for new developments, thus enhancing the value to shareholders. On occasions, particular companies were criticised publicly in relation to other companies, who were perceived to be more helpful in offering cheap trips, for example complaints about the Lancashire & Yorkshire Railway in Preston in 1850.[53] Similarly a writer in *Household Words* in 1851 compared the South Western with the Great Western Railway company policies on excursions.[54] Public perceptions of company motives changed; while in the early days the provincial press generally expressed gratitude for the 'liberality' of directors in allowing such traffic, they later commented critically on the profitable nature of excursion traffic, for example comments on the Sheffield & Lincolnshire company in 1850 as 'up to the dodge of "small profits and quick returns"' in running excursions.[55]

Profit should of course have been a key factor in a company's business portfolio, but railway companies for many years found it difficult to understand the economics of traffic operation, mainly from the lack of appreciation of overhead costs.[56] Some contemporaries thought that on the Brighton line in 1844 the new excursions were not only profitable but they barely affected income from regular traffic, such was the demand.[57] In 1850, the London & South Western Railway half yearly gross receipts from newly offered excursion traffic were over £10,000, with over 200,000 excursionists carried, of which £4,000 was produced by Sunday excursions. It is likely that this was misleading, their calculation of extra working expenses here was £223, and porters and clerks were not rewarded for the extra work.[58] When later questioned about the economics of this activity in government committees, many directors and managers would say that they lost money, particularly on trips over several days (because of the necessity of running empty rolling stock back to the original station) and especially as excursions were perceived to displace traffic on normal trains at higher prices.[59] Perceptions of profitability appear to have been variable;

perhaps in some cases it might be assumed that continuing to run excursion traffic was seen as a public relations exercise. It might enable a railway company to be reflected in a good light to the general public which would encourage public support for other more profitable initiatives, something which became more important in the 1860s, when companies came under increasing scrutiny.

To make the best use of existing resources in running excursions, railway companies often adopted a strategy of economies of scale, keeping their costs low by crowding the most passengers they could into long, heavy and dangerous trains. The newly amalgamated Midland Railway (from 1844) had built up a reputation for excursion trains under the chairmanship of George Hudson, despite not having direct access to London until 1857, but its excursion trains were often far too long for safety. They carried huge crowds in carriages hauled by several engines, leading to complaints in the Leicester press in 1844 about conditions on these.[60] The heavy loads caused couplings to break and led to collisions when sections of trains rolled back down inclines. There were sometimes insufficient guards to work the brakes. Extremely long trains exceeded platform lengths, at times stopping on viaducts, leading to passenger falls. This characteristic lack of safety management grew to typify the excursion in the eyes of the public, but it failed to act as a deterrent in the face of exciting new journeys.[61]

Competition, and a company's response, played an important role in shaping the market, for example some contemporary analysts welcomed the competitive effects of steamboats on the new excursions in keeping railway excursion prices low.[62] The price war in the summer of the Great Exhibition in 1851 demonstrated how far competing railway companies would go in bringing prices down to retain business. A closer look at one year, 1846, sheds more light on the effects of competition on excursion crowds.[63] Both Liverpool and Manchester generated working-class crowds when compared to the skilled artisan/middle-class crowds of Birmingham, but for different reasons. In Liverpool the London & North Western Railway had a railway monopoly until the mid-1860s. As a result, in 1846, almost all the excursion trips from Liverpool were cheap steamer trips, many on Sundays, to nearby coastal destinations, with relatively small crowd sizes. The London & North Western would not offer Sunday trips so they had difficulty in competing against the steamer, and they failed to innovate by offering trips to inland locations. Steam excursion fares were low; the timings and destinations reflected the interests of working-class people and it may well have been that in Liverpool a high proportion of unskilled and low paid working classes featured in excursion crowds, compared to other cities such as Birmingham. By contrast Manchester had a range of competing companies in 1846, as, including Salford, it had four terminus stations serving five lines. Routes were available in all directions by 1846: south to the Midlands (on the Manchester & Birmingham line which opened up pleasure traffic to Alderley Edge); to London on the London & North Western Railway; east to Sheffield on the Sheffield, Ashton-under-Lyne and Manchester Railway (opened 1845); and to Leeds on the Manchester & Leeds Railway from 1840, with a branch to Halifax opening in 1844. A further link with Bolton opened in 1845. Opportunities were available for excursionists to travel north to Scotland using strategic links to Preston, Fleetwood, Ardrossan and Glasgow. Other resorts were reachable in 1846, for example Lytham and Blackpool via Fleetwood, the Isle of Man and the Lakes via steamers from Fleetwood.[64] In 1846 there was a large-scale close-down of the factory workplaces at Whitsun in Manchester, which offered a ready market for competing railway companies to offer affordable trips to working people in all directions during the week. This compensated for the lack of Sunday trains, thus the railway companies were dominant in innovating and shaping excursion crowds, assisted in some cases by excursion agents. Together these demonstrated a huge spectacle of mobility in Manchester at Whitsun, around 400,000 people, with large numbers of the working-classes free to take holidays using excursion trains over a lengthy period at this time.[65] The *Manchester Guardian* commented on the spectacle:

'These various means of transit make Manchester during Whitsuntide the scene of an extraordinary ebb and flow of population. Fast as our citizens pour out by every iron outlet, and by the waterways and roadways, in search of rural enjoyments, – as rapidly as they rush out of this immense brick Babylon, "to seek fresh fields and pastures new," so rapidly does the influx of visitors from the country for thirty miles round roll a still larger human tide into this great town. Then the stream that pours forth every noon towards Kersal Moor, and flows back at night, its lifesprings almost choked with the dust of that dustiest spot in Her Majesty's dominions, is a scene not without a deep interest of its own, for the intelligent stranger, the philosopher, the statist, and the philanthropist…

… So far as we can judge, the railways are promising greatly both the increased influx of country visitors to Manchester, and the rapidly spreading efflux of those who prefer some rural haunt, or a tour to some distant part of the kingdom, to the noisy sports of the racecourse. Thus, in very opposite ways, the railways are mighty agents in promoting the holiday enjoyments of the people.'[66]

Directors and managers of most early railway companies inevitably had wide social and commercial contacts, a form of social capital, because of the nature of their role and activity in developing business opportunities, and those taking advantage of these would reap results in working with voluntary and church groups to generate large-scale excursion business. The Midland Railway (and its predecessors) has featured often in the history of railway excursions because of its relationship with Thomas Cook; however it is important to recognise that one of its predecessors, the Midland Counties Railway, was running excursion trains as early as 1840, encouraged by Secretary John Fox Bell.[67] It pioneered mass excursions as soon as it opened, working with publishers Allen and Allen of Nottingham and Leicester, who produced a touring guide, a *Railway Companion* in 1840, a cooperative venture which recognised the value of supporting promotional material.[68] The railway company offered four large-scale excursions between Leicester and Nottingham in the summer of 1840, and it was later claimed that these were 'the first trains of this character ever run on English railways.'[69] The company clearly recognised the benefits of working with local organisations; the first trip on 20 July 1840 was organised by the Nottingham Mechanics Institute Committee, who took names before guaranteeing the sale of tickets to the railway company.[70] There were however missed opportunities. Companies failed to see the potential demand for the expansion of excursions, as there might have been more coordination and cooperation between transport and accommodation providers.[71]

The railway company was unusually seen as public property, an organisation which provided such an important new service that people felt that it was owned by all, despite being a private company. The railway employed and carried local people with a range of incomes, it transported their families and their goods, supported local traders and negotiated with local landowners, thus its role was very visible and the public felt they could demand of it features which suited their own interests. The railway was seen as a kind of social service and thus its consumers felt they had the right to claim a better experience as well as excursion fares. As a result the railway company suffered constraints which shaped its business strategies, especially in relation to Sunday services, shaped by the nature of its business structure. In contrast to other commercial companies, for example manufacturers, banks and insurance companies, it had to react constantly to public demands, as noted in a report by the directors of the Lancashire & Yorkshire Railway in 1848:[72]

'Railways are often spoken of, and even openly claimed, as the property of the public; and unfortunately, have too often been dealt with as such, instead of being regarded in their true light – that of a private commercial enterprise, depending for its success upon the amount of benefit conferred on the public.'

Joint-stock companies such as the London & North Western Railway were effectively operating as 'political institutions…with some degree of accountability to a 'public' composed of shareholders, customers, and workers,' and needing an aura of legitimacy to survive.[73] Unfortunately the railway mania of the mid-1840s dented the reputation of the joint stock company, and they were subject to a number of legislative changes in the 1840s and 1850s.[74] The widespread perceptions about the role of the railway company led to much public debate which influenced the way that management responded to excursion traffic potential, for example in debates about Sunday services. The stance of the chairman and directors of a railway company on Sunday services was key. Sunday was usually the only day available for the masses to participate in leisure activity, ensuring or losing immense levels of business. For example the Stockton & Darlington Railway was a Quaker railway and therefore did not run services on Sundays.[75] Importantly, therefore, the profit motive was constrained by wider cultural and social norms. The Sabbatarians were the most powerful opponent of a profitable business strategy, and this perspective was so pervasive that often the railway decision-maker also opposed Sunday travel (see Chapter 5).

However, another important factor driving and shaping the way that excursions developed up to the 1860s appears to have been the presence in the company of key personalities, who used their energy and enthusiasm to develop a strategic approach to opportunities. They needed sufficient social capital to harness resources effectively – engines, carriages, workers and publicity – in the face of stiff competition for resources from within their companies.[76] Without such drive excursions would have been extremely limited. It was only after 1850 that a few railway companies started to standardise their executive structure, headed by a general manager. Before then a variety of people might take the lead: these could be 'traffic managers, engineers, secretaries, solicitors and occasionally committees of directors.'[77] These would have little overall executive responsibility, which had implications for entrepreneurial activity. Those in the lead were responsible for coordinating a team of departmental specialists, a structure which lasted for the rest of the century. Some major companies were very slow in following the general manager approach, for example the Great Eastern, Great Western, London & South Western and London, Brighton & South Coast. As late as 1865 the Lancashire & Yorkshire lacked a general manager, although in their case other factors ensured the relative success of their excursions (see pages 30). The departmental approach dominated until 1920, causing great difficulty for railway companies in assessing realistic net revenues for an operation, and in persuading departments to cooperate as a team. While it might be thought that a railway company would act with one voice, there were times when the directors, the managers and their staff might support or obstruct excursions in different ways, depending on their role, especially arising from the differences in executive responsibility. The fact that railways were internally quite different made it difficult to focus on devising and promoting excursions, a key tool in ensuring that public needs were anticipated and met.

Individual directors and/or managers could make a personal difference to strategic decision-making, depending on their power base, both within the company and within their community, and their professional background. Some were able to use their charisma and energy to enhance their power. George Hudson was equivocal about cheap fares. After he gained control of the North Midland Railway in 1842 excursion traffic was developed, with Whit Monday trips from Leeds to Ambergate, connecting with boats for Matlock, and cheap weekend tickets to London.[78] Hudson also saw the appeal of Sunday excursions for the working classes as a moneymaking exercise, when other companies were deflected by the Sabbatarians.[79] However he recognised in 1844 the need to judge these in the context of a particular line catchment area, whether a line was a 'pleasure line' or a 'business line'. He commented on the need to balance low fares, populous districts, travelling habits and shareholder dividends, and acknowledged that his railways could not compete with the cheap fares offered by steamboats.[80] Hudson recognised the risks of low fares. On giving evidence about his lines to a Select Committee in 1846, he claimed that company income had been reduced as a result of offering day tickets at a fare and a half, extended over the weekend when issued on a Saturday. At the same time he referred to his strategies for increasing traffic, for example by excursions, 'we carry 2,000 to York from Birmingham, 140 miles, for 3s 6d,' but suggested that in general, increased traffic on his lines was due to factors other than low fares. It seems he was worried at this time about being forced by the government to reduce fares, preferring to be selective about this, and about competition from competing lines. However his influence was powerful in showing others how to innovate by carrying excursion traffic.[81]

There are other examples of managers, directors and chairmen playing a leading role in generating excursion traffic. Peter Clarke, manager of the London & Brighton Railway, was proactive in using press advertising in 1845 to encourage Sunday school and voluntary associations to take advantage of special trains at low fares to Brighton on weekdays, with a minimum of 400 passengers required.[82] The chairman of the London, Brighton & South Coast Railway, Samuel Laing, was a supporter of cheap travel for the poor, presenting a clear economic and moral case in 1850 for the success of excursion trains. His was the first London company to use excursion traffic as a regular source of income.[83] Laing argued that the poor needed a change of scene on Sundays and that the staffing involved for a train – four – was minimal to enable 600 people to visit Brighton. His arguments, however, deliberately ignored the safety issues involved in running large trains with minimal staffing, and the need for staff at stations to cope with crowds. He stressed that people in towns should not be 'hermetically sealed' on a Sunday, and that the Scottish evidence following cessation of Sunday transport suggested that this had led to much drunkenness. He calculated the running costs of an excursion train at 2s a mile, but based this only on the non-fixed costs such as coke; thus his estimation of the running costs per head at 1/25th penny a mile for 600 passengers was not realistic. He influenced thinking on excursion traffic publicly, by presenting data showing that while excursion traffic generated much income, in his view it did not displace income from regular traffic on other days. However it was not until the London, Brighton & South Coast offered reduced fares to the Exhibition that they were able to improve their financial results.[84]

By taking a closer look at one individual it is possible to demonstrate the role that key personalities played in developing excursions for the masses. When they left their respective companies, changes in policy led to a diminution of excursion traffic. This suggests that the success of excursion strategies depended on factors such as the structure of the company, and the drive of an excursion 'champion', to harness resources.[85]

The Lancashire & Yorkshire Railway (which had changed its name from the Manchester & Leeds in 1847) was a company which gained powerful benefits from connecting areas of high population. The north west regional rail network was more or less complete by 1850 and also functioned as part of the route between London and Scotland (the map on Figure 9 shows the lines connecting regional towns and cities in 1851).[86] There had been a culture of operating excursion trains in the area, as one of its predecessors, the Preston & Wyre Railway (which opened from Preston to Fleetwood in 1840), had offered cheap trips from an early stage. It had been encouraged by the level of interest in road trips by cart to the coast, with contemporary commentators even in 1849 describing the sight of thirty to forty large carts leaving Preston for Lytham every Sunday, around 12 miles away, each laden with around twenty passengers.[87]

With regular cheap Sunday trips from 1844, the Preston & Wyre stimulated the development of Fleetwood as a resort and led to steamers using the port for a service to Ardrossan, with onward travel by railway to Glasgow. Although short, this line was strategically important because it linked up with the sea and rail route to and from London. The opening of branches to Blackpool and Lytham in 1846 led to huge numbers of working-class excursionists visiting these resorts by rail.[88] The Lancashire & Yorkshire developed a reputation for its prominent excursion traffic, especially as it was able to hold out against the Sabbatarians, although it eventually abandoned Sunday excursions in 1856.[89] Several directors had resigned over the issue and a number of strategies had been discussed to avoid excursion trains clashing with church services. At least one director suggested that the issue, being a moral one, should not be considered by the board alone but by all the shareholders. It appears that the obvious success and profitability of its Sunday trips encouraged the board to continue these, especially as those directors most vehemently opposed had left.[90] Importantly however it had a passenger superintendent, Henry Blackmore, who played a crucial focusing role in encouraging

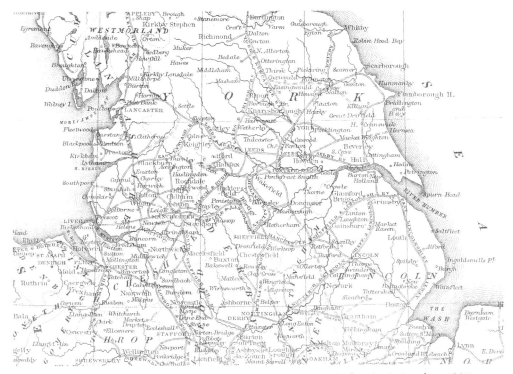

Figure 9. Section from map in Edward Churton, *The Rail Road Book of England*. (London, 1851)

and supporting excursions over a long period. Blackmore had become the Lancashire & Yorkshire divisional passenger superintendent for Lancashire in 1850 under general manager Captain Laws, along with two others for Manchester and Yorkshire. When the Manchester passenger superintendent resigned in 1853, the company was divided into two, with Blackmore responsible for the Western division.[91] The Lancashire & Yorkshire amalgamated with the East Lancashire Railway in 1859, when an East Lancashire division with its own passenger superintendent was included. In 1871 divisional management was discontinued, and Blackmore became line superintendent.

Henry Blackmore was later described by his London & North Western Railway colleague Superintendent Neele as 'a regular attendant at the Clearing House and Excursion meetings, the very apostle of cheap trips for workpeople and Sunday school children, an excellent organiser, and a thoroughly blunt, straightforward fellow.'[92] It appears that his success owed much to his taking his responsibilities seriously, in working cooperatively with other Railway Clearing House members, and, importantly, his ability to generate support from his colleagues, who held him in high regard. Blackmore's entrepreneurial strategy seems to have focused on supporting excursions in two ways, by working with various groups and also by running speculative excursions to popular resorts.

Blackmore used cooperative networking to encourage voluntary societies and church groups to generate guaranteed business. He was the principal contact for a Manchester Mechanics Institution trip to Blackpool from Manchester in September 1849, when in order to offer a price of 1s return for a 100 mile round trip (together with an option of a next day return for an extra shilling), he secured a guarantee from the Mechanics Institute that they would sell 1,500 tickets. From the press description it appears that Blackmore organised the trip very efficiently and proactively, taking particular care to manage the crowds of operatives, in a very mixed group, as the Athenaeum Club and many mechanics institute members would have been rather more middle class in status.[93] Blackmore was proactive in encouraging group excursions where he knew there was untapped demand. This advertisement in 1851 invited business from any group involved in making arrangements for cheap trips at Whitsun (Figure 10). Again, in 1855, he advertised that the Lancashire & Yorkshire was willing to make arrangements with Sunday school conductors for Whitsun trips around Manchester, alongside similar advertisements from the London & North Western, the Manchester, Sheffield & Lincolnshire, and East Lancashire (Figure 11).[94] The 1855 advertisement was unusual at the time, in that Blackmore was by now adopting an interesting advertising strategy, using very positive words to market the experience, such as 'unlimited numbers', 'delightful Sea-bathing places, at very Low Fares...all in covered carriages,' an approach which railway companies normally tended to avoid in their very plain and factual advertisements. It demonstrates an early marketing approach, using particular words to whet the appetites of groups, but Blackmore might have been inspired by his company's introduction of new carriages, affording accommodation for more passengers.[95]

Some evidence for Blackmore's business policy appears in a press report of an inquest in 1858. This relates to a serious accident involving a very cheap Sunday school excursion train on the Oxford, Worcester & Wolverhampton Railway near Dudley, where he was called as an expert witness on the practice of excursion trains. He stated that his own company advertised that they were prepared to 'furnish trains' to Sunday schools, as opposed to advertising trains for Sunday schoolchildren. After providing the trains 'they never allowed their station masters

LANCASHIRE AND YORKSHIRE
RAILWAY COMPANY.

BLACKBURN DISTRICT.

WHIT-WEEK.

THIS Company is prepared to make arrangements, on liberal terms, for CHEAP TRIPS, on MONDAY, TUESDAY, and WEDNESDAY, in WHIT-WEEK, from any part of the Blackburn Line, to MANCHESTER, LIVERPOOL, WHALLEY, CLITHEROE, or CHATBURN.

Parties are permitted to visit the beautiful Ruins of Whalley Abbey, Clitheroe Castle, and Sawley Abbey, every day (Sundays excepted).

Early application is requested to either Mr. BLACKMORE, Superintendent, Salford Station, Manchester; or to Mr. YEO, Darwen Street Station, Blackburn.

BY ORDER.

May 20th, 1851.

Figure 10. Advertisement in *Blackburn Standard,* 4 June 1851. (*British Library*)

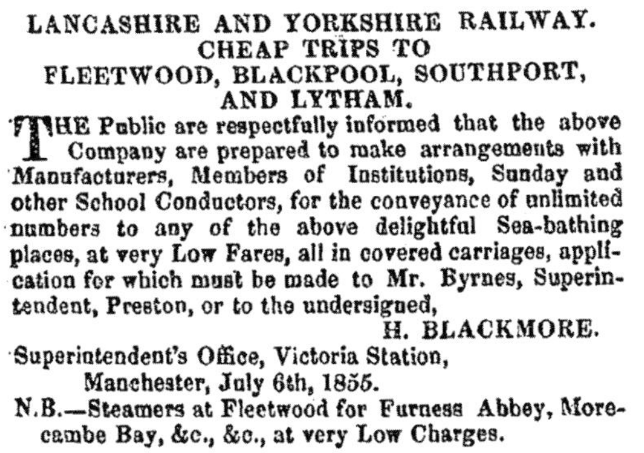

LANCASHIRE AND YORKSHIRE RAILWAY.
CHEAP TRIPS TO
FLEETWOOD, BLACKPOOL, SOUTHPORT,
AND LYTHAM.

THE Public are respectfully informed that the above Company are prepared to make arrangements with Manufacturers, Members of Institutions, Sunday and other School Conductors, for the conveyance of unlimited numbers to any of the above delightful Sea-bathing places, at very Low Fares, all in covered carriages, application for which must be made to Mr. Byrnes, Superintendent, Preston, or to the undersigned,

H. BLACKMORE.

Superintendent's Office, Victoria Station,
Manchester, July 6th, 1855.

N.B.—Steamers at Fleetwood for Furness Abbey, Morecambe Bay, &c., &c., at very Low Charges.

Figure 11. Advertisement in *Preston Chronicle*, 7 July 1855. (*British Library*)

to issue tickets indiscriminately to people who were not connected with Sunday schools…', their practice was 'to issue the tickets in the mass to the persons who engaged the trains.'[96] This appears to be an effective way of distancing himself and his company from the work involved in selling individual tickets for such excursions, and a way to control passenger numbers too.

There is further evidence, however, from accident reports that Blackmore and his colleagues pushed for economies of scale in the running of Lancashire & Yorkshire excursions, by minimising staffing and rolling stock costs. A goods train had collided with an excursion train of factory operatives returning to Wigan from Liverpool in 1857, and one of the reasons for this collision had been a delay at Kirkby.[97] There is some disparity between the press report of the accident and the inspector's report. The former suggested that only one man and a boy were collecting the tickets from the 1,100 passengers (which was the reason for the stop at Kirkby) and that the collision occurred after twenty minutes, when the ticket collecting was not 'half over'. The inspector reported that three guards as well as the station master and a boy were doing this, for a period of only five to eight minutes before the collision. Wherever the truth lay, it was this unwieldy process in passenger handling which contributed to the collision, which was mainly attributed to the goods train driver and guard ignoring signals, together with timing discrepancies. However Blackmore took care of his charges where possible; he personally visited the injured and arranged for money to be given on this occasion.

It has been suggested that the Lancashire & Yorkshire Railway was generally an 'ill-run company', dominated by profits, and there is clear evidence that the company took advantage of its passengers.[98] In 1849, working-class excursionists were herded into open cattle wagons without even a seat, with experiences recorded of a six hour journey out and five hours back, mainly caused by repair stoppages, standing all the way.[99] The same policies were still in practice in October 1859, when a government inspector objected to the line's passengers being left unprotected from the weather, and temporary roofs were fitted.[100]

The enormous growth in excursion traffic on the line had led to the use of carriages withdrawn from regular traffic and station porters having to work as guards. In 1853 the Company was heavily criticised by a Select Committee for unsafe practices in respect of the running of its excursion trains.[101] This was partly due to the use of excursion agents. It was found that where an excursion agent was used to sell the tickets, such as Joseph Stanley, paying him 10 per cent commission on gross receipts, the company could not predict the demand. Frequently these trains were insufficient for the number of passengers, leading to a dangerous overloading of engines, which were attempting to haul too many carriages or wagons. Where the excursion was commissioned directly from Blackmore by a large group for a specific amount of people, then these were slightly safer, in that the size could be predicted. By 1860, Lancashire & Yorkshire Superintendent Normington suggested to the company that they dispense with excursion agents, to save money, and presumably to aid the prediction of demand, with safer loading. The directors decided to leave the 'guaranteed' excursions 'such as millhands, schools, institutions and day trips to Belle Vue', the easy business, to the district officers, and only use agents for the speculative ventures – the advertised excursions – with commission of 4 per cent on net earnings up to £9,580 and 7½ per cent on all earnings above that.[102]

Blackmore's second strategy was to develop his own speculative excursions to seaside resorts, still using economies of scale, and following on from the success of Blackpool. In July 1855, the Lancashire & Yorkshire and the North Eastern Railway offered special cheap return trips from Manchester to Scarborough, with further trips from Lancashire to Scarborough, Bridlington and Hull four years later.[103] Blackmore's role in stimulating excursion traffic to Blackpool was recognised in 1860 when he was presented with some silver plate by the leading men of commerce there.[104]

The importance of key figures was apparent in a climate of rapid change on the railways, where they could still shape strategy despite alternative views held by other railway companies. The Lancashire & Yorkshire Railway continued to support excursions throughout the 1860s, when other companies were no longer keen. By 1867, J. Smithells, their Traffic Manager, was reporting to the Royal Commission on Railways that they had a large amount of profitable excursion traffic over their lines, especially at Whitsun, and that they were keen to encourage it.[105] This traffic was short distance, around 10 miles, over the company's lines.[106] The company changed their policies however in the early 1870s, significantly around the time that Blackmore retired in 1875.[107] One of his colleagues has suggested that the discontinuation of divisional management caused a drop in the success of excursion traffic, with a move to centralisation in 1871, when enquiries from local groups seeking arrangements were diverted to the Manchester headquarters, delaying responses. The company also increased excursion fares, which led to passengers favouring other companies with cheaper fares.[108] Blackmore's role in developing excursions for his company had focused on business strategies which were sensitive to some social goals, and it appears that his focus was a major factor in the company's success with this business.

However the company's approach to exploiting economies of scale generated a negative reputation as a result of the very poor conditions under which the masses travelled.

The railway companies provided the means for the new excursions, but it was a particular section of society which stimulated demand for these from the masses, the rapidly expanding voluntary societies, which, with church groups, mobilised large parties of excursionists.

Chapter Three

Voluntary Societies and Church Groups

'MANCHESTER AND LEEDS RAILWAY. — A special pleasure train left Wakefield for Hull on Monday, consisting of ninety-seven carriages, with the extraordinary, and we believe, unprecedented number of 4,000 passengers, composed of the "Ancient Order of Foresters", other lodges and their friends. Not the slightest accident occurred, and the parties returned at night within half an hour of the appointed time, the whole highly delighted, and grateful for a cheap and pleasant trip. The management upon this line appear to wield their monster trains with the same facility as they do their ordinary ones. Numerous similar excursions are in contemplation; indeed there will be scarcely a week during the summer in which the manufacturing operatives will not be afforded similar means of recreation at a trifling cost.[1] (1844)'

In the mid-nineteenth century it was the voluntary societies and church groups who played a large part in developing a demand for the new railway excursions. These included Sunday schools, mechanics institutes, temperance societies and friendly societies, and their 'respectable' image meant that their activities were supported by the middle classes as an appropriate way to improve working-class leisure opportunities. They featured ready-made groups with a desire to travel and an ability to negotiate as a body with the railway companies. In this respect they were also able to represent the users in this activity, unusual in the history of nineteenth-century travel. The *Manchester Guardian* commented in 1844 that it was demand by religious groups that was shaping cheap fares on excursions, rather than the railway companies themselves.[2] Voluntary societies had a mixture of motives in encouraging excursions; they could be treating the poor, looking to expand their membership or promoting their reputation as a moral force. They might even be hoping to raise funds; there are many examples in the provincial press in the 1850s of voluntary societies offering trips for fund-raising purposes, encouraging excursionists to take part in a trip to benefit a good cause with any profits.[3]

Sunday schools were an important feature of the childhood experience in the mid-nineteenth century, with 38 per cent of the English population under fifteen enrolled in a Sunday school in 1851. This was at a time when fewer than one in ten people attended church or chapel in the large industrial towns and cities.[4] Edward Baines of Leeds calculated in 1843 that there were 158,528 Sunday school scholars in the manufacturing districts of Yorkshire, 218,412 in Lancashire and 30,591 in Cheshire and Derbyshire, a total of 408,531, thus around one in five of the population in these areas attended Sunday school, the majority linked to Dissenting congregations. At the same time there were only around 210,592 scholars at day schools in these manufacturing areas, only half of the above total.[5] There are some variations however. Baines suggested that while Sunday school scholars in Manchester, Leeds and Preston vastly outnumbered those at day schools at the time, this was not the case in Liverpool, possibly because of the number of Catholic children, increased by Irish immigration, although Preston also had a large Catholic population.

Most of the children and young people attending Sunday schools were working class, indeed in some areas such as Manchester, the Sunday school was the club for the young people of the working classes, to some extent true in the twentieth century too.[6] Traditionally in the area Sunday schools had used canal packets (boats) on the short journey to Dunham for outings, with a capacity of up to 300 passengers, before the railway made mass travel possible. It is clear that the numbers of Sunday school scholars, and the desires of their leaders and reformers for rational recreation, led to a new group of entrepreneurial middle-class Sunday school managers, who were able to use their organisational muscle to develop and promote excursions to a huge market. These were a major component of railway excursions in the 1840s and 1850s, shaping the profile of and demand for trips. These were often advertised as a way of removing large groups of children away into the country from potential scenes of debauchery, such as race weeks. Such trips had been commissioned as early as 1831, when the Liverpool & Manchester Railway allowed a Sunday school trip with 150 passengers from Manchester to Liverpool and back, at a third of the usual fare.[7] An infrastructure developed around the demand for holiday railway excursions, for example the '*Half-Holiday Hand-Book*' was published in Manchester in 1846, to help Sunday schools to plan their excursions in the area.[8] During the Whitsun holiday of that year around 14,000 Sunday school children took part in railway excursions on the Sheffield, Ashton-under-Lyne & Manchester Railway out of Manchester, with a further 3,000 children left disappointed as the line was at capacity. There were also 12,000 scholars on trips on the Manchester & Leeds line, with their carriages all attached to regular trains, for safety reasons.[9]

The press supported the Sunday school movement in emphasising the railway excursion as an element of rational recreation. Reporters and commentators had a tendency to wax lyrically over the sight of Sunday school excursionists, describing it as a kind of pastoral idyll:

'The managers and teachers of Sunday schools gather together the whole of their interesting flock, and, having engaged a train for the purpose, take the children into the country, where they are feasted in the open air with buns, cakes and milk, and where they are permitted to enjoy themselves in almost any manner that their fancies dictate. The traveller on the railway will frequently see some beautiful wooded field dotted over with numberless parties of these delighted Sunday school children.'[10]

At the same time, correspondence in the Leeds press in 1848 about trips around Manchester highlights the variation in the nature of Sunday school trips; whereas some trips would be purely for Sunday school scholars, controlled by their superintendents, others included the general population, and led to the scholars being subject to the occasionally rather more disreputable behaviour of a large mixed crowd.[11] Trips could sometimes turn out to be dangerous affairs and often enormous crowds were generated; a scholars' trip in September, to York in fifty-four carriages, by St George's and St Philip's Schools in Leeds, emphasised that children under six had to be accompanied by a parent or friend.[12] The idea of children as young as six or seven taking part in these activities with minimal supervision is shocking in comparison to modern day practice in Britain, but then following the 1842 Factories Act, children as young as eight could be legally employed in textile mills at the time.[13]

In 1858 a shocking accident occurred just south of Dudley, on a very cheap Sunday school excursion from Wolverhampton to Worcester, on the Oxford, Worcester and Wolverhampton Railway.[14] At the time this was the worst railway accident that had ever occurred. The low return fares (1s for adults and 6d for children from Wolverhampton) had attracted many adult excursionists, with around 2,000 people filling 45 carriages. As a result the train was divided into two separate trains. The accident happened on the evening return journey. The first train had struggled on a steep incline; subsequently some of its rear carriages uncoupled and rolled back at high speed, colliding with the front of the second train. Fifteen adults were killed and over eighty were injured, many seriously. The guard was convicted of manslaughter soon after the event, as a result of failing to apply his brake correctly.

Sunday school excursion organisers presented the outing as a kind of crowd performance, expressing the power of their organisations in the context of moral reform. When children were involved it was usual for them to be organised as a formal procession, both at their home neighbourhood and at the destination, to highlight their good behaviour to the watching public. Processions were of course a traditional activity for children on festival days even before the development of excursions, but excursions meant that these processions would take place in areas far away from their normal living spaces. Importantly, the right to walk the streets of a community, which has traditionally had a significant meaning, claiming attention, showed that such groups had a legitimate right to display themselves in this way.[15]

A writer in *Fraser's Magazine* in 1856 described a Sunday school outing from Manchester to Wortley in 1856.[16] While he was a middle-class observer in a first-class carriage, his description captures the noise and bustle of a typical trip. Some of the carriages were uncovered cattle wagons, leading the young boys to low and bleat like animals. He talks about the dense crowd at the destination station – 'a human stream' branching off in different directions into 'rivulets'. The teachers engaged a room for twelve hours, where they were able to take advantage of 'a good wash' before making tea. A further tool used by Sunday school organisers in managing their excursion crowds was the singing of hymns on their travels, again reinforcing the idea of moral reform. The Leeds Sunday school trip to Scarborough in August 1846 took around 2,540 people, including 870 scholars, in two massive trains of fifty-four and forty carriages. Leaders took the opportunity to employ a moral motif by encouraging the children to sing *The Spiritual Railway*, a rousing and somewhat threatening hymn composed a few years earlier by the American poet J. Adams in response to railway development (see Plate 6). It suggests that only those who kept the faith would be on the upward lane to Heaven, those who did not repent would be on the downward line to Hell.[17] Thus the railway line represents a good life, but sinners would be left at the station. The idea was to reinforce the outlook and behaviour of the schoolchildren. On this trip, however, the large numbers involved made it difficult to control the crowds; it had been intended that the children process to the Scarborough schoolroom on arrival, but plans had to be abandoned because of the anxiety of many members of the party to get to the sands, 'to many of them for the first time.'[18]

Sometimes church trips involved older excursionists. William Quekett, Rector of Warrington, organised an excursion from Warrington to the Crystal Palace at Sydenham in 1857, in which 415 of his parishioners travelled.[19] Quekett had spent much of his earlier career in the East End of London, where his pioneering activity led to his work being described by Charles Dickens as that of a model curate.[20] The Crystal Palace trip, known as 'The Rector's Trip', was noticeable for the high level of preparation which went into its organisation. Twelve months before, Quekett encouraged excursionists to start a savings club, with weekly subscriptions to pay for their trip. He set up a series of lectures on the chief objects of interest at the Crystal Palace exhibition, and gave them a note of the important sights in London. Early in the morning on the day of departure a bugler sounded his horn to wake the travellers at 4.30 am, and at the station Quekett organised them into carriage groups of thirty people, each led by a 'captain'. On arrival in London they kept in formation, process to the Crystal Palace. After two nights in London seeing a myriad of sights and scenes they returned to Warrington.

Many voluntary societies were developing in the 1830s and 1840s in manufacturing towns, a complex mixture of diverse groups. They were inextricably linked with the growth of urban culture and the desires of middle-class elites to react to economic problems in society. At the same time they were also responding to worries about radicalism. Towns and cities offered a viable catchment area for societies, and their presence indicated a level of stability in a community. These organisations populated a natural market and driver for excursions, being large groups with urges for sociability and the development of experiences further afield. It has been argued in Leeds, for example, that it was in fact voluntary societies which showed greater powers to innovate and experiment than the state, and they certainly influenced railway companies to experiment in using their rolling stock for this new kind of traffic.[21] Leading opinion formers were keen to encourage trips for members as a form of rational recreation, and at the same time members were keen to share ideas and break down barriers with other communities.[22]

There are examples of societies in smaller places organising excursions. Samuel Robinson, who founded a village library in Dukinfield to the east of Manchester, was a keen supporter of mechanics institutes, although concerns about growing Chartist influence led him to urge workers to cooperate with employers while distributing knowledge. At a meeting in 1839 Robinson toasted:

> 'our village Travellers and much pleasure to them in their excursions; and may the easy and rapid and economic communication effected by railroads and steamboats induce many to employ their holidays in forming an acquaintance with the beautiful scenes of nature, and curious monuments of art which abound in their native land.'[23]

It seems here that Robinson was keen to use the power of the voluntary association to support the excursion as a kind of cleansing agent, giving workers an opportunity to take advantage of the beauties of the sights. At the same time he was concerned about the power struggle between workers and their employers, seeing excursions as a kind of 'sweetener' to take away any thoughts of class conflict and demands for workers' rights.

Most voluntary associations were designed to underline the power and identity of a leading urban elite and the majority of these organisations were dominated by the middle class.[24] Sir Edward Baines Snr played a significant role in leading the Leeds Mechanics Institution and also in the Yorkshire Union of Mechanics Institutes, as well as publishing the *Leeds Mercury*.[25] An example of the way in which voluntary societies might wield a certain amount of power occurred in 1846 in Blackburn. When the Whit Monday Procession Committee in the town was unhappy about the lack of hospitality support from local traders for benefit societies' Whit celebrations, it threatened to commission an excursion trip elsewhere the following year.[26] There are also many examples of middle-class leaders taking great pleasure in negotiating access with the aristocracy to country houses for excursion visits by well-behaved voluntary societies.[27]

In some locations it appears that the lack of a powerful middle class able to organise societies to commission trips led to others taking this role, such as in Hull in 1846, despite the presence of a Mechanics Institute, and a Literary and Philosophical Society.[28] All but two of the excursions from Hull reported or advertised that year were organised directly by railway or steamer companies. Hull's middle class was generally small and voluntary societies did not appear to play the powerful role in arranging excursions as in Leeds and Birmingham for example.[29] In Birmingham there were many savings clubs and benefit societies aimed at working men and their families. In 1851 it was reported that 'there is perhaps no town in England in which the principle of association for mutual benefit, real or supposed, is carried to so great an extent as in Birmingham.'[30] There were any number of clubs for the family there:

'The father of the family clubs for his Trade Society, or for the Odd Fellows, or for a Sick and Burial Society, or perhaps for the Freehold Land Society, or for a Money Club, or for a Watch and Seals Club, or for an Excursion Club. The mother joins a Medical Attendance Club, or a Coal and Coke Club, or a Flour Club, or a Shawl Club, or a Silk Dress Club, or, at Christmas time, a Pudding Club, or a Goose and Gin Club; while the children, if at school, bring their fortnightly halfpence to a Sick Club, or a Clothing Club…'[31]

The example of such clubs meant that it would be perfectly normal to save for an excursion trip. While most voluntary organisations had middle-class origins, friendly societies were often essentially working-class organisations, for example those in Manchester. These were attacked by the middle classes for a number of reasons, not least because they met in public houses. Many societies organised railway excursions, for example the Oddfellows and Foresters from Leeds to Scarborough in 1846, with a further trip by the Ancient Order of Foresters from Leeds to Hull in September 1846.[32] Similarly the report on page 36 describes a large crowd of 4,000 Foresters, in a 'monster train' from Wakefield to Hull in 1844.[33]

Mechanics institutes played an important role in the history of the railway excursion. Concerns about rapidly growing towns in the 1820s had led to instability and worries about working-class unrest, and philanthropists were keen to fund mechanics institutes as a possible solution to these problems. The laudable aim was to attract 'the humbler classes of a town or locality' to their membership and to 'instruct members in the science, literature and the arts.'[34] The first mechanics institutes were founded in London and Glasgow in 1823 and in Birmingham in 1825, and by 1849 there were 204 mechanics institutes in England and Wales. It is not clear how far mechanics institutes ever attracted ordinary workers, as they tended to be dominated by the well-meaning middle classes.[35] It was suggested that most Manchester Mechanics Institution members were 'clerks, warehousemen, small tradesmen and shopkeepers rather than manual workers.'[36] It appears that mechanics institutes in Manchester, Liverpool and London were beyond the reach of ordinary people and that in Lancashire, Cheshire and the Midlands, few MIs were attended by 'considerable numbers' of the working classes.[37] However in Yorkshire the position appears to be different, and it has been suggested that the Yorkshire MIs did support the educational needs of working men, and were in many cases managed by them. For example Bradford MI had 1,203 members in 1858 of which 65 per cent were 'mechanics, labourers and warehousemen'.[38] The reasons for a lack of working-class participation in other areas appear to include the absence of attractive topics and exclusion of party politics, the need for more basic education, and power play by the middle classes to control the working class.[39]

Excursions by mechanics institutes developed with several objectives, depending on the interests of their major players. They welcomed the potential for using the new railways, seeing these as an enlightened way of taking workers out into the countryside, or of introducing them to cultural experiences. In general these excursions by members and their friends and families served the broader purposes of the MI and in doing so spread the word about their role.[40] Excursions were encouraged, not only in the interests of rational recreation, but also 'to enlarge the sphere of observation, to improve the intellect, and to nurture all the kindly and benevolent principles of our nature.'[41] Banker Benjamin Heywood of the Manchester Mechanics Institution (founded in 1824) suggested that trips might be made to 'places of geological, botanical or zoological interest' or to see railway sectional cuttings, coal mines or salt mines.[42] He also encouraged members to visit Blackpool, where he had a house and strong associations, surprisingly not for light amusement, but to view the setting sun over the sea and revere 'the Almighty power which formed the universe and which controls the elements.' He did not achieve this ambition until 1849 however.[43] Heywood was inspired by the new steamships and had proposed the idea of a mechanics institute excursion as early as 1827, but it was not until 1833 that Manchester Mechanics Institution organised an excursion to Liverpool, and then there were no more until the late 1840s.[44] Leading speakers hailed the power of steam in creating such mass excursions for their groups. As early as 1838, York Mechanics Institute had organised an aquatic excursion on the new steam packet *Ebor* along the Ouse from York to Naburn, with 220 participants, aiming at a combination of relaxation and amusement with the 'intellectual and moral culture of the mind.'[45]

Some MIs wanted to help their members to experience fresher air in rural areas. Loftier purposes included the aim of breaking down barriers between communities.[46] It was partly the idea of developing relationships with other mechanics institutes that drove excursion traffic. There were few mechanics institutes in agricultural districts, but excursions could be used as a form of missionary activity, to expand mechanics institute coverage from urban to rural areas. The Yorkshire Union of Mechanics Institutes (one of whose founders was Edward Baines of Leeds) organised a trip to Flamborough Head in June 1849, and encouraged the Flamborough people to open an institute.[47] One of the participants was said to be a young manufacturer from Wadsworth, employing nearly 300 people, but it is unclear how many workmen were involved in this visit. A speaker on this trip reflected on how the reputation of Yorkshire had changed in his view from 'being beyond the pale of civil society' and that now 'strangers are not afraid to visit us.' Excursions such as these allowed visitors to compare the landscape of the West and East Ridings of Yorkshire. Importantly they played a role in spreading a message about mechanics institutes, with key people urging local fishermen to form such a body.[48]

It was the mechanics institute trips in 1840 which caught the eye of the press and the public, with their huge crowds, and inspired others to follow suit.[49] It has been suggested that the first 'monster' train ran in August 1840 from Leeds Mechanics Institute to Hull, with 1,250 passengers in 40 carriages, the first of many monsters, with Nottingham and Leicester following suit.[50] There are many examples of annual excursions by mechanics institute groups in the 1840s and 1850s. Leeds Mechanics Institute organised trips to Wentworth Park (1846), Castle Howard (1847), Bolton Abbey (1848), Chatsworth (1849), the Lakes (1850), Whitby (1852), and Manchester Art Treasures Exhibition (1857). Huddersfield Mechanics Institute organised trips to York (1844 and 1846), to Liverpool (1845) and became ambitious in 1847, journeying to Fleetwood, Blackpool, the Lakes and the Isle of Man. Clearly this had become a tourist activity rather than a visit to another mechanics institute. Interestingly such trips were said to have been organised to 'give the rising generation a distaste for "large feudal orgies",' local feasts which might last up to a week and lead to 'serious excesses'. Bradford MI organised a trip in 1846 to Wentworth Park. Keighley MI's first excursion was in 1850, when 700 members and friends went to Studley Royal, Fountains Abbey, Ripon and Harrogate. At Ripon, 'they were very much surprised at the quiet appearance of its streets, compared with the bustle of a manufacturing town.' There were some joint excursions: Beverley, Bridlington and Driffield Mechanics Institutes joined in a trip to Flamborough Head in July 1847, with over 200 people in forty-seven carriages. Bridlington MI commented on the 'splendour of the day, the bold and beautiful scenery, the novelty of the experiment, and the union of mind, and its harmonising influence in the field meeting.'[51] At a visit to Ripon by

200–300 members of the Stockton Mechanics Institute, the visitors so enjoyed their visit to Studley pleasure grounds and Ripon Cathedral that they omitted to attend a special 'soiree' and tea party arranged for them by the Ripon MI, who apparently made a serious loss on the refreshments provided.[52]

The trip to Wentworth Park in South Yorkshire in July 1846 by Leeds MI was shared with four other MIs, as it was offered to members, subscribers and friends including neighbouring Mechanics Institutes at Bingley, Bramley, Kirkstall and Garforth, and they were later joined by 200 members of Bradford MI.[53] Two long trains were 'decorated with Flags' and a capacious 'Teetotal Kettle' provided tea in the park, 'in the shade of the noble elms', with the Mayor in attendance and bands playing.[54] The Leeds MI was a large and powerful middle-class led group, with 1,500 members and subscribers, with Edward Baines playing a significant role. They were able to use their influence to organise a trip to the home of Earl Fitzwilliam. Reports of the outing show how the press persisted in presenting such trips in a positive and glowing light, describing an 'idyll', but at the same time ignoring a tragically fatal accident which had occurred.[55] A separate report of this accident, which happened near Barnsley, describes how a young man, a cloth dresser, had been standing on the seat of a third-class carriage with another man, looking at the landscape with a printed guide. It must have been an open carriage and unfortunately a sudden jerk threw both men out into the gap between it and the next carriage, resulting in their deaths. They were both working class; the other victim was a former tailor, later keeper of the 'tap' at a Leeds hotel. The accident was regarded as caused by their own indiscretion. Although the young men were not members, the directors of the MI subsequently paid for the education of the son of one of those killed. This goodwill gesture did not extend to the children of the other unfortunate traveller, as his children were mere girls.[56]

This trip had originally been proposed for a Monday, but a potential clash with another Midland trip from Derby to Leeds led to a change of date to a Wednesday. Three classes were offered – the cheapest at 2s – and 1,800 tickets sold. In the event the first train set off with thirty-six carriages, mainly third class, and then, half an hour later, the second train set off with a first and second class of thirty-one carriages, each accompanied by a band and flags. This seems to indicate a determination to separate the middle classes from the *hoi polloi*, of which there might be presumed to be roughly equal numbers judging by the number of carriages, but neither date seems suitable for the ordinary operative. However it was not always just the working classes who travelled third class, the middle classes were not averse to saving money by doing so, despite the basic level of amenity. Participants were offered dancing, cricket and bowls at the Park, and could bring a picnic – most did this – or buy a tea ticket in advance, or eat at 'a respectable inn' near

Darfield Station. A band performed en route and at the venue. In common with other visits to country houses much walking was expected. For example, at Darfield Station, most people alighted to continue on foot (around 5 or 6 miles), others proceeded by train to Masborough (around 4 miles to the park). The group were joined by Holmfirth Mechanics Institute at the park, bringing the total number of visitors to around 5,000. The house itself was only open to the party of dignitaries, but people could see the park, gardens, aviary and menagerie.[57]

There were usually lengthy and detailed newspaper accounts of MI trips as leading press figures were often involved in MIs.[58] Their advertisements also had a tendency to be verbose, for example in 1848 Bradford MI took a lengthy and presumably expensive advertisement in the *Bradford Observer,* to announce their trip to the newly opened station at Skipton, including a third-class fare of 1s 6d. A penny guide was available and a free lecture on the area to be visited, and the advertisement included a paragraph from Wordsworth about the beauties of the area. On this occasion the trip was unsuccessful. Only 348 tickets were sold, with twelve third-class carriages out of a total of sixteen, and the press commentator assumed a loss by the MI.[59] The lack of success seems to be due to a number of reasons. The weather was unsettled, with rain on the day; there were worries about large crowds as a result of Chartist militancy in Bradford; and economic conditions were poor, with much unemployment among textile workers, which would have impacted on traders in the town. A report in the *Leeds Mercury* illuminates another aspect which the *Bradford Observer* failed to mention, which was that the MI had wanted to hold this trip during the Whitsun holiday, which was the following week, but was prevented by the railway company (the Leeds & Bradford Extension), who 'refused to enter into arrangements' for some reason, thus it was held on a normal working day, when many people could not travel. It also faced stiff competition from other trips at Whitsun, for example to the Lakes.[60] A surprising feature was that the full details of the trip on 5 June 1848 were only advertised on 1 June, with a twenty-four hour deadline to apply for tickets. There are other examples of short deadlines in advertising, and it appears therefore that MIs either depended on other means of promotion, such as word-of-mouth or handbills, or they were accommodating a market used to making short-notice decisions about participating, a risky strategy for the MI to adopt.[61]

A report of a mechanics institution trip to Blackpool from Manchester in September 1849, with 1,555 passengers on the Lancashire & Yorkshire Railway, features a number of typical elements.[62] Firstly it was held on a Monday, 'Saint Monday', when many workers chose to take a day off work (see page 69). It was very cheap, at 1s for a day return and 2s for people who wished to come back the next day. The streets leading to the railway station 'presented a thronged and animated appearance – young and old, male and female – with joyous aspect, and in eager haste to obtain a "good place" in the carriages – some laden with umbrellas, shawls, over-coats, sticks, bundles, baskets…even hampers and bottles… substantials for the adults, and pastries for the children.' There were forty-seven carriages in one train and seventeen in another. There was no difference in payment for class of carriage – all were used, but no open carriages because of the weather. People in Blackpool were 'astonished at this immense stream of human beings pouring into the town from the railway station.' Trippers took part in a number of seaside activities, including some who 'were scientifically engaged in examining the beach for shells, geological specimens of stones, and exploring the sand hills for botanical and entomological objects.'

In general it seems that MI trips were usually successful, and it is possible that the commissioning of an excursion by a mechanics institute led to a far wider group of people participating compared to those who went to classes and lectures, as members were often encouraged to involve their family and friends in excursions, and trips were advertised to the general public. Mechanics institutes played an important role in generating and organising demand for excursions in this early period, sometimes in the face of economic risk, creating crowds which accelerated the reputation of the excursion as an acceptable leisure activity.

The temperance movement, which had its origins in societies starting in the 1820s, with around 150,000 members of the movement by 1833, was another powerful entrepreneurial group driving the development of excursions.[63] The movement also had links to Sabbatarianism, Dissenters and Chartism.[64] Concerns about crowd behaviour, including drunkenness, led commentators and reformers to hope that well-organised railway excursions would help reduce these problems. Once more, most transport histories have focused primarily on the role of Thomas Cook. There is no doubt that his networking links with the temperance movement drove the development of his distinctive tours, whose branding made his excursions visible, and enabled the press and the public to see how desirable this new kind of leisure mobility could be. However it is important to recognise the role of the temperance movement itself.

Temperance societies consisted of large groups of men, certainly working class in the early period, with radical undercurrents in Manchester for example. It was not until the 1860s that they came under middle-class control.[65] The temperance movement was riven with class struggle, the working classes complaining that temperance reformers were seeking to deny them their beer shops, but at the same time allowing the middle and upper classes to drink wine at home and in hotels. The movement had varying approaches to the issue of drinking, with some advocating a total ban and others barring only spirits. The Leeds Temperance Society had brought in a teetotal pledge in 1836 but this was opposed by the elite founding members, who eventually had to leave the society.[66] These societies had a fiercely evangelical approach and a burning desire to spread their aims across the country. This created a natural market and driver for mass excursions on the new railways, further promoted by regular accounts in the press in the 1840s and 1850s. Temperance societies saw the advantages of the new railway trips as a kind of natural advertisement which could not be ignored; their enthusiasts could be seen 'en masse', in the same fashion as the mechanics institute crowd, passing through the countryside. The demand for these immense temperance groups to travel increased, because they regularly held conventions in large cities and towns, which also generated profits for the railway companies prepared to offer trips. A Great Temperance Festival was held at Derby in 1841, when thousands of visitors arrived from Birmingham, Burton, Tamworth and Nottingham.[67] A similar event in Hull in 1850 attracted over 6,000 visitors by train.[68] It might be said that the temperance excursion was an expression of the group's potential power, by showing the hosting destination their strength as a large crowd. Such excursions based on the movement's structure could be much more far-reaching in pursuit of the aims of the movement than the activity of one excursion agent, Thomas Cook.

Some Temperance Committees actively organised cheap trips for workers and the poor. In Preston the Temperance movement was behind an annual Poor People's day trip to the seaside, organised for twenty years. It was sometimes referred to as the Buttermilk trip, as a large amount of milk was carried with buns for passenger refreshment. Cheap tickets at eight pence a head, including refreshments, were bought by charitable people and employers, and distributed to those whom they considered in need.[69] It wasn't all plain sailing however: a letter writer in July 1849 to the *Preston Chronicle* complained that the charity trip to Fleetwood from Preston had been a 'melancholy pleasure… the day being … exceedingly wet.'[70] This was in contrast to the official report of this trip, organised by the Temperance Committee through the Lancashire & Yorkshire Railway, which strikes a very positive note and again seems to be designed to make the benefactors feel good.

In August 1846 a trip was organised by the Leeds Temperance Society to Castle Howard, courtesy of Lord Morpeth, with permission to view the house as well as the grounds and gardens. Three classes were offered and 2,000 excursionists travelled in two trains of seventy carriages.[71] The station was 3 miles away from the house and, although some transport was available, others had to 'pedestrianize the distance.' Further visitors also arrived from neighbouring towns and villages. The temperance theme was prevalent, with a Temperance Band and addresses, and there was also cricket and food stalls. On this occasion visitors were trusted to see the house in groups of forty, supervised by stewards and domestic staff. The Countess of Carlisle and her family were seen walking too. It was reported that there was 'no trespass or damage' and this was later confirmed by a letter from the family published in the press. There were no accidents on this occasion.

Others organised trips for fund-raising purposes; Bradford Long-Pledged Teetotal Association reported in 1849 that they had organised day trips to Liverpool and Skipton with various railway companies, with profits channelled into the debt repayment for the cost of their hall, although a later trip to Kirkstall in 1858 proved loss-making.[72]

The temperance movement was therefore particularly significant in driving the development of the excursion crowd in this period. It created a natural market, recognising the advantages of the new railway trips as a kind of living advertising vehicle which could not be ignored. Regular conventions in large cities and towns increased business by attracting members to travel, and supported the profits of the railway companies involved.

Finally, a further example of a 'projector' of trips is worth highlighting, not least because he fails to feature in historical accounts, but also to demonstrate the power and drive of individual personalities in making a success of the railway excursion on a very local level. The Reverend Joseph Brown, of Bethnal Green, London, was remarkable for his abilities and indefatigable efforts to improve conditions for the poor of his parish. An 1850 article in *The Leader* noted that he 'truly lived among his people…entering heartily and thoroughly into their ways of life.'[73] Brown recognised the value of affordable holidays for people with little resources, organising heavily subsidised large-scale annual railway excursions for local working men and the poor for twenty years until 1865, firstly from his Bethnal Green parish (from 1844) and subsequently from his parish of Christchurch, Blackfriars, London (from 1849). These excursions usually took place on a July Monday and involved thousands of people, for example 1,500 to Richmond (1851), 7,000 to Brighton (1859), and 2,500 to Hampton Court (1865). They were funded partly from his own resources, partly from benefactors, partly from low fares negotiated with railway companies and partly by a contribution from those in work. He harnessed the wealth of his numerous contacts and sponsors to fund them – he had an extensive circle of 'noble and wealthy friends'. This was not his only focus: his other philanthropic initiatives included the Albert Institution in Blackfriars (comprising ragged schools, a reading room and lending library, dormitories, bath and wash houses), the Cholera Orphan Home at Ham in Richmond, and the Female Servants' Home Society for servants 'out of place', with two homes in London.

Brown's excursions involved workhouse inmates, tenants of almshouses, and charity school children and their families. Trips involved several railway companies – the London & South Western, the London, Brighton & South Coast and the South Eastern. While some excursionists paid a small contribution, others, such as those from the workhouse, benefited from free places. Fares were very low, for example 6d for the Richmond trip, and refreshments were provided, including tea and cakes, with extras of beer and tobacco for the older people. Occasionally details of the fares were provided in press accounts, for example in 1859, for the trip of nearly 7,000 people to Brighton, the fare for the working participants was 1s 2d (apart from the free places), with Brown reportedly paying the London, Brighton & South Coast 2s 6d, thus meeting the difference from his own purse and from subscriptions from benefactors, a total of around £430 in subsidy for one trip.[74]

A press account in 1850 gave a vivid description of the excursion crowds on his Richmond trip:[75]

'never had Richmond Station disgorged such heaps of humanity… "they are welling out sir, oozing out like a flood", cried an admiring traveller. And so it was – a strange living flood – waves of cleanly children – billows of grey shawled women from the workhouse, gushes of smiling girls more blooming than might have been expected.'

The writer suggested that this unusual annual activity generated a greater understanding between the working masses and the poor of the parish:

'its easy affluence was confronted with its destitution; and perhaps for the first time in its history, it knew itself in a new aspect, recognised influences at work unseen, and learned to respect its own troubles, its own sorrows, its motives, and its better dispositions. Signs of that awakening knowledge were not wanting at the close… the parish had learned to regret its divisions, and had learned to know its common interests and common feelings.'

It seems that this was one of Brown's objectives, the idea that using the excursion to create opportunities for the deliberate mingling of classes led to a more compassionate understanding of social conditions experienced by others living in their neighbourhoods. In 1852 he was presented by the working classes with a testimonial at Richmond as a result of his renowned trips, an event celebrated in the *Illustrated London News*.[76] Brown appears to have been an exceptional, entrepreneurial person, demonstrating how resources could be exploited by an enthusiastic and well-connected man in the cause of leisure mobility for the poor. He died in August 1867, seemingly unrecognised otherwise since for his achievements.

It was another type of individual however that was to harness the more widespread adoption of railway excursions across the country, the excursion agent. And while most people are aware of Thomas Cook, it was other agents who were to stimulate the movement of the Million at this time.

Chapter Four

The Excursion Agent

'Mr Marcus may be said to be the father of cheap trips as the late Mr Stephenson was said to be the father of railways. Certain it is that millions of the working classes are indebted to the exertions of Mr Marcus for a great accession to their health, their enjoyment and their instruction.[1] (December 1853)'

Excursion agents were private individuals working in combination with one or more transport companies, and these people were to have a tremendous impact on mass mobility. While most railway histories of Britain focus on Thomas Cook when discussing the birth of the railway excursion, other agents were operating at the same time, forging their business with a much larger working-class market. This is illustrated by the remarks made above in the testimonial recorded in the press to Liverpool-based excursion agent Henry Marcus. However it is the reputation of Thomas Cook which has prevailed, completely overshadowing that of other agents, because of the longevity of his operation.

The independent excursion agents sought to use excursions for profit, but in doing so achieved social goals which enhanced their reputation in the eyes of the public. They might even be classed as social entrepreneurs, mixing economic and social goals. Many excursion agents built up their powerful reputations during the 1840s and 1850s as 'friends of the masses', especially in the north of England, using a mixture of entrepreneurial, marketing and organisational skills to extend the mobility of huge crowds of ordinary working people. They recognised what we now describe as the power of branding to enhance the reputation of their offering. Some also developed guidebooks and other mechanisms as marketing devices to support their excursionists. Thomas Cook is the most well known of these excursion agents today, almost always appearing as the 'first' excursion agent, 'the originator' and representing the sector, with his first tour in 1841.[2] But other railway excursions had taken place before this, organised mainly by railway companies. Furthermore Cook served a middle-class market, albeit lower middle class and provincial, and there were others equally as important at the time, especially in the north of England, such as Richard Stanley, Joseph Stanley, Joseph Crisp, John Cuttle, and John Calverley, Joseph Dearden and Henry Marcus. In the Midlands other examples were John Houlston (Houlston's Cheap Excursions) of Wellington and Oakengates, and Mr Booth

Figure 12. Handbill for Christmas trips from Leeds, Normanton and Castleford, 1850.

of Walsall.[3] The handbill in Figure 12 promotes Christmas trips organised by Mr T. Clapham of Leeds in 1850, to Hull, York and Scarborough. Typically it makes no mention of the railway companies involved in transporting passengers. Many of these agents were well known to the masses and well used by them.

Advertisements in the provincial press in 1846 show clearly that a variety of railway excursion agents were in evidence in the 1840s, in the north and the Midlands especially.[4] Henry Marcus was advertising trips from Preston, Liverpool and Manchester, Richard Stanley advertising from Manchester, and Thomas Cook and one other unnamed agent from Leeds. In Birmingham there were Jones & Co., J. Gardener and Sansum Day & Sutton. Thus Thomas Cook was only one of a number of agents operating at the time, and he was operating at a rather more expensive end of the market, with first and second-class tickets only, although his fares reflected the longer distances travelled, and in 1846 were comparable to those of Stanley and of Marcus for longer trips.

The business practices of excursion agents are rarely described. Sometimes agents appeared to buy up tickets in blocks on ordinary trains, offering discounted sales; more often there were special excursion trains. At the same time there were issues about economic risk, level of commission and guarantees to the railway companies. Certainly the ability of a major railway company to give exclusive rights to an agent made sure that such agents were major players in this arena. Early agents were frequently commercial people who had other roles in the trade of a town, although some appeared to operate on a full-time basis. In Wakefield in 1846 Mr Hepworth, a printer, and Mr Oldfield, an accountant, sold excursion tickets to Scarborough.[5] There were certain key factors which helped excursion agents to develop their traffic, and these were discussed by a journalist writing in 1853.[6] Firstly the availability of a single gauge across most of the country made long distance travel possible without necessarily changing trains, secondly the Railway

Clearing House system (see Chapter 2) enabled the through booking of passengers across multiple lines, and thirdly the low fares charged were appealing to the masses.

Thomas Cook owed his initial success to his ability to make use of a network of temperance colleagues to forge strong relationships with key people in railway companies. His background as a travelling village missionary in his youth would also have helped him to engage with a range of people at short notice, sometimes using preaching techniques to generate business. A diary of a Ripon tradesman in 1851 records how Cook arrived there in 1851 to announce his Great Exhibition excursions and, when he found no-one at a pre-arranged meeting, he went outside and stood on an ale barrel to drum up interest.[7] It can be argued, however, that Cook and his tours were irrelevant to day trips for the masses, as they were aimed at other classes, taking costs and timings into account.

The dominant focus on Cook conceals the role of the Midland Counties Railway and the later Midland Railway in organising early excursions, as they were doing this at the same time as Cook.[8] The Midland Counties 'monster' mechanics institute excursions in 1840 are likely to have influenced him to embark upon his enterprise. Furthermore, John Fox Bell of the Midland Counties organised other trips, for example from Preston and Liverpool to London, and excursions to Ambergate to connect with boats for Matlock in June 1842, from Leicester to Rugby and from Nottingham to Derby, and onwards to Liverpool in 1843. At this time, when a railway company was not proactive and there was no commercial agent involved, people interested in organising a trip in the early 1840s had to collect names and negotiate with the railway company, without the support of an entrepreneur, and this involved an element of risk to the individual(s) concerned. For example, a group of 'ordinary persons' booked a train in 1846 to take 600 people from Brighouse to Liverpool, and only 100 went as the weather was poor, generating substantial losses.[9]

The story of Thomas Cook has predominated in history because he was perceived to be the first in initiating tours as an individual on a commercial basis in 1845 and subsequently his enterprise developed into a large-scale operation which remains today. The presence of a substantial archive has also generated much work on his importance. However other commercial agents operating at the same time, such as Joseph Crisp of Liverpool, have been long forgotten because they were relatively short-lived.[10] Crisp was offering trips in the early 1840s, advertising in a variety of cities around the country and pioneering excursions to the Continent from 1845. Crisp's advertisements for London trips in the *Liverpool Mercury* and *Preston Chronicle* in May 1843 included accommodation. These advertisements also referred to trips the previous year (1842) thus Crisp started early, working with a Mr Healey, and contracting with the Grand Junction Railway and the London & Birmingham.

Cook's role in the invention of excursions is significant, but it is as one of the first creators of 'tours' as a rounded experience and combined tickets, rather than cheap trips, pioneering, for example, annual tours from South Wales through Birmingham to the north of England and to Edinburgh. Such tours were very much a middle-class experience, because of the costs and time needed away from work. Interestingly even the way that trips were described reflects class: while the working classes went on 'trips', the middle classes went on 'excursions' and the upper classes went on 'tours'.[11] Certainly organisational ability was key to the success of Cook's tours, and, when added to his networking skills and temperance connections, this led to commercial success. His importance in mass mobility is that along with other agents he was able to demonstrate to railway companies how such business could work, although in some cases companies were already running excursions themselves.

To many people in the north-west of England, excursion agent Henry R. Marcus was known as the 'father of cheap trips' and 'the originator of railway excursion trains', from the mid-1840s. This was emphasised in a testimonial notice from grateful customers in the *Liverpool Mercury* in March 1869, when the London & North Western Railway finally dispensed with his services after twenty-five years.[12] Born in Holborn in London around 1804, Henry Marcus moved to Liverpool and was living in Newton St in Liverpool in 1841, where he was described as a tobacconist. He married local girl Theodosia Fazakerly in 1843, and appears to have started working as a 'conductor of excursion trains' around this time.[13] Marcus focused on the working classes, in contrast to Cook's middle-class tourists, and some of his trips were directly promoted as such – 'a grand treat for the working classes'.[14] (Figure 13). He ran excursions to London and other destinations with the London & North Western Railway, being appointed as their agent from the railway's formation in 1846. Working on his own from home in Liverpool (at this time in Leigh Street), he received a percentage from both the London & North Western and other lines at the end of the season for publicising excursions, selling tickets and 'conducting trains'.[15] By April 1849 he was offering extension trips to Paris and Brussels, and supported his excursions with 'a book of instructions' which included information on 'places of amusement'

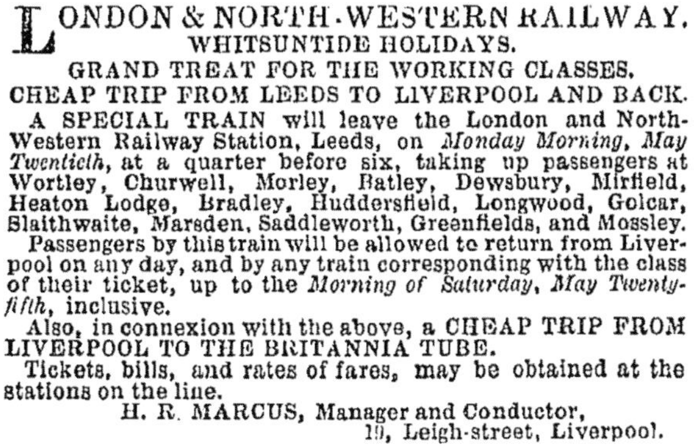

LONDON & NORTH-WESTERN RAILWAY.
WHITSUNTIDE HOLIDAYS.
GRAND TREAT FOR THE WORKING CLASSES.
CHEAP TRIP FROM LEEDS TO LIVERPOOL AND BACK.
A SPECIAL TRAIN will leave the London and North-Western Railway Station, Leeds, on *Monday Morning, May Twentieth*, at a quarter before six, taking up passengers at Wortley, Churwell, Morley, Batley, Dewsbury, Mirfield, Heaton Lodge, Bradley, Huddersfield, Longwood, Golcar, Slaithwaite, Marsden, Saddleworth, Greenfields, and Mossley.
Passengers by this train will be allowed to return from Liverpool on any day, and by any train corresponding with the class of their ticket, up to the *Morning of Saturday, May Twenty-fifth*, inclusive.
Also, in connexion with the above, a CHEAP TRIP FROM LIVERPOOL TO THE BRITANNIA TUBE.
Tickets, bills, and rates of fares, may be obtained at the stations on the line.
H. R. MARCUS, Manager and Conductor,
19, Leigh-street, Liverpool.

Figure 13. Advertisement in *Leeds Mercury*, 18 May 1850. (*British Library*)

and 'respectable hotels and lodging houses'.[16] The use of handbills was clearly important in publicising his trips, known as 'Marcus's Cheap Excursions' (Plate 7).

Marcus tried to keep his prices low, for example from Liverpool to Birmingham return 7s and to London return 18s in 1852.[17] Most cheap trip fares were very reasonably priced; these worked out at around ½ pence a mile, compared to the London & North Western average in Jan-Jun 1851 of .92 pence a mile for third-class travel. Liverpool dock labourers earned 18s-24s, and shipwrights 20s weekly in 1850, thus a return trip to London around this time would have cost the equivalent of a week's wage for a male worker. This might still seem quite a lot, but careful saving on a weekly basis may have achieved this amount, for what was to many people the experience of a lifetime. Marcus' role in achieving social goals was recognised publicly as early as 1853, when a committee of gentlemen was organised to promote a testimonial for Marcus, highlighting the value of his work in the Liverpool and Manchester area.[18] Between 1846 and 1850 it was reported that he had carried over 100,000 people on his trips, advertising excursions extending over a period of days from London to Edinburgh and Glasgow, Dublin, Liverpool and Manchester, Bangor and Conway, Chester and Shrewsbury, Birmingham, Carlisle, Penrith, Windermere, Kendal, Lancaster, Preston and Huddersfield.[19] By the end of 1851 it was claimed that he had carried 200,000 persons to London, including the immense traffic to the Great Exhibition in 1851[20] (by comparison Thomas Cook announced that he had carried 15,246 travellers during the 1850 season[21]). Marcus was remembered for his push and energy in promoting excursions to the Great Exhibition in 1851 and his trips to the Duke of Wellington's funeral in 1852, and the Manchester Art Treasures Exhibition in 1857.[22]

Marcus was a successful businessman making good use of rolling stock. A press correspondent in 1853 described Marcus' trips as being available both ways, which meant that both Londoners and northern people could benefit, and trains would carry a 'double series of pleasure seekers – the one going out and the other returning home.'[23] He was at the same time perceived as bringing social benefits, referred to as 'the grand mover of the whole…general benefactor of the community at large.'[24] He also had a reputation for taking care of his charges, for example a correspondent to the *Liverpool Mercury* refers to an unfortunate occasion on returning from a day trip to Windermere, when, at Liverpool Edge Hill station, staff ordered excursionists out of the train far away from the platform in the darkness, and Marcus was at hand with a lantern to show them the way to the steps.[25] The press in 1850 reported on his 'indefatigable exertions in catering for the amusement of his passengers.'[26] Marcus recognised the importance of his business reputation in the media and was keen to defend any criticisms about adverse experiences in the press about his trips. There are occasional press reports of county court cases against Mr Marcus, brought about by an excursion passenger with a ticketing problem, and he would respond with a careful and detailed refutation of the points raised.[27]

Marcus was also an early example of a businessman who used his own name to great effect. Marcus clearly decided to position his business for the mass market, using advertising copy – 'cheap excursion for the working classes' – and price, whereas entrepreneurs such as Cook and Crisp focused on middle-class targets, with longer, more expensive tours. Excursion agents such as Marcus cleverly developed a continuous relationship with their customers, encouraging them to ask for their excursions by name and running annual trips at certain times, in contrast to most railway companies at this time. The latter, possibly because of their monopolistic activity in relation to many destinations, did not feel the need to promote their excursions beyond stating factual details, apart from occasionally promising 'covered carriages' and emphasising the low cost. It appears that railway companies realised that the organisation of a cheap and fast means of transporting large numbers of ordinary people would be sufficient to generate demand, and this was true.

This emphasis on his own name was ultimately unfortunately to contribute to Marcus' downfall, due to a conflicting relationship with the London & North Western, who objected to the prominence of his name compared to theirs. A press record of a meeting in 1869 organised by his supporters, following his dismissal from the company, sheds an interesting light on the commercial arrangements between Marcus and the London & North Western in the 1840s and 1850s.[28] It records that he carried nearly a million and a half excursion passengers during his time as agent, a substantial number. It appears that arrangements between 1843 and 1850 were satisfactory, but then opportunities arising from the Great Exhibition of 1851 changed the temperature of his dealings with the company. There were changes to railway company management and policies, and growing misunderstandings. A competitor had offered to take over the business for 12½ per cent (of gross receipts), but in response Marcus suggested to General Manager Mark Huish that he would carry out the work for a 'discretionary remuneration' together with reimbursement of his printing and advertising costs. He was appointed sole agent for the Exhibition by the London & North Western and the Lancashire & Yorkshire, and clubs and societies were requested to contact him with commissions on their lines.[29] Unfortunately the London & North Western took advantage of this and, although they took £65,000 worth of business in the four months of the Exhibition, they apparently only paid Marcus £300 for his services. The following year they attempted to recruit him directly to their staff to conduct excursions, which he refused. Subsequently he carried on as an independent excursion agent under the direction of Huish, bearing the printing and advertising costs himself, conducting the excursion traffic and receiving 16 per cent of the gross receipts. Unfortunately Huish left the company in 1858, although it was reported that he provided a very positive commendation for Marcus to the new manager, William Cawkwell. So Marcus was able to continue on the same basis until 1862, when the second Exhibition was staged. (By 1861 the family were living in Cecil Street, St Clement Danes, Westminster.)[30]

Marcus appears to have suffered by not negotiating a clear agreement with the company over the terms of their business at this time. A misunderstanding led to him receiving a minimal amount of commission for the traffic which he generated, and it was reported that his subsequent profits were very low, around £50 a year, especially when set against the costs of producing and distribution handbills, around £1,500 a year, because the most profitable business had been taken away from him. This might well reflect the changing policy of the London & North Western with regards to excursions at that time. Cawkwell took issue with the way Marcus described the excursions in his advertising, placing emphasis on 'Marcus's Excursion Trains' rather than London & North Western, and even complained that Marcus was able to get printing done more cheaply than the company, using his accomplished business skills. Superintendent Neele of the London & North Western reflected the official stance in his reminiscences, recording that 'it was with regret that at last we had to part company with excursion agent Mr Marcus, but some little want of discretion on his part brought about the final dissolution of the arrangement.' When the Company dispensed with his services in 1869, there was a huge groundswell of public support for the shabby way he had been treated. Sadly Marcus was eventually killed by a train in 1875, when, due to his deafness, he failed to heed a warning as he was walking along a line at Rainford.[31] The notices recorded that at the time he was a director of the Victoria Colliery Company at Rainford.[32]

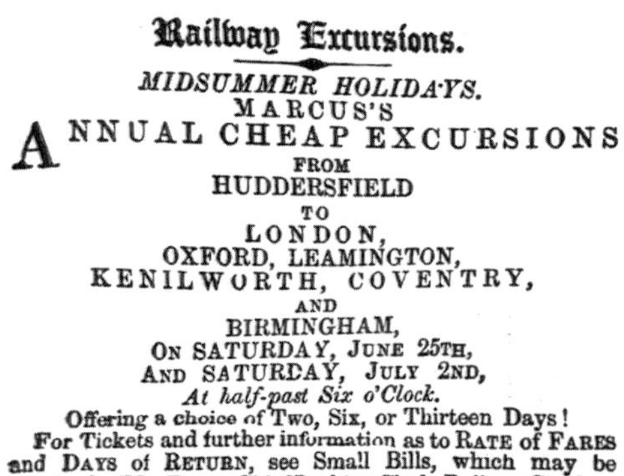

Marcus' promotional techniques relied heavily on handbills and newspaper advertisements. This example of one of Marcus' advertisements shows how his own name sometimes took prominence, something which annoyed the railway company, but which he recognised as of great value in successfully promoting his services (Figure 14).[33] Marcus used terms such as 'Midsummer Holidays' and 'Annual Cheap Excursions' to consolidate

Railway Excursions.

MIDSUMMER HOLIDAYS.
MARCUS'S
ANNUAL CHEAP EXCURSIONS
FROM
HUDDERSFIELD
TO
LONDON,
OXFORD, LEAMINGTON,
KENILWORTH, COVENTRY,
AND
BIRMINGHAM,
ON SATURDAY, JUNE 25TH,
AND SATURDAY, JULY 2ND,
At half-past Six o'Clock.
Offering a choice of Two, Six, or Thirteen Days!
For Tickets and further information as to RATE of FARES and DAYS of RETURN, see Small Bills, which may be obtained of Mr. HIRST, Chief Booking Clerk, Railway Station, Huddersfield.
HENRY R. MARCUS,
Manager and Conductor of Excursion Trains to the London and North Western Railway Company.
19, LEIGH STREET, LIVERPOOL.

Figure 14. Advertisement in *Huddersfield Chronicle*, 25 June 1853. (*British Library*)

the idea of a regular outing at a particular time, with his own name prominent. He offered flexibility, both of destination and length of stay. Cook and Marcus both used their own names with great success. In using his name consistently Marcus was developing reliance and trust between himself and his customer in a marketing relationship, although it could not be said that he was actively developing or marketing his 'brand' in the modern sense. It appears that Marcus trod an uneasy path. The more he met the needs of his market for excursions, with a tremendous impact on the mobility of the working classes, the more he threatened his relationship with his major business partner, London & North Western. In the end however they had the controlling power to destroy that relationship.

Excursion agents operated throughout the nineteenth century. In 1894 it was reported that 'the ubiquitous excursion agent has once more networked the whole Kingdom.'[34] In the mid-nineteenth century they had little direct power and they were at the mercy of decisions made by railway companies. However, their public relations strategies rewarded them with a tremendous amount of influence, because of public perceptions about their social role and the manner in which their activity matched the values prevailing at the time. In the case of the Lancashire & Yorkshire Railway, when Superintendent Normington complained that the excursion agent for Yorkshire was not doing as well as expected and persuaded the directors to give him notice, this agent was able to use his influence with the directors to be reinstated.[35] Excursion agents therefore used this influence to harness the railway systems to the interests of mass leisure mobility, while at the same time developing successful business for themselves.

The excursion agents were remarkable agents of change. They were social entrepreneurs, enabling the masses to break away from their home areas for leisure. But there was a tremendous obstacle which prevented people from enjoying a trip away on Sundays, their one day off work. Sabbatarians, supporters of Sunday observance, led a great battle against these trips, using their influence to limit opportunities.

Chapter Five

Never on a Sunday

'Now, do Sunday excursion trains, and such inducements to recreation on Sundays, turn from attendance at church any who would not otherwise be absent from the sanctuary? Those flaming posters in divers colours, describing marvellously cheap trips to places which the walled-up citizen delights to think of, do they seduce the regular worshippers at church from their holy and laudable employment? We say, unhesitatingly, that of all those who go systematically to church on the Sunday, there is scarcely one who is even tempted to break his custom under the pressure of any suggestion of pleasure, however enticing.[1] *(1857)'*

The most fervent public debate about the railway excursion in the mid-nineteenth century focused on Sunday leisure, between those in favour of leisure pursuits on Sunday and the Sabbatarians, who denied the working classes these opportunities. Sunday was the only day free from work outside the home, but the Sabbatarians were an immensely powerful force at this time, using potent arguments, designed to appeal to the emotions, to restrict Sunday leisure.

Sabbatarianism was a powerful ideological force which reached its peak in the mid-1850s. It was based on an evangelical movement devoted to the observance of rest and worship on Sundays. After the Lord's Day Observance Society was founded in 1831, it played a leading role in shaping the provision of Sunday railway excursions. In the north east of England there was a particularly outstanding period of Sabbatarian activity before 1850, when campaigners made great use of petitions and memorials to railway boards, with debates at railway shareholder meetings. These often started in smaller towns and villages, where the clergy could use their influence on individuals personally known to them. In the north east it was not just one religious group behind the Sabbatarian movement, it included the Church of England in York, the Methodists in Hull, the Quakers in South Durham, and the Church of England and Non-Conformist Union on Tyneside.[2]

Sabbatarian arguments featured Sunday observance, but also to a lesser extent Sunday as a day of rest (however the arguments that all work and recreation cease on a Sunday did not appear to extend to women's work in the home). Sabbatarians claimed the moral high ground; for example a typical debate on Sunday travelling was recorded at a North Union Railway meeting in Preston in July 1845, where it was argued that Sunday excursions lowered the 'moral and religious tone of the community', and were an example of 'a desecration of the Sabbath.' There were concerns that Sunday would be seen as a holiday, with associated mental and physical freedoms, leading to 'vicious indulgences' and 'unsettled habits'. It was further suggested that Sunday excursions only benefited publicans at destinations and railway company shareholders. At the same time it was noted that the people complaining against the practice most vehemently were the local beer shop owners, who had lost trade as a result.[3] In the case of the North Union Railway, however, on this occasion it was decided that the benefits outweighed Sabbatarian concerns and that Sunday excursions should continue on the line.

Certain religious figures painted a very negative picture of Sunday excursionists, suggesting that excursion trains brought 'idlers and prostitutes' into the countryside.[4] It seems there was a genuine fear that such Sunday travelling would bring about the end of organised religion. A congregational minister at Banbury, Joseph Parker, referred to excursionists in 1856 rather outrageously as including the 'dirtiest, silliest, laziest and poorest of the toiling population.' He suggested of women who travelled on Sunday excursions: 'with very few exceptions they are accustomed to licentiousness, robbery and drunkenness.' These comments generated fierce debate at the time, with many people complaining about Parker's expressed views.[5] Opposition to Sunday trips on the Newcastle & Carlisle line was particularly strong, from energetic Sabbatarian organisations in Newcastle and in Carlisle. The young Reverend W.C. Burns of Kilsyth protested vigorously against a Sunday trip in 1841, with a vehement poster announcing, 'people taken safely and swiftly to Hell! next Lord's Day.' Possibly the success of Scottish policies on this issue just over the border played a part in encouraging the rebels.[6]

Intriguingly, a press report in 1857 about Sunday services in India on the Madras Railway highlights the moral issues involved for British railway directors in imposing Christian practices on a population with a different religion. There was considerable discussion about how far the native population should be able to take advantage of the railway on a day of the week which was not sacred to them. Sabbatarian policies had the effect of telling them that they must submit to the religious views of the governing power, but there was no majority in favour of changing these rules.[7]

In Britain, Sabbatarians argued that railway workers were stopped from observing the Sabbath themselves as they were forced to work on it, although it seems this was not always the case. Supporters of Sunday excursions suggested that few workers were needed to run these Sunday trains, as tickets were bought in advance and excursionists had little luggage.[8] A heated correspondence developed on this issue in 1859 in the *Hampshire Advertiser* between Charles E. Mangles, Chairman of the London & South Western Railway, and Archdeacon Wigram of Southampton. Wigram claimed that he had been told by some railwaymen in Southampton that they had been unable to attend

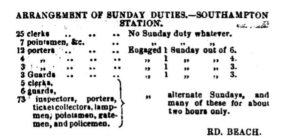

Figure 15. Press extract from *Hampshire Advertiser*, 19 November 1859. (*British Library*)

divine service for six years, because of their work on Sundays. Mangles refuted this claim with evidence from Southampton Station (Figure 15). But the Sabbatarians were not without a lot of influence: it was announced in June 1860 that the London & South Western would no longer be running excursion trains on Sundays, as a result of pressure from the Winchester clergy. In a further twist, however, a subsequent notice declared mysteriously that these trains would be running after all.[9]

Those in favour of Sunday excursions, who opposed Sabbatarians, argued that it was the only day that the working class could travel, and that it could not become habitual as they could not afford this, being poor. Advocates suggested that excursionists tended to be prudent and that the cheap train was seen as a means of 'social and intellectual gratification', which would 'exalt, rather than deprave, the minds and habits of the parties.'[10] Rowsell, the writer on page 58 in 1857, suggested that church going was a habit unlikely to be broken by a cheap trip and that those on trips would not be churchgoers anyway. He unusually promoted a view at the time that people could be non-churchgoers, with no religion, and still be moral and law-abiding, and that the occasional trip was good for the health of sickly artisans.[11] There were some other surprising supporters, as the chief of the Manchester Police Force made the case for the benefits of rational recreation on a Sunday excursion.[12]

There was much conflict in the 1840s between the railway shareholders, who were seeking to make good profits from Sunday excursions, and the Sabbatarians, with some people belonging to both groups. Members of the public who were Sabbatarians also put pressure on railway companies, museums and galleries, and other Sunday attractions. Excursion supporters highlighted social progress and rational recreation as a key goal for the working classes. The Sabbatarians, concerned about Chartist crowds, warned of the dangers of uprisings on Sunday trips, with the potential for inciting the 'humbler classes', and whipping up concerns about the dangers of the crowd.[13] In an unsuccessful attempt to add a clause prohibiting Sunday travelling to the Railway Clauses Consolidation Bill in 1845, Mr Plumptre, MP for East Kent, expressed a typical fear of the crowd, complaining about hundreds and thousands of people travelling into towns and suburban districts on Sunday excursions, 'fearful to contemplate in a Christian country.' In the same vein, a colleague reported on 'an immense train of persons entered into a quiet country place just as divine service was about to commence, much to the annoyance of well-disposed persons.'[14] The Chartist newspaper, the *Northern Star,* poked fun at Plumptre and his colleague Spooner.[15] Plumptre had said that this type of 'desecration of the Sabbath' was 'quite horrid'. He had sometimes, as he was riding by in his carriage, seen several people walking about on Sunday, breathing the country air, who must have come down by the railway' and 'shuddered at the impiety.' He particularly objected to the pleasure trains, disregarding business trains as these might be necessary, for 'pecuniary interests might be at stake.' The paper reported his views that 'pleasure trains, for a parcel of people who only had recourse to them for relaxation, were an abomination.'

Press commentators often highlighted the class inconsistencies, pointing out that Sabbatarians were trying to stop the masses doing things while unfairly ignoring richer people who could choose their own time of travel.[16] Legislators saw the irrational nature of the position on Sunday travel. A clause to prohibit railway travel on the Newcastle to Carlisle line on Sundays had been debated in 1835, when Lord Wharncliffe argued in favour of Sunday excursions, saying that it was illogical to ban travelling on Sundays by rail but at the same time to allow travel by road, and that for people who were working all week it would be good for their health to relax in this way on a Sunday. The Earl of Roden, however, suggested that allowing Sunday travelling would promote riots in trips from Carlisle to Newcastle. But the Duke of Richmond responded that it would be better for Newcastle people to take a railway trip on a Sunday than to pass their time in beer shops. He compared railway trips to travelling by posthorse or by steamboat, and questioned why only the railway traveller should be denied. Some took a patronising view of the needs of the working classes; the Bishop of London claimed in 1835 that there had been no complaints from the poorer classes of Newcastle or Carlisle nor the agricultural districts en route about lack of recreation opportunities on the Sabbath. At the same time he was against the profanation of the rich in travelling on Sundays. The clause was finally rejected.[17]

There were many attempts to add clauses into railway bills to prevent Sunday trains, such as with the Great Western Bill in 1835.[18] Opponents were indignant about the class discrimination aspects of this and proposed that if it was accepted then they should also have a Bill preventing Sunday travel on turnpike roads, as was the case in Scotland, which was said to have led to drunkenness and idleness at home on that day. Where railway companies tried to include clauses in their bills prohibiting Sunday trains, the Chairman of the Lords Committee struck these out, as he favoured a general act for this purpose, in effect a powerful move to support Sunday services.[19]

In 1841, the Whig *Examiner* argued against the Sabbatarians who opposed Sunday trains between Glasgow and Edinburgh, pointing out inequalities: while the 'well-appointed carriage' was acceptable for travelling on a Sunday, the railway train was denounced as 'a freight for Satan'. The writer suggested that the 'use of legs' on Sunday should be denounced as a sin and was amused by the Reverend Bagot's implication that people travelling by the Sunday trains must be thieves.[20] In 1844, Gladstone's Railway Bill proposed that railway companies would have to run a third-class train every weekday on its lines, later amended to compel them to run these every day that passenger trains ran, including Sundays.[21] During the debate, the Bishop of London tried to prevent railways having to offer third-class carriages on Sundays, while at the same time retaining first and second-class carriages. His motives were heavily satirised by *Punch* in 1844, in their piece on the 'Railway Moral Class Book'.[22] This cynically contrasted the morals of the three classes, implying that as the rich were used to pleasure during the week, it would be cruel to deprive them of this on Sundays, whereas the poor suffered 'toil and hardship' during the week, therefore enjoyment on Sundays would make them 'discontented with their lot'. This may well have been a fundamental concern behind the Sabbatarian strictures, with anxieties about the generation of large uncontrollable crowds on that day.

A third-class passenger writing to the *Preston Chronicle* in 1844 pointed out that when the Bishop of Chester came to preach at Preston on a Sunday morning, on that occasion travelling only a matter of 200–300 yards, he required a carriage and a pair of horses plus two or three servants. He complained that this could be compared to a Sunday excursion train employing twelve to twenty people but carrying 2,000 to Fleetwood.[23]

Class-based discrimination against Sunday excursionists raised its head again in 1854, when an Act was passed limiting Sunday opening hours in beer houses, except for 'bona fide travellers', a subject of great public interest, as it implied a class distinction, where an excursionist was somehow not a 'traveller' (see Chapter 9). The Act was later repealed and, by the mid-1850s, there were some moves to encourage Sunday recreation for the masses. The National Sunday League was founded in 1855, and played a role in developing excursions, when it campaigned for the opening of parks and museums on Sundays, later promoting railway excursions on that day. However, a move to persuade London venues to open on Sundays was rejected in 1856, and the Lord's Day Observance Society set up a Central Committee for Securing the Cessation of Sunday Excursion Trains in 1860.[24]

There were differences in the way that people viewed Sunday observance between steamboats and railways, with steamboats being allowed practices based on custom, while the railways suffered powerful constraints. This may be because boats were regarded as older and more traditional vehicles for leisure, and it might have been felt that as the railway companies were new, it would be possible to adopt a principle from their opening, to prevent Sunday trips from starting. Steamboat practices had varied: Lewis Gilson, agent and secretary to the New Gravesend and New Margate Companies, gave evidence in 1832 that the New Gravesend Company ran trips on Sundays (with profits three times that of other days) but not the New Margate Company, whose shareholders and banker were opposed to Sunday excursions.[25] His company provided a service on Sundays to artisans, mechanics and people in business unable to go on other days, and these were described as mostly 'lower classes'. Although Sunday working by crews might have deprived them of the opportunity of attending divine service, they apparently gained a share in the profits from the sale of beer and spirits, a major incentive. Mr Rowland, shipping agent to the Liverpool Bootle Waterworks Company, described how increased facilities opening up in Liverpool had encouraged Sabbath breaking, for example the increase in steam vessels plying across the Mersey, with the 'lower orders' taking advantage of the small charge for this on a Sunday. The steamboat did encourage Sunday outings and it might well be argued that the steamboat excursion helped to secularise Sundays in support of popular tourism.[26]

From the first stages of railway line development there were excursion trains commonly running on Sundays, although the Liverpool & Manchester had agreed in 1830 not to run Sunday services between 10 and 4pm ('the church interval'), and that Sabbatarian shareholders could donate the dividend earned by Sunday traffic to a charity. However the Post Office insisted on running mail trains on Sundays and railway companies carried passengers on these. In 1847 almost every railway in England carried Sunday services, but only a few in Scotland.[27]

It is clear from the press in the 1830s and 1840s that the Sabbatarian interest reduced the availability of trips on that day, effectively denying a major opportunity for companies to expand their business. The Chairman of the Midland Railway, John Ellis, confirmed in 1855 that they never ran Sunday excursion trains, although they did run some other types of train on that day. However, it was not a straightforward battle between companies who wished to offer Sunday services freely and Sabbatarians who refused to support any such services, as each side had some flexibility in their stance on this issue. But few entrepreneurs followed George Hudson in seeking to make money by harnessing the appeal of cheap Sunday excursions for the working classes.[28]

Sabbatarianism was such a controversial issue that several directors resigned in the 1840s in protest against Sunday trains, for example various directors from the Lancashire & Yorkshire and George Leeman from the York & North Midland. Until Hudson took over in 1845, the Hull & Selby line was strongly opposed to 'unnecessary' Sunday services. In 1835 they were keen to prevent all Sunday trains, a view promoted by two prominent figures in Hull: Avison Terry and the Reverend John King. At their general meeting in October 1835, Sunday travelling was heatedly debated, with concerns by a merchant that excursionists would otherwise use the steamers and would be able to drink all day on these. Eventually a resolution against Sunday travelling was carried, with the aim of including this in their Bill, but during the third reading in March 1836 it was unsuccessful by a very large margin, with strong arguments from those who claimed it would deny cheap travelling to the poor. Later the Hull board did manage to pass a resolution banning Sunday excursions, but in return, on seeing the demand, they offered more weekday trips.[29]

Railway companies adopted a number of strategies. The Leeds & Selby in 1838 offered reduced fares only on those Sunday trains leaving Leeds before 9am, to avoid conflicts with Sunday worship, but by the summer of 1840 their manager, Peter Clarke, was arranging a number of Sunday trips.[30] The Lancashire & Yorkshire asked its line superintendents to investigate the possibility of running trips from Saturday evening to Monday, but this was said to be impracticable as the trains would not be available on Saturdays and the mill hands would not be free from work on Mondays.[31]

Other companies devised strategies to limit Sunday services to avoid the times of divine service; in 1849 the East Lancashire line decided to ensure that cheap Sunday trains arrived before 9.30am and left after 5pm.[32] In 1852, Henry Tennant, Traffic Manager of Leeds Northern Railway, only allowed excursions to the coast on condition that they reached the sea before church service.[33] In moves to avoid criticism from the public and many directors, rather than offering cheap trips on Sundays, some companies used differential pricing and other means to discourage Sunday travel, echoing the approach of tollbars which would previously charge double tolls for road traffic on Sundays.[34] The *Manchester Guardian* noted in 1845 that fares from Manchester to Liverpool and back other than Sundays were 2s 6d, whereas Sunday trains cost 4s for the return journey.[35] The Stockton & Darlington Railway board were strongly religious and always refused requests for Sunday excursions. They apparently charged 'double duty' on Sundays to dissuade the public from travelling.[36] Sabbatarians were sometimes responsible for creating absurd rules, for example in 1854, excursion visitors to Dudley Castle and grounds were informed once they were inside that they could not leave between three and five o'clock, but would have to wait until after divine service.[37]

There are examples of lines managing to hold out against pressures, where a threatened resignation was not enough to defeat those planning Sunday trips. For example the London & Birmingham Railway refused to close their lines on Sundays, despite protests by director Joseph Sturge, who was a leading Birmingham Quaker and moral radical, and who later resigned on this issue.[38] The Manchester, Sheffield & Lincolnshire Railway ran Sunday excursions and was criticised by correspondents.[39] The Manchester & Leeds ran four trains each way on Sundays from 1841, but the chairman and various directors resigned over this issue.[40]

The influence of George Hudson showed how a powerful and charismatic leader could use his authority to hold his own against the inroads of Sabbatarianism. The York & North Midland left the issue of Sunday services to the discretion of their Board rather than trying to include a clause in their legislation, and services started to run on Sundays in 1839.[41] In York public opinion was roused against this at the general meeting in July 1839 by Sabbatarian leaders James Meek and Samuel Tuke, who attacked George Hudson on the issue. Hudson defended the policy on the grounds that banning Sunday services would only affect the poor, winning the argument, and therefore the York & North Midland continued to offer Sunday services.[42] When Hudson resigned from the York, Newcastle & Berwick and the York & North Midland in 1849, the loss of his championship of Sunday excursions was soon felt. In 1849 the York, Newcastle & Berwick directors resolved to run no more Sunday excursions, offering Saturday to Monday trips instead, and the York & North Midland Board took a similar stance on excursions. When the North Eastern Railway was formed in 1854, these policies were retained, influenced by the Quaker Pease family. A subsequent review of lines in England in 1864 which were closed on Sundays found that almost half were NER owned.[43]

There were sometimes opposing views between the directors and the actions of managers and railway workers in operating services. At the North Midland Railway half-yearly meeting in August 1840, the liberal reformer Edward Baines had urged the company not to consider Sunday trains and the Chairman, George Glyn, agreed that the company's position was not to run Sunday excursions. It appears that this was not just a response to public pressure, but a personally held conviction by Baines that Sunday excursions were morally wrong (see page 67).[44] However, a week later it was discovered that a Sunday excursion had in fact taken place the previous week, from Leeds to Sheffield, with 63 carriages taking 2,000 passengers at half fare. There was outrage that tickets had been sold with the apparent knowledge of the board of directors, despite rulings to the contrary by the Court of Proprietors in March, but it seems that this activity had apparently arisen from a misunderstanding about approvals.[45]

The press played their part in influencing the policies of railway companies on this issue. In 1850 the *Morning Chronicle* leader writer came out in favour of Sunday excursion trains, when reporting a meeting in Bath where Sabbatarians denounced Sunday excursionists who were 'cooped up for seven hours in close carriages, indulging in *trivial conversation.*' The writer playfully suggested that the conversation might be equally light 'in the sylvan bowers of Osborne House'. Reports of drunken disorder at the excursion stations highlighted the class implications, with working-class speakers denying the disorder which had been hinted at by middle-class Sabbatarians. The writer finally advocated an occasional trip on an excursion train as good for the health of the mechanic.[46] In 1851 the

Essex Standard was particularly incensed that the Eastern Counties Railway was not only running cheap trips from London to Cambridge on Sundays, but promoting them in *three languages* in the *Times* (English, French and German).[47]

In some cases railway companies adopted what might now be described as public relations strategies to persuade opinion formers of the value of Sunday trips. In 1850 the Great Western Railway started cheap Sunday excursions out of London and the Great Northern ran trains on Sundays in the 1850s. The Great Western Railway secretary published a very carefully argued letter defending its policy on Sunday excursions, on the grounds that a reversal of their decision would withhold 'social and moral benefits' from working people.[48]

By focusing on one year, 1846, it is possible to see the effects of Sabbatarianism on early excursions. That year Birmingham featured no Sunday excursions, pointing to an important constricting role in the city by local Sabbatarians.[49] Many of the trips there were on Mondays, 'Saint Monday' (see page 69), suggesting that it was the artisans, the skilled workers who were taking part, as well as the middle classes, as they were not reliant on Sunday trips because they could travel on Mondays due to their traditional flexibility to celebrate 'Saint Monday' on that day. However recent research on some other towns, for example Leeds, Hull, Preston, Liverpool and Manchester, demonstrates some surprising differences which have not previously been highlighted in railway history.[50]

In Liverpool and Preston in 1846 Sunday trips were common, and seem to have arisen for two reasons. Firstly Sabbatarian pressure groups had not been powerful enough to stop the Preston & Wyre Company and steamer companies from operating on Sundays. Organised religion had never been a strong influence in Lancashire, only five English counties had a lower proportion of people attending church or chapel in the religious census taken in 1851. For the Church of England, Preston 'had the lowest overall attendance figure…of any English town in 1851.'[51] There had been some attempts to stop Sunday cheap trains from Preston in May 1846, when objections were raised at the half-yearly meeting of the Preston & Wyre Company, seeing them as leading to 'scenes of riot' at Fleetwood 'as would not be seen in any other part of the country.' Objectors favoured working people coming for a week in summer instead, to encourage 'the proper preservation of order', but a responding minister observed that 'people would travel, and that they would not be good.' He suggested that the train times be changed to allow people to get to Fleetwood in time to attend church services there. This was rebutted with the argument that although most of the passengers were working class, they had been commended for their orderly conduct. Others agreed, pointing out that on one occasion 5,000 passengers had arrived and they had been seen to be very orderly.[52] The Lancashire & Yorkshire Railway finally ceased running Sunday excursions in 1856, ostensibly down to reduced profits, but their minutes also recorded their regard for the views of the train crews, and there had also been ongoing campaigns by Sabbatarians against such trips.[53] Secondly, and importantly however, it is possible to see the effect on excursions of the concentration of Catholicism in areas of Western Lancashire around the middle of the nineteenth century, supported by Irish migration through Liverpool, and comprising around a third of worshippers in Preston.[54] It has been noted that there were 'two wholly different attitudes towards Sunday recreation: benevolent in Catholic districts, restrictive and grudging wherever Protestantism prevailed.'[55] Local Catholics would have been able to attend a vigil mass on Saturday as an alternative to Sunday churchgoing, leaving Sundays free for trips. The availability of Sunday trips in those two towns meant that it was more likely that industrial workers could take part in cheap trips, unlike the other towns.

In Leeds, as in Birmingham, the fact that there were no Sunday excursions from Leeds in 1846 might be seen as surprising, as some railway companies serving Leeds (the Manchester & Leeds, Midland and York & North Midland) were running a few limited Sunday services around the time. But the new middle class was able to exert a powerful influence on working-class leisure in Leeds, as the Sabbatarian pressure from men such as Edward Baines shaped the timetable. In August 1840 Baines had urged the North Midland Railway not to consider Sunday trains, and the Chairman, George Glyn, agreed that this was the company's position.[56] In June 1846, Baines' *Leeds Mercury* emphasised the need to avoid 'desecrating the Sabbath' in a report on a Temperance Gala.[57] This also reflected the traveller Granville's experience in 1841, when he found that Sabbatarian pressure had forced the closure of the Leeds Zoological Gardens on Sundays, the only day when the industrial classes were free from work.[58] It is surprising that George Hudson's York & North Midland Railway and Midland Railway appeared to offer no trips on Sundays from Leeds during 1846.[59] However, in his evidence to the Select Committee on Railways in 1844, Hudson expressed the view that most people from Leeds were not willing to travel much from home, and even if he provided free travel 'they would remain stationary'.[60] At the opening of the Hull & Bridlington line in 1846, Hudson did his best to avoid discussing the issue of Sunday railway travelling.[61] Peter Clarke, who was close to Hudson, had been appointed general manager of the newly amalgamated Midland Railway in 1844, following his role at the North Midland, but left in April 1845 to go to the London & Brighton Railway, where he played an important part in promoting controversial Sunday excursions. Thus a potential champion of Sunday trips was lost to Leeds by 1846, although the prevailing mood against Sunday trips there would have almost certainly prevented him from offering such trips and may have contributed to his departure.[62] The absence of Sunday trips leads to the conclusion that ordinary working people may not have had the opportunity to participate in most excursions there, despite their low cost.

The picture was similar in Hull, as the Hull & Selby line had banned Sunday excursions in the early 1840s. Hudson had in theory been in favour when he took over in 1845, although there were still strong Methodist Sabbatarian pressures against this activity and this seems to have shaped policies in favour of trips on other days.[63]

In Manchester there were no Sunday trips advertised in 1846, indicating the power of the Sabbatarian groups there. Manchester was a centre of nonconformity at this time, with only 39 Church of England churches out of 137 churches and chapels in Manchester in 1844, and nonconformists were particularly opposed to Sunday leisure.[64] Railways associated with Manchester were running Sunday services in 1847, but this did not apply to excursions, despite evidence from the police at that time that Sunday excursions were beneficial in improving behaviour.[65] There was conflict between leading reformers in Manchester over the running of Sunday excursions in the early 1840s (see page 79) and this appears to have limited such trips in 1846. An old Manchester operative looking back from 1857 commented that any religious observance among the lower orders was mainly confined to Catholic churches, and that many of this class could be found on a cheap trip on Sundays.[66] This could not be true there of the mid-1840s however because of Sabbatarian pressures on railway company policy. At the same time however there was a strong Unitarian presence among the middle class in Manchester, which traditionally did not agree with Sabbatarianism.[67]

The growth of excursion crowds and new forms of leisure was shaped to a great degree by a railway company's stance on Sunday excursions in the face of Sabbatarian pressures. The Sunday travellers had some powerful supporters, with the Duke of Wellington writing to Gladstone in 1844, in the context of debate on the Railway Bill that year, expressing the view that it would be most unfair on the poorest travellers if legislation to enforce new cheap trains caused companies to cease offering third-class carriages on Sundays.[68] Where Catholicism was dominant or at least strong, as in Liverpool and Preston, then Sunday trips were frequent, allowing many more working-class people to take part, whereas in towns such as Birmingham, Leeds, Manchester and Hull, it seems more likely that the Sabbatarians restricted trips to skilled artisan and middle-class participation, because of their greater flexibility to travel on other days.[69]

Overall, during much of the middle of the nineteenth century, the Sunday excursion was not seen as acceptable in many eyes, including the press, and it would take a considerable period before Sunday trips became acceptable again from the late 1860s.[70] The only religious groups which were rather more relaxed about Sunday leisure were the Unitarians and the Roman Catholics. Many people were thus prevented from participating in this mass mobility because Sunday was their only day away from work. Others benefited from the strategies which companies adopted to overcome Sabbatarian pressures, or where a few companies ignored such pressures. There were, however, other groups and bodies which were to play a further role in supporting or restricting trips.

Chapter Six

Shaping Excursions

'No one can have seen the thousands and tens of thousands of men, women, and children belonging to the labouring classes, whom the cheap trains have brought down to Liverpool during the present summer, without being convinced that they and the class to which they belong are prosperous and happy. From Whitsuntide to the present time there has been a constant succession of cheap trains from different places within a hundred miles of Liverpool. Each train has brought several hundreds, and some upwards of a thousand of these pleasure-seekers. Saint Monday is the favourite day for the arrival of the trains, and every resident of Liverpool must have noticed the crowding of our streets, on at least a dozen Mondays, during the present summer, with the mechanics and artisans of Lancashire, Yorkshire, Staffordshire and Shropshire, and their wives and children.[1] (Liverpool Times, August 1850)

While the new social entrepreneurs were working on their ambitious and innovative schemes to move the masses around the country, there were other important and powerful groups at work. They were using their influence to shape the way that excursions developed, either by encouraging these or by limiting them. Sometimes there was direct pressure, sometimes indirect, to offer opportunity or close down possibilities.

Timing was a key factor in the development of cheap excursions, as employees needed leisure time to be able to spend a day on a trip. Many only had Sunday off, and Sunday excursions were the subject of ferocious battles with Sabbatarians. However it was the observance of 'Saint Monday', still rife in many areas in the nineteenth century, which was significant to excursions. Until 1850, most employed workers in England were certainly working between 6am and 6pm, Tuesday to Saturday. Some workers took Mondays off, too, while others worked on Mondays.[2] Saint Monday was the 'avowed and self-constituted holiday of the pleasure-loving portion of "the million"', when it was traditional in an area for employees to refuse to work on Monday, usually where specialised craft workers had enough power over their employers to give them the upper hand.[3] It could only be celebrated with the collusion of the employer however. It was particularly prominent in Birmingham, mainly with better paid working men in urban districts, who even took Tuesdays and Wednesdays too. The public house interest was very strong in Birmingham, and the city was prosperous at this time, with many small manufacturing masters who paid good wages to their men.[4] The Saint Monday pattern was also reflected in other Midland areas; an anonymous potter working in Tunstall in the Potteries in the early 1840s described how there was little work done on Mondays and Tuesdays, but the men worked like 'galley slaves' the rest of the week, from 'four and five in the morning to nine and ten at night.'[5] This contributed to railway company policy, as when the Shrewsbury & Birmingham line opened in 1849, the company planned excursions every Monday throughout the summer, to the Wrekin and Wales, for artisans and their families.[6]

The Midland region was quite different to Lancashire in holiday observance, regarded as much less 'civilised' for a longer time, as a result of irregular working practices, lower wages and less thrift.[7] Saint Monday was waning in Lancashire by the 1840s in both spinning and weaving, and the process of 'civilisation' of holidays was underway, aided by the policies of local magistrates. However, a correspondent to the *Preston Chronicle* did complain about the 'vast numbers of working men lounging about the streets' in Preston on Saint Monday in 1841.[8] The comments on page 69 indicate that Saint Monday was still being observed widely in 1850 by mechanics and artisans from Lancashire, Yorkshire, Staffordshire and Shropshire.[9] There are further examples of Saint Monday leisure practices in Bolton, and in other regions of England, for example trips to the seaside at Yarmouth and Lowestoft were usually taken on Mondays by operatives from Norwich during the summer season of 1856.[10]

Even in 1867 engineer and social commentator Wright noted that 'numerous day trips…are run every Monday during a great portion of the year.' He based his comments on his considerable experience of tramping around the manufacturing centres of the North, the Midlands and the south of England.[11] He divided the working-class celebration of Saint Monday on excursions into several types. Firstly he suggested that day trips to the seaside, to suburban recreation grounds and parks were patronised by the more 'affluent and sedate Saint Mondayites', who were generally young mechanics and their 'young ladies', doing 'all in their power to contribute to the successful doing of the genteel during their day out' by dressing fashionably and eating in tea gardens. Older couples and family parties might go to the resorts but take their own provisions to establishments there, which offered 'the kettle boiled at twopence a head', and share out anything left over with their fellow excursionists on the way home. Lastly the young unmarried mechanics style on these excursions was 'jolly', they travelled in groups and were attracted to dancing venues. Wright noted that alternative activities to an excursion on Saint Monday included sport and drinking, and the group he refers to as 'loafers', who, if they lived near excursion destinations, took advantage of the trippers as 'camp followers', taking their money and their food. Wright considered that those people using Saint Monday for excursions made it a commendable day, a contrast to their difficult working conditions, enabling them to be invigorated the next day, a view shared with others. But he was concerned about those who went on excursions but could not really afford them – the 'improvident' ones, who left their families ill-supported, and their labouring workmates unable to work because the mechanics were off.[12]

Railway excursions for the masses were expanding dramatically in the 1840s and 1850s among factory workers in the north of England. People there had migrated relatively short distances following industrialisation, into factories in rapidly growing towns and cities.[13] These new factories were concentrated in Lancashire, Cheshire, and the Yorkshire West Riding at this time, as well as parts of the West Midlands, and parts of central and lowland Scotland.[14] However, in 1841, even in Manchester only a quarter of the adult male workforce were textile workers, and of these only half were working in factories. At the same time forty per cent of employed women over twenty were textile workers, and two-thirds were in factories.[15] Thus the market for excursions was not necessarily primarily from factories, but factory workers were an important component. In general, employers in the industrial manufacturing districts paid higher wages than the agricultural south. While the average wage of men, women and children in the cotton mills around 1843 was 10s 6d a week, this included a large proportion of women and children, and some men were earning as much as 20s to 30s a week.[16] This contributed to a substantial family income, when compared to male agricultural labourers who might only earn 10s a week. Thus these employers helped cotton workers in the industrial north to take part in the new excursions, generally day trips, without the need to pay for accommodation.

Were they affordable? Calculations of changes in the cost of living in the nineteenth century in relation to earnings are fraught with difficulties and complex. Any averages will mask circumstances in particular towns or rural areas. Leeds weekly wages in the woollen industry in 1839 ranged from 20s to 24s 6d on average, compared to 16s for tailors and 14s for shoemakers. In one Leeds spinning mill in 1840, weekly wages were reported as 21s 8d for men, 5s 11½d for women and 2s 5¾d for children, and therefore a day's income for a spinner and his wife with two working children would have easily covered the cost of an excursion, if the timing were suitable.[17] In general real earnings rose steadily during the 1840s, with a dip in the mid-1850s, recovering their former levels towards 1860.[18] There were cyclical depressions, for example in Manchester in 1841–2 and 1847–8, with dramatic fluctuations in employment and short-time working.[19] However, wages do appear to have improved significantly for Lancashire workers between 1820 and 1850.[20] By 1861 the average weekly wage of a higher skilled male labourer in England and Wales was 28s-35s, and that of a lower skilled male labourer 21s-25s, with unskilled labourers earning 10s-20s weekly. Thus a 100 mile cheap trip at a cost of around 4s 6d would have been manageable, given careful saving.[21]

A reduction of working hours could also help people to take part in excursions. By now employers were reacting to popular activism and government reforms on this, shaping new forms of leisure.[22] Women and children working in textile factories benefited from the 1850 Factory Act, which prohibited them from working after 2pm on Saturdays. However this did not apply directly to men or to the many people in other workplaces, such as shops.[23] Birmingham's industrial base of small workshops rather than large factories was not covered by this until much later, but following representations by groups of working men, engineering employers eventually granted the half-day in exchange for the discontinuation of Saint Monday and for working extra hours each day in the 1850s. Some commentators suggested that 'evil habits' were more likely to take place on Saint Monday than on Saturday afternoons and evenings. In Liverpool it was only the elite employees who gained the Saturday half-day in the 1850s. The dates of other towns and cities differed widely in gaining the half-day, for example Sheffield 1840s, St Helen's 1857, Nottingham 1861, and Barrow-in-Furness late 1860s.[24]

Some argued that the labour needed in the new factories was comparatively light, compared to much agricultural work, as it involved watching machines, and therefore workers were not too exhausted to enjoy trips away, even though their hours were very long.[25] The passing of the Ten Hours Act in 1847, and the development of new mechanical inventions, also contributed to improvements in the physical condition of textile factory workers.[26]

Some railway companies responded to changes in working hours. In 1844, when commercial firms in Manchester allowed their employees Saturday afternoons off, the Manchester & Leeds Railway offered special excursion rates on trains leaving on Saturday afternoons, to return either Sunday evening or early Monday morning, to give workers the 'opportunity of visiting their friends'.[27] However this was not available to all workers, as unfortunately, despite intensive campaigning activity over a period of sixty years by the Early Closing Movement, retail shop workers in Manchester were denied a half-day and were still working excessively long hours, around eighty-five weekly, on average, until after the turn of the century.[28] However, longer holiday periods such as Whitsun, when some workplaces closed down, generated much excursion traffic, especially in smaller towns in the Midlands and North of England, where, with small units of production, holiday patterns were focused around traditional carnivals and feasts.

As well as trips organised by railway companies there were works railway trips, which began as early as 1840. These were a common feature during the 1840s and 1850s, designed often as a public relations exercise by paternalistic employers to motivate their workers and emphasise the position of an employer in the local community.[29] Some employers used the works trip in an attempt to develop a closer relationship with their workers. It was not always a positive experience. A police report in 1858 records a dispute between an operative, a sweeper in a Preston worsted mill, and his employer, over whether he should be forced by his employer to buy a 1s ticket for a cheap works trip on a Saturday. He bought the ticket despite straitened circumstances, but in the event he did not go on the trip and was summonsed by his employer for stopping away from work. He claimed, 'I was obliged to go [on the trip] or be bagged [sacked].'[30] Typically employees would assemble in the factory yard and walk to the station for a trip, sometimes headed by a band. Workers from cotton spinners J. Paley took a trip from Preston to Fleetwood in August 1844, marching in procession to the station, with assorted flags, a band and mottoes fixed to the sides of the carriage, and a procession on their return plus the obligatory three cheers as they went past their employer's house.[31] Press correspondents were keen to emphasise the positive and moral nature of such activities in support of employers: reports from Preston in August 1849 detail a number of works outings to Fleetwood, with the reporter at pains to record these as an expression of 'masters and men…all enjoying themselves in one boat – no differences, no contentions, no jealousies', showing mutual respect. Here the writer suggests this was unprompted, for example Mr Grundy's men welcomed him loudly but 'with no slavish shouting'.[32]

While many employers' trips typically featured factory workers, especially from Lancashire and Yorkshire, on a few occasions other types of employer became involved in this activity. There were reports of a Scottish agriculturalist, Mr Cowie, from Mains of Haulkerton, organising local agricultural employers to send their rural farm servants on a railway excursion in 1854, when 2,000 farm servants from Angus and Mearnshire in Scotland travelled to Aberdeen. Cowie was particularly keen on the moral and physical improvement of farm servants, and the role of education in developing this, and had arranged for tickets to be presented to the men by their employers.[33] The men were formed into marching order, four abreast and made 'a triumphal entry into the Granite City, preceded by the Forfar Band.' Mr Cowie gave them a personal guided tour of a number of buildings, works, docks, barracks and a shipyard, followed by lunch in the Union Hall – a pound of wheaten bread, half a pound of cheese and a 'chopin', or half a pint, of beer. Mr Cowie expressed the view that people on excursion parties sometimes became excited, foolish and offensive to others, mainly down to the consumption of spirits, and he hoped that by providing the workers with a small amount of beer, this would dissuade them from going elsewhere for more liquor. He also hoped that they would show their gratitude for the trip by 'increased diligence'. A similar excursion took place two years later in August 1856, combining leisure activity with more worthy pursuits, when again Mr Cowie organised another excursion of farm servants to Perth. Only 500 workers, male and female, took part this time, and the day was rainier, reducing the potential for outdoor activities. In the City Hall they were subjected to possibly less exciting activity, a competition featuring 'arithmetic, farm bookkeeping, reading, the history of Scotland, the history of the Covenanters etc.' In mid-nineteenth-century Scotland, rural children were obliged to attend parochial schools between October and March, as education was valued rather more than in England, and therefore farm servants were sometimes able to read.[34] The report notes that many of the farm servants exhibited 'a very creditable acquaintance with the several subjects.' When the weather had cleared sports and games were held, followed by a prize-giving.[35] The excursion was used by the employer here as a tool for the moral reform and education of workers, a particularly Scottish concern. The motivation for this seems to vary from that of the employers from Preston, who were seeking to bring their employees closer together, rather than to educate them.

This press report goes on to show the effect of an excursion crowd on society. It notes that the physique of these farm servants was prepossessing and that townspeople had been known for a prejudice against the agricultural population, arising from 'the licence which they too generally took some years ago, on their visits to towns.' However the new visit created a more favourable impression of such hearty and open people, as 'fresh looking and stalwart fellows, representative of the sinews of a country's existence.' The labourers expressed admiration and wonder, and were an object of curiosity, with large crowds coming to see them off on their return home. Again, in 1860, Mr Cowie organised a trip on the Scottish North Eastern Railway to Aberdeen and once more this featured a procession, band, games and prizes. Once more he was keen to add the need for 'instruction and improvement' to 'pleasure and recreation'.

Taking 1846 as an example shows the effects of differing employer practices across varying cities, particularly in relation to 'Saint Monday'.[36] In Leeds that year there was a predominance of day trips leaving on a Monday or Wednesday, and trips lasting a few days, suggesting involvement by the middle classes or by better paid artisans, or self-employed tradesmen with the flexibility of celebrating Saint Monday. This is similar to Birmingham.[37] By contrast, in Manchester, the introduction of steam power meant that manufacturers had to keep their machinery working to routines and so could not accept workers taking time off on Mondays. Manchester was ahead of Birmingham in the development of this technology and thus Saint Monday had lasted longer in the Midlands.[38] However, it was reported in 1850 that the LNWR were offering cheap trips to Alderley Edge on the first Monday of each summer month, amid complaints from workers that this may have suited shopkeepers rather more than industrial workers who would have preferred Saturdays.[39] In Hull in 1846 there were a number of Monday trips, both day and staying. The preference for Saint Monday is usually associated with towns and cities where skilled artisans worked flexibly in small craft units, but Hull's economy at this time featured import and export shipping, seed crushing, cotton manufacturing, trawlfishing and related industries, such as transport.[40] A survey there in 1839 found that employment was not regular, often seasonal, and there was little work for women and children when compared to Lancashire for example. Importantly there was no 'aristocracy of labour' which drove the observance of Saint Monday in other towns at the time. There was a large lower middle-class of small business owners, and also clerks, but this sector was unstable.[41] It may well be that in this case, rather than employment practices, it was the influence of competing steamboat trips that shaped the profile of railway excursions in Hull, as these traditionally took place on Mondays and Thursdays. Importantly, Liverpool and Preston did not need Monday trips as Sunday excursions were available (see page 66), when the masses could participate.

Many workers were only able to go on excursions during the annual Whit holiday, and railway companies ran many excursion trains at that time. There were however exceptions, for example in 1846 in Leeds there were none advertised or reported on in the press. The Whit weekend was hot that year, with temperatures of 72°–76°, but there appeared to be no clear tradition for Leeds people to be able to or wish to take holidays in celebration of Whitsun. There was no universal shut-down of industrial employment in Leeds. A few events were recorded at this time – a large gala organised by the Leeds Temperance Society at the Zoological Gardens in Headingley on Whit Tuesday, which attracted large numbers of visitors from the West Riding, and a train of teetotallers from Leicester.[42] By comparison, in Manchester in 1846 almost all the excursions (ten out of twelve trips reported or advertised that year) took place at Whitsun, the most important holiday of the year there, 'the one week in the year when, by mutual consent, almost everyone ceases from labour.' Again the weather in Manchester was much hotter than in earlier years, with a spell of fine, dry and warm weather at the end of May, reaching 78° in the shade on Whit Monday and 81° on Whit Tuesday.[43] Manchester people had traditionally enjoyed a mobile leisure experience during Whit week, even before the advent of the railway, with excursions, either on foot or in vehicles.[44] It is not clear how comprehensive the shut-down was, as a correspondent noted that some Sunday schoolchildren were unable to join the Whit Monday procession because of their employment in the mills, which did not stop working until Tuesday evening. The *Manchester Times* however claimed that there was little work and very little business carried out during the whole of Whit week.[45]

The railway was not the only mode of transport for such excursions at this time. There were Whit week outings in 1846 from Manchester to Dunham Park, when thousands of Sunday school children and other people travelled along the roads or the Bridgewater Canal, using farmers' carts, large wagons, canal boats (forty-seven boats engaged on the Thursday), Swift packets and omnibuses, with an estimated 50,000 people visiting the

Park between Tuesday and Saturday (3,000 scholars on Wednesday).[46] It was estimated that the canal boats carried nearly 12,000 people on the Thursday alone. (It was not possible to make this journey by railway in 1846 as the Manchester, South Junction & Altrincham Railway did not open until 1849.[47])

Strikingly, excursions around Manchester meant that two opposing forces were in motion – country people ventured into the great town and town people ventured out into the countryside. There were also many visitors from surrounding towns, as in the 1840s Manchester was surrounded by a web of population centres, each connected by the railway to the centre: Oldham (43,000), Bury, Rochdale and Halifax (24,000 to 26,000 each), Bolton, Preston and Chorley (totalling 114,000), Stalybridge, Ashton, Dukinfield and Hyde (80,000), Stockport (50,000), Wigan (26,000) and Warrington (21,000).[48] As a helpful estimation of the sheer crowds involved in this feast of Whitsun mobility for the masses in 1846, the *Manchester Guardian* summarised the traffic for the week conveyed on lines which terminated in Manchester, including double tickets, day tickets and Sunday scholars, in carriages and in wagons:[49]

Excursion crowds in Manchester at Whit 1846

Railway company	Sunday to Saturday	Notes
Manchester & Leeds	103,000	(20,000 more than 1845)
Liverpool & Manchester	60,000	(around 17,000 in wagons)
		(increase of 400% on 1845)
Sheffield & Manchester	101,600	(including 21,458 scholars)
		(32,000 more than 1845)
Manchester & Birmingham	85,300	(almost 100% increase on 1845)
Manchester & Bolton	45,800	(only very slight increase on 1845)
Total	395,700	

In this way Whit excursion traffic in the Manchester area contributed to the mobility of almost 400,000 people, a huge spectacle, with large numbers of the working-classes free to take a holiday over a lengthy period at this time.

Apart from employers, there were other powerful men in cities who played a surprising role in shaping the development of railway excursions for the masses in the early days. Some had a hand in controlling both the press and the local railway network, for example Edward Baines in Leeds. Baines saw the railway excursion as a solution to the need for rational recreation, although his strong Sabbatarian views conflicted with the timing of such trips.[50] While he was incensed at the way that metropolitan prejudice against the manufacturing districts in the early 1840s painted pictures of 'scenes of vice, ignorance, sedition, irreligion, cruelty, and wretchedness' in the north, and campaigned to present data which showed a more realistic picture of urban life in these areas, he still saw the need to promote excursions as a means of rational recreation. Baines' liberal views only stretched so far, he also argued that the new railway communication could be used to enable military forces to travel quickly to quell disturbances of the peace.[51]

Visiting crowds needed refreshment and by 1858 in Liverpool there were, unusually, many free public drinking fountains, installed gradually by the philanthropist and temperance enthusiast Charles Melly at his own expense since 1854. Their value to excursionists was recognised in the press.[52] Melly was a practical reformer, born in Tuebrook, Liverpool, in 1829 to a well-off family of merchants.[53] His younger brother George became a well-known MP (George's great-grandson was the jazz musician George Melly). As well as working in the family business Charles quickly became a liberal philanthropist, supporting the working classes from his early 20s. In 1852 he established a night school in Beaufort Street, and he also supported the Domestic Mission in north Liverpool, with ragged schools providing free education for poor children. Following one of his visits to Geneva, where there were numerous fountains, Melly, a temperance enthusiast, acknowledged the benefits of a free supply of drinking water not only to emigrants at the Liverpool docks, but 'to people from the manufacturing and rural districts, who fill the street as excursionists' especially as an antidote to drunkenness when beer at the public house was the only other refreshment option, or water from horse troughs.[54] Melly funded the first Liverpool fountain on 31 March 1854, at the south end of Princes Dock, then six more the same year, and fourteen more by 1856. They were usually made of polished Aberdeen granite, although a few were cast iron, and were linked to the town council water supply, which Melly arranged to be provided free of charge. Each had two galvanised iron ladles attached by a chain to the wall on each side, and they were ornamented by a bronze head of a lion, child, satyr or similar.[55] He estimated later that fountains cost around ten pounds each.[56] These were tremendously successful: on two days in July 1856 it was estimated that more than 2,500 people had drunk at each per day. Melly also paid for fountains elsewhere, such as for the fishermen in the Isle of Man in 1860.[57] He was dedicated to his causes: much later in 1864 he wrote to the council complaining that the style of tap used in some of the fountains led to them freezing up in bad weather, and he asked for changes to be made.[58] By 1859 there were forty-six fountains in Liverpool, of which thirty-five were paid for by him. He inevitably became known as Fountain Melly.[59]

Melly served as a Liberal on the Town Council, and was also instrumental in developing open air playgrounds/gymnasia in Liverpool so that the working classes could exercise in the fresh air, with poles, ropes, ladders and chains, and trees.[60] In his speech at the opening of the first of these he urged: 'Let good humour and good temper prevail. Let there be no quarrelling among yourselves: and allow no stone throwing, or fighting among your younger members.'[61] These gymnasia took the traditional practice however of closing on Sundays, which was unfortunate as this was often the only day of leisure for ordinary people at this time.[62] Melly also provided wayside benches and supported Sefton Park. He was President of Liverpool Athletic Club, and supported the Grand Olympic Festival in Liverpool in the 1860s.[63] The value of his work was recognised by a testimonial from the working men of Liverpool, first mooted in 1858, which resulted eventually in £1,000 being raised to buy an ornamental piece of silverware to present to him in 1861.[64] Tragically he suffered from depression and mental problems, gradually becoming irrational and changing his views around 1879/80. There were signs of this in 1879, when it was reported in the press that he moved an amendment at a Liverpool meeting against the proposed closing of public houses on Sundays, suggesting that until provision was made for the opening of cocoa-rooms, reading-rooms, museums, and picture galleries on Sundays, it was undesirable to curtail the present short hours during which the public houses were open. While this aligned with his views about supporting working-class leisure, it seems an unlikely stance from someone who had been a keen temperance enthusiast. The amendment was supported by very few of his colleagues at the meeting.[65] In 1880 his wife, Louisa, petitioned a jury about the 'alleged insanity' of her husband.[66] His colleagues had noted changes in his behaviour from 1879, complaining that this man, who had been held in such high regard by all during the past thirty years or so, had become very excitable, and was quarrelling with his family and the leading men of Liverpool, over money and philanthropy. At the time he was being housed in the Liverpool Asylum (of which he was a manager) because his doctor reported that he was suffering from chronic mania and delusion. Melly professed to be worried that assassins were out to kill him and refused to take his soup as it might be poisoned, barricading his room at night. He was declared insane and incapable of managing his own affairs.[67] At some point in the 1880s he came back to live in the family home at Riversley, supported by an attendant. On Saturday, 10 November 1888 he shot himself in the head with a pistol.[68] Melly left an important legacy however as, following his lead, other towns began to carry out similar initiatives, sometimes funded by councils, sometimes by individual benefactors, for example Leeds, Hull, Derby, Chester, Leicester, Sunderland, Aberdeen and Glasgow.[69] This initiative also inspired the foundation of the Metropolitan Free Drinking Fountain Association in London in 1859.[70] Interestingly a report of a meeting of the working men's auxiliary committee of this organisation in 1859 notes that it was the working classes and the aristocracy who gave the most support to their fund-raising efforts; they met with indifference from the middle classes.[71]

Religious views in society had a major impact on how far Sunday train services were allowed or campaigned against. It is illuminating to look at Manchester, which had a background of concerns about large crowds. There had been social disturbances in 1831–2, generated by restless hand-loom weavers, and it was identified with agitation. For example the Anti-Corn Law League was founded there in 1839 and the Chartists generated high levels of support in the town in the late 1830s. It also became known as the centre of non-conformity.[72] Memories of the horrors of Peterloo inhibited cooperation between the factory workers and the middle classes, and increased concern among the latter about the power of working-class crowds, leading to views that rational recreation was important in controlling the masses.[73]

Certain features of Manchester in the 1830s supported the influence of powerful elites. These include its large size, which diminished the powers of traditional local leaders, the structure of its industry, with wealth held by certain people who had to be listened to, its relative newness which reduced traditional bonds, and lastly the level of squalor, which led to social segregation and low life expectancy. A government report in 1842 stated that the average age at death of mechanics, labourers and their families was only seventeen, for tradesmen and their families it was twenty and professional people thirty-eight.[74] Manchester suffered from an economic depression after 1836, and the development of the power-loom transformed its employment profile, leading to a reduction of males in the textile workforce from 35 per cent to 25 per cent between 1841 and 1861.[75] The employment of many women and children in factories, however, had the potential to increase the disposable income of families for spending on excursions, at the expense of male textile workers. In common with most other major towns, there was nowhere for local operatives to spend their leisure time healthily, because of the disappearance of common land.[76]

Manchester had a powerful middle-class elite at this time, owning a large number of warehouses, shops and banks, giving them power over land and the labour market. This enabled them to act in unison, for instance from the mid-1840s commercial and public offices began to close at noon on Saturdays in Manchester, allowing a half-day for workers, stimulating the market for excursions. At the same time this supported the Sabbatarians by replacing the need for Sunday excursions. Some railway companies responded by running extra trains on Saturday afternoons. A correspondent to the *Manchester Guardian* in June 1844, however, complained that the railways were slow to react to this potential market, and that he had to persuade the Manchester & Leeds Railway to run a cheap weekend trip on their line.[77]

Middle-class philanthropists, worried about the potential for agitation in Manchester and the lack of open spaces, were able to use their networks to promote excursions for the masses as a tool for rational recreation. Powerful figures frequently combined railway affairs with cultural and municipal activity. Edward Watkin was a Manchester railway promoter who was involved with a number of civic organisations from his youth. A director of the Manchester Athenaeum, he helped to start the Saturday half holiday movement in Manchester for clerks, extending their leisure time for excursions. There were two pleasure gardens, Belle Vue Gardens and Pomona Gardens, and these offered a variety of entertainments and attractions, especially at Whitsun. But Watkin promoted the need for public parks, three of which eventually opened in Manchester and Salford, following complaints in 1844 that there were no parks or open spaces in the city for workers to spend leisure time, leaving them only the street for open air leisure. The new spaces offered by the public parks were, however, a long way from the most densely populated working-class areas, and there were rules about opening hours and behaviour which restricted their popularity with the masses.[78]

Watkin's views on leisure opportunities for the masses influenced his policies in his railway career. He worked as assistant to Mark Huish at the London & North Western Railway and then became general manager of the Manchester, Sheffield & Lincolnshire Railway in 1853, playing a leading role in negotiations with the Great Northern, London & North Western and the Midland railways.[79] He had strong views about the working classes and rational recreation, proactively supporting this, but concerned about Sunday observance. He recognised the conundrum that the masses needed to access new spaces and to gain the benefits of associating with other classes, but they could only do this on their day off on Sundays, and this would involve the railwayman working on the Sabbath. As a result Watkin ran excursion trains on Sundays, but as little as possible. Thus, in the 1850s, Watkin typified the dilemma of reformers on how to square the circle of promoting rational recreation for the masses to prevent class conflict developing, alongside religious observance. There was however not much evidence that the masses attended church even when they were not tripping, especially in the northern industrial towns.[80]

At the same time, while the middle classes might have been keen to support the working classes in their cultural and artistic self-expression, this did not extend to political self-expression.[81] An account from Manchester in 1844 sheds light on the absence of Chartist railway excursions. In this case it was a canal excursion but it demonstrates the attitudes involved. It reported that when Manchester Chartists tried to hire a boat from the Irwell and Mersey Navigation to take Sunday school scholars along the canal to Barton-upon-Irwell, as they had done the previous year, they were refused, and told that orders were 'not to let the Chartists have a boat on any account.' In addition if anyone else lent them a boat, 'the moment it was found it was to be tied up.'[82] The radical *Northern Star* newspaper mentions just one Chartist excursion by railway between 1838 and 1852, a four shilling Sunday trip from London to Brighton in August

1845, when 3,000 people took part in three trains, and the trip proceeds were used in support of the Chartist Land Society.[83] However several other types of Chartist excursion are recorded over the period, using either horse drawn 'vans', carts, or steamboats, on rivers or canals.[84] Several reports mentioned the novelty of a Chartist pleasure trip.[85] The capacity of vans and boats was surprisingly large, with reports of trips involving 400 people in several vehicles. From London, steamboats were used along the River Thames or vans on the roads, for example to O'Connorville, the Chartist estate in Hertfordshire. Some trips took place in the north east and in Scotland. Many would run on Sundays, recognising the suitability of this day for the working family, otherwise they tended to take place on Mondays. Many trips were organised as fund-raising activities, sometimes to distribute Chartist material too. Mass walking processions to Chartist events played an important role as a dramatic demonstration of strength.[86] At times individuals might have travelled by train to events, but there is conflicting evidence about this, depending on the political slant of the newspaper.[87] The absence of railway trips reflects the mutual antagonism between Chartists and railway companies, especially as trains had been used to move soldiers during Chartist disturbances in 1842.[88] Railway companies at times opposed Chartist activity, encouraging employees to volunteer as special constables, and accommodating soldiers in station buildings, thus it is not surprising that the use of the railway for Chartist trips did not develop.[89] If it had, the enormity of the crowds taking part and the variety of destinations would have done much to spread the political ideas of the Chartist movement during the 1840s.

The press played a key role in shaping excursions, especially the provincial press. Usually controlled by members of the urban elite, it played a powerful, progressive and significant role in advertising, reporting and commenting on railway excursions, stimulating and encouraging business, and commenting on these new crowds, which might be seen as a potential threat to public order. The provincial press was mainly produced, consumed and distributed in towns and cities, supporting a sense of regional identity.[90] It used railway networks for distribution and thus the large concentration of population in its catchment areas enabled excursion advertisers to reach a big audience which was relevant to their services. Newspapers played a hand in highlighting the success of excursions or otherwise, to future entrepreneurs and social groups for example, and in persuading or dissuading potential excursionists. A writer in the *Liverpool Mercury* in May 1855 sought to explain the lack of excursion visitors that year in Liverpool at Whitsun. He was concerned that there was only one London & North Western excursion by Mr Marcus to London, and felt that the number of Whit excursionists was a barometer for the 'social condition of the working classes in the manufacturing and surrounding districts.' In his view the main cause was the long and severe winter that year, which had the effect of reducing workers' disposable income. However, in emphasising the lack of providers, the press might be seen to be encouraging other entrepreneurs to enter the market.[91]

There were frequent advertisements on the front pages for both rail and steamboat excursions (generating a substantial source of income for the newspapers). These helped readers to compare modes and make judgements about value. At the same time of course excursion promoters made heavy use of handbills to distribute information effectively, targeting the masses who might not have access to a shared newspaper or whose standards of literacy would have discouraged the use of the press. In supporting this new mass mobility, the press also provided some useful 'statistical collations', a key feature of Victorian writing. The *Leeds Mercury* expressed excitement in 1846 that, 'special pleasure trips from Leeds have become quite the order of the day.' The paper published the following table showing the reduction in fares and mileage travelled for five forthcoming trips.

Costs of selected cheap railway trips from Leeds in 1846[92]

Destination	Usual cost of third-class ticket	Third-class excursion fare	Distance out and back (m)	Usual cost per mile (d)*	Cheap cost per mile(d)*
London	34s	15s	408	1.00	0.44
Scarborough	16s	3s 6d	146	1.32	0.29
Castle Howard	9s	2s 6d	94	1.15	0.32
Sheffield	6s 6d	2s 6d	76	1.03	0.40
Liverpool	21s#	5s 3d	184~	1.37	0.58

* extrapolations from data

Bradshaw indicates a fare of 19s at the time

~ mileage adjusted using Bradshaw, as the paper used an incorrect figure of 108 miles here

This table highlights how the new excursions suddenly became affordable for the masses. The anonymous writer expressed a typical view by the urban elite at the time, recommending trips not just on economy grounds, but as a tool in the moral reform of the masses: a 'desirable means of recreation to a great mass of persons who would otherwise be debarred from the benefits.' It was suggested that the 'humbler' classes could use them to see scenes and places for their 'magnificence, antiquity, or historical or commercial association.' They were regarded as a source of 'healthful enjoyment' and 'calculated to improve and gratify the taste and enlarge the views of those who participate in them.'[93]

There were other more indirect ways in which the press influenced excursions. It played a major role in supporting the development of voluntary societies, frequently involved in commissioning trips, for example the *Liverpool Mercury* and the *Leeds Mercury* both promoted mechanics institutes.[94] Some newspapers were particularly proud of their role in enforcing Sabbatarian practices on the working classes, as recorded for example by the political editor of the *Manchester Times* in 1825.[95] The press often used rational recreation as a theme, and felt able to allay the fears of the public about the crowd, frequently with comments on the nature and behaviour of the excursion crowds, well aware of public concerns about drunkenness and debauchery, and the potential for uprising, especially in the 1840s. There were some concerns however about the way that the new mobility might be perceived as a threat. Some papers, such as the Tory *Morning Post*, written for the upper classes, supported this new leisure activity for the masses, but suggested that critics saw such advances as 'a weakening of their political fulcrum.'[96] In 1851 the *Economist* hailed the railway as the 'Magna Charter' of the motive freedom of the poor, in providing much needed recreation, reporting that the number of people enjoying cheap trips from Manchester had risen from 116,000 in 1848 to 150,000 in 1849 and 202,000 in 1850.[97] A report in the *Era* in 1857 suggested that the excursion train could be responsible for 'lengthening out the lives' of ordinary people by allowing them more time to enjoy activities which previously took a long time. It acknowledged the role of the Saturday half-holiday in encouraging this, and urged employers to offer more works outings too.[98]

The term 'monster train' appeared in the press as early as 1840 and was soon commonly used in relation to excursions in the 1840s, attached as a descriptive label to the new phenomenon and giving it a distinctive aura. *The Standard* decided these were 'all the rage' in 1844, like a 'monster quadrille.'[99] In 1844 the American magazine *Living Age* suggested that 'monster' excursions of 3,000–4,000 people were common in the northern manufacturing districts.[100] A perceptive reporter in the *Bradford Observer* wrote that these 'monster' trains of 'pleasure-seeking denizens' were becoming so common that they were hardly noteworthy, but reflected that they may be of interest at some future time.[101] In 1844 the experience of watching two monster trains converging on York, from Newcastle and from Leicester, was compared to a marvel from the *Arabian Nights* by a reporter.[102]

There were many occasions where the press summarised the social benefits. A *Chambers' Edinburgh Journal* article in 1844 suggested that cheap trips reduced drinking opportunities, by taking people away from public houses and racecourses for example.[103] The *Standard* in 1857 even proposed that the drunken artisan had been changed into a 'reflective being' with the advent of excursion trains, by spending drinking money on trips for his family.[104] It was believed that excursions would encourage thrift and savings to displace money potentially spent on drink. A Manchester commentator in 1849 reported that a publican had told him that cheap Sunday trips (and teetotalism) were ruining his business and those of his colleagues, as people were saving their money for excursions.[105] It was suggested that prejudice might be reduced, especially that supposedly of the rural population, accused by commentators of being 'ignorant and selfish'.[106] This was a common theme, suggesting that rural people were ignorant and could learn from town dwellers by taking excursions to urban areas, that people who have not travelled much have their minds 'contracted and weakened by prejudices and self-sufficiency', had very low morals, and indulged in vice and profligacy. As a result it was proposed that railways were the 'great civiliser of society' and would produce 'an assimilation of manners and customs'.[107] Even the Chartist *Northern Star* suggested that 'the petty prejudices and local errors sure to accompany isolation, or a limited field of observation, are dispelled.'[108] Excursions were perceived to assist in the breaking down of class barriers, especially as all classes were known to use the cheaper third-class option: 'the iron bond' bringing people together.[109] They were even featured as 'dissolving national antipathies', in the case of cheap trips to France.[110]

Improving health was a further theme, by access to fresh air and countryside for town dwellers living and working in cramped and unhealthy conditions, supported in Manchester at Whitsun by several afternoons of business closure. The advantages of the 'freshening influence of nature' and the 'dream land' of the seashore were highlighted.[111] In 1853 it was argued that the decreasing number of applications to the Manchester Infirmary was evidence of the improved physical condition of local people, arising from a number of factors including the popularity of outdoor exercise such as 'cheap trips by rail and omnibus'.[112] It was suggested that cheap trips improved morality and behaviour, with the removal of people from the 'evils' of cities, diminishing the attractions of brutal sports in favour of excursions, and 'exchanging the haunts of low and vicious indulgences for the railway excursion to some attractive landscape.'[113] As early as 1841 the *Manchester Guardian* reported that local leaders were keen to keep children and others away from the racecourse at Whitsun.[114] Excursions were often judged as 'innocent' recreation.[115] There were simplistic attempts to correlate the rising number of railway excursions with a decrease in crime; an article in 1853 attributed the fall in the number of prisoners in Manchester to excursion activity, as it reported that there were 12,147 prisoners in 1843 (when the excursion trains started), declining to 7,620 in 1846 and 4,578 in 1850.[116] Commentators also encouraged orderly and 'proper' behaviour by Sunday school visits to country estates.

Trips were perceived at times to encourage educational and intellectual pursuits. In 1851 Charles Knight referred to the excursion train as 'one of the best public instructors', although the *Morning Chronicle* grumbled about this in its review of his guide, on the grounds that such trains caused accidents and got in the way of 'legitimate business traffic'.[117] Some of the more unusual trips were seen as a way of developing employment potential, by disseminating knowledge about agricultural improvements and industrial processes.[118] Excursions were reported to improve morale for workers, by support for works trips and Sunday trips supposedly replacing a need for workers to take their traditional Saint Monday away from work.[119]

By 1850 the *Standard* was arguing that excursion trains were becoming 'a necessary portion of our domestic and moral economy', and the same year the *Illustrated London News* also highlighted the fact that, while normally anything 'for the million' was used as a disparaging reference, in this case it was 'productive of good'.[120] The press were very careful not to link excursion activity with a potential for generating working-class crowds for political motives. However, in the *Manchester Times* in 1850, Liberal philanthropist John Passmore Edwards, who had Chartist sympathies, noted the potential of an excursion for 'refining the tastes, improving the habits, and quickening the aspirations of the people', subtly suggesting a call for reform. In his final paragraph he hints at this with:

'the secret of excursion parties is their cheapness, and cheapness is the result of association. I see in the principle of association, as applied merely to the transmission of persons from one part of the world to another, an important instrument to progress, and a fresh triumph of civilisation.'[121]

There was occasional editorial commentary opposing the railway excursion, apart from Sabbatarian criticism. While supporting the new excursions in general, in a colourful report, the *Daily News* in 1849 expressed tremendous anger about trips from London to Norwich for a public execution:

'what a moving Pandemonium the locomotive is doomed to drag after it… The squalid inmates of the lowest haunts of lazar infamy in the metropolis, may, thanks to the reduced fares, enjoy tomorrow's spectacle at Norwich. The raffish finery of the swell mob, male and female, will impart a shabby splendour to those pilgrims to the shrine of callous curiosity… The brutal jest, the callous glee of the hanging holidaymakers as they pass along, will resemble a moral Simoom sweeping along the railway.'[122]

There were major and valid concerns about the safety of excursion trains. Following the report of Captain Galton into railway accidents in 1858, a *Times* editorial compared the railway deaths (276) and injuries (556) to those of the battlefields in Italy. It suggested that excursion trains were in particular danger of collision and portrayed them as the 'comets of the railway system. Their orbits are irregular, their appearance uncertain, and their aspect equally portentous.' It pointed out that they were usually large and travelling at unusual hours, leading to confusion and collision.[123] There were a few other criticisms: an article in *Leisure Hour* refers to the cheap trips in 1857 taking the Protestant masses away from religious observance, unlike Catholic lower classes for whom church attendance was much higher.[124] There was a high level of critical coverage featuring the Sabbatarianism perspective on Sunday excursions, for example Great Western Railway Sunday excursions in 1850.[125]

Taken overall, the role of the press in shaping the new railway excursions cannot be overstated, in particular encouraging their readers and opinion formers to support the excursion by making it acceptable. A sustained campaign outlined the benefits of these in relation to moral reform, aligned to the needs of their advertisers, together with general support for Sabbatarian views opposing Sunday trips. Newspapers provided constant reassurance about the behaviour of the large crowds which were generated, and the close relationship between the press and the urban elites engendered a developing role for the voluntary societies who were responsible for expanding the market for trips in this period.

Finally, central government played a part in determining the shape of the excursion crowd at this time. Railway development in Britain had been largely left to the private sector rather than planned by the state, as was the case with other countries such as France and Belgium. Central government only constrained activities where there was cause for serious concern, although Gladstone would have been keen to bring the railways into state control, similar to the General Post Office.[126] Many members of parliament however played roles in the fast developing railway industry in the 1840s, known collectively as the 'railway interest', a very powerful group which included landowners and lawyers who grew rich as a result of railway development. The 'railway interest' was able to influence legislation, particularly in the early days, but growing pressure and legislation from the Board of Trade gradually shaped operational and safety issues from the 1840s.[127] Despite its relatively light hand on the control of the railways, government moves in the 1840s dramatically shaped the development of excursion trains.

Firstly there was the level of government duty, originally imposed in 1832, at ½d a mile for every four passengers carried, leading to various strategies by companies to minimise the effects of this. For example, in August 1840, the Newcastle & North Shields Board gave permission for a Saturday excursion trip at half price, described as free in one direction (to reduce the duty), to Tynemouth for pupils of Gateshead Fell National School.[128] The Manchester & Leeds Railway was in favour of promoting excursions at this time, but in 1840 Captain Laws, their manager, reported on the problems with passenger duty in relation to a requested cheap trip for 40,000 charity children from Manchester, to 'remove them from the scenes of vice and debauchery' during race week. Approaches to the Treasury to reduce the duty in these circumstances met with a stony response and the company finally decided to reduce the duty payable by selling 10,000 tickets and giving away 30,000.[129] In 1842 the passenger duty was changed from a mileage system to 5 per cent of gross receipts from passengers, and this was again seen to discourage some companies from offering excursions. Throughout the 1840s railway companies complained bitterly about the bureaucratic hoops they had to negotiate to secure remission of duty, constraining their flexibility to promote excursion trains at short notice.

The Parliamentary trains brought in by the Railways Act of 1844, the 'earliest and most drastic interference with railway companies in the conduct of their business', were associated with the remittance of passenger duty on third-class travel.[130] This led to a debate between government departments about whether excursion trains should be classed as Parliamentary trains and therefore remitted from duty, and whether this remittance should extend to classes on excursion trains other than the cheapest.[131] Several companies achieved remission from duty of all of their third-class traffic, despite their carriages not fulfilling the specification laid down in the Act.[132] There was a disagreement between the Railways Department and the Board of Inland Revenue, as the former approved excursions trains as exempt, sometimes even sanctioning open carriages for excursions. However, application had to be made for remission of duty and this had the effect of discouraging companies from responding to demand by putting excursions on at short notice. Companies had to complete a form in advance of running an excursion train, specifying the hour of departure, class of carriages and fares, in order to claim exemption, which caused them some problems, as for example the Lancashire & Yorkshire complained that sometimes an excursion train needed to be organised at less than twenty-four hours notice.[133]

In 1850 there was a dispute between the Railway Commissioners and the railway companies, when it was reported that passenger duty was remitted on 'all excursion trains' where fares were less than a penny a mile, except with certain companies such as the London & North Western Railway, and where proper notice had not been given (there was also a government circular reminding companies that trains needed to keep to their starting times to qualify).[134] Transport policy was inconsistent: a writer in 1851 compared the tax on railway excursions, which had been remitted, to that on omnibus travel, which was still three halfpence a mile.[135] Over the next few years there were legal moves between the Board of Inland Revenue and companies, especially the London & South Western Railway, who did not include excursion trains in their returns to government for duty, as they considered them exempt, and the government sought to reclaim the duty payable on these. It appears that by 1852, however, railway companies, including the London & South Western, *were* paying duty on all excursions, presumably because of the threatened legal action by the Inland Revenue.[136] In 1855 Captain Galton, in his report to the government on the railways, indicated that 19,000 excursion trains had been approved for exemption from duty, mostly from London and 'towns in the manufacturing districts', but that was an underestimate of the total excursions running.[137] Thus a very confusing picture is painted of the status of the excursion train with regard to passenger duty in this period, but nevertheless the system for authorising exemption from duty reduced the flexibility of the railway companies to respond speedily and flexibly to fluctuating market needs.

Central government also played an important part in responding to safety concerns, which received extensive press coverage in the 1840s.[138] In 1844 Captain O'Brien of the Board of Trade issued a circular highlighting the dangers of working excursion trains with multiple engines, and recommended a maximum of two engines per train. He also emphasised punctuality, the lack of which caused a number of accidents.[139] This circular was generally supportive of the new excursions, expressing a view from the Board of Trade not 'to suppress excursions of this character' and highlighting their 'useful influence' on the community. After a number of well-publicised accidents resulting from the unmanageable size of trains, the high speeds and lack of guards, Pasley, the government inspector of railways, produced a report in 1846, which was more prescriptive than supportive of excursions.[140] It discussed two alternative means of conveying excursions, either carrying all passengers in one train with a number of locomotives, or dividing them into several trains following at intervals. As the first option was regarded as having too much potential for fatal accidents, the report made a number of recommendations relating to the second option, which could still give rise to collisions unless it was properly managed. Firstly that no monster trains should be drawn by two or more engines, successive trains to be used with one engine each although a second engine could be used for steep inclines, and intervals to be not less than three minutes, corrected by signal at every station. Secondly he recommended that there should be no goods wagons used to carry passengers. Thirdly there should be not less than one guard per eight carriages and passengers should not be allowed to sit on the roof of first or second class, or on the side or end of open third class. And fourthly that trains should not be allowed to carry more passengers than their capacity. These recommendations had important implications for the way that excursions were handled from that time, although some were frequently ignored, such as the use of goods wagons.

While the government played no direct part in the provision of the excursion trains, because of its responsibilities for safety it was obliged to observe their operation closely.

Each accident was investigated by the government in great detail, with interviews with railway staff and passengers. From 1854, reports were published earlier after an accident, with attendant press publicity, encouraging public opinion to put pressure on railway companies as a result.[141] During the 1850s there were around six accidents a year involving excursion trains, often contributing around 10 per cent to the total number of accidents to passenger trains, with around 20 per cent in 1859.[142] In 1857 and 1860 in particular there were a large number of excursionists injured, almost 40 per cent of the total of all those injured in passenger train accidents. The figure of 19,000 excursion trains approved for 1855 (see page 88) could be compared with the overall traffic data for that year, when 64 million third-class passengers were carried, from a total of 119 million passengers overall. If an average of around 500 passengers per excursion train is used, then this suggests that in 1855, around 9.5 million passengers were travelling in excursion trains, 8 per cent of the total traffic.[143] Excursion passenger deaths and injuries almost always contributed a proportionately greater number of deaths and injuries when compared to the total of passenger traffic, demonstrating the large numbers of passengers conveyed on these trains and unsafe conditions.[144] The dangers extended well into the 1860s.

Central government played a constraining effect on excursions, but the important and enduring effect of the 1844 Act was to improve the comfort and convenience of services across the board, including excursion trains, for the masses who could not afford first- or second-class fares. Although these only created a limited number of improved 'Parliamentary' services, the move stimulated the railway companies to focus on the importance of third-class travel more generally.[145] The Board of Trade recommended a certain quality of third-class accommodation under the Act for Parliamentary accommodation, advising on aspects such as light and ventilation, weather protection, night lamps, seats with backs, sufficient doors and also windows for 'look-outs'. While these were good intentions, the influence of the government was not strong enough to force companies to comply, and the carriages which tended to be used often failed to live up to these standards. On a pleasure trip people might expect a window view, but most windows were very small and high up, with no glass, thus it is not surprising that third-class passengers were said to prefer open carriages. Carriages would be packed with excursionists, for example the Great Western carriage had a capacity of fifty-nine passengers, with limited ventilation usually provided by fixed louvred shutters. Lighting was rare: only the Manchester & Birmingham had night lamps; most third-class carriages in the 1840s and 1850s were unlit, as gas lamps were not used until the 1860s, and there was no heating.[146] To make matters worse, as this only applied in theory to the Parliamentary traffic, at times excursion traffic might be carried in goods wagons and trucks. Thus the excursion carriages were either open trucks or cold, dark and stuffy carriages, with bare boards to sit on, and these did not improve until after the 1860s.[147]

Despite the uncomfortable conditions however, the government legislation had the effect of changing how people felt about travel at this time, when thousands of ordinary people realised the potential of the new services in enabling them to travel away from home. While transport histories have focused on the technology and on the buildings, the locomotives, bridges and stations, there has been little to date on how ordinary people experienced the new excursions.

Chapter Seven

What Was It Really Like?

'and now what Bedlamitish sounds meet my ear! Singing on every hand, shouting on every hand, swearing on every hand, whistling on every hand, and the mad iron monster at the front rearing away like nothing else.'[1] *(Manchester, 1860)*

Lancashire handloom weaver Benjamin Brierley painted a vivid picture of his cheap railway trip from Ashton to Worksop in 1860. Embarking in a crowd on a railway excursion, possibly for the first time, will have been memorable and pleasurable for those who took part in early trips in the 1840s and 1850s. Certainly for the mass of ordinary people, being part of a large excursion crowd was remarkable, with a significant impact on how they saw new things and how they behaved. While in some areas steamboat excursions were still providing an alternative option, for many people the railway train was the only way in which they could escape temporarily to new places and landscapes. As a result their perceptions of time and landscape, people and places would change.

There were a few brief accounts of railway excursions in the press in the 1840s, but longer articles started to appear in the late 1850s, featuring male travellers writing about a trip, often for the first time, and mostly taking a positive attitude to this new experience. By 1860, excursion trains had become commonplace, and the characteristics of the crowds which they created were to give rise to an element of snobbery by other people caught up in such occasions. *Punch* featured humorous and often cynical accounts of tours undertaken by middle-class travellers who encountered working-class excursionists around this period. One correspondent described catching an excursion train full of 'pleasure-seekers' when he was returning from a holiday in North Wales back to London. It was the day of the Oswestry fair and the excursion train was extremely overcrowded:

'drawn by a very wheezy and feeble-bodied engine, and invariably arriving everywhere half an hour after its time: thus providing to passengers the additional excitement of arising from the probability of being run into by the next express; which conveying wealthy people on business cannot of course be retarded by any paltry considerations for the lives and limbs of poor people on pleasure… I was a good deal gnawed about the legs by a pig, which travelled with us in a sack, under the restraint of which garment it seemed not unnaturally impatient. Its companion and proprietor seemed highly to enjoy the little diversion afforded by his four-legged friend. I was also much poked in the face by the umbrellas and parasols of unprotected females tumbling into the carriage in a state of excitement…nor was my enjoyment materially heightened by the playful humour of several large and energetic young gentlemen, whom I found to be ironfounders in various ways, and who, no doubt from habitually talking against the roar of blast furnaces and the clang of steam hammers, had acquired the practice of invariably roaring at the top of their voices, and who made me an involuntary confident of their amours, adventures and achievements during the fair…'[2]

Etiquette guides were produced, advising how the middle classes might come across this new species. *The Railway Traveller's Handy Book*, published in 1862, advised that excursion trains, while useful for 'the humbler classes and the economically inclined', were 'not best calculated for the ordinary traveller':

'The confusion and bustle, the irregular times of departure and arrival, and the boisterous company into which one is thrown, although of very little moment to the person who only has a travelling bag, and who sets off for a few days' jaunt, are ill-calculated for the railway traveller who has a sober journey to perform, and is burdened with its attendant responsibilities and cares.'[3]

The emphasis here is of course on the 'traveller', regarded as a higher status than trippers or excursionists, and almost always based on class distinctions.[4] Thus the middle-class 'traveller', forced to mix with working-class excursionists, might be prevented from being 'serious' on such a journey. Furthermore, it was assumed that only the higher status traveller could appreciate in sufficient depth what he or she was seeing on their travels.

There are accounts which offer a sensory description of the experience, in comparison to the flat reports of observers. One appeared in the *Daily News* in 1855.[5] Entitled *An Excursion Train*, this is an anonymous account of a cheap trip from London to Portsmouth on the London & South Western Railway, and was originally published in *Household Words*. It appears on the surface to be an amusing account of a personal experience. However an exploration of the anonymous writer is revealing: Robert Brough, journalist and poet, was celebrated as a parodist who supported working-class causes and held a 'deep vindictive hatred of wealth and rank and respectability.'[6] It is actually a semi-fictional satirical piece, he wanted to highlight stereotypes and mock prevailing attitudes to excursions at the time.

Unusually the writer's focus is on the journey itself: 'we are not going to write a guidebook…all we have to do with at present is the excursion train.' He asserts his class perspective by defending the 'dense crowd of pleasure seekers' waiting at the station, as no less unmannerly than those at the opera. He highlights the wide range of travellers who might be found in an excursion carriage, with the effect of a mixing of classes in close proximity which had not previously occurred. He portrays his fellow excursionists as 'all very common people, doubtless' but then suggests that they needed to enjoy themselves and so 'acquaintances were quickly formed'. Typically all were soon in friendly communication, 'chattering away as busily as though we had been friends for years', and he deduces that 'there is some hidden excitant in excursion trains to conversation.' He compares his new experiences to those of the past, recalling previous long journeys in a first-class carriage, where there was hardly any conversation. He satirises that travel 'in an open carriage by an excursion train' is 'horribly plebeian' and 'low', especially so because it is so 'disgracefully cheap' – around 2s 6d per hundred miles. The use of 'vulgar' open carriages for excursions, even in 1855, is confirmed here, while at the same time he criticises the alternative third-class carriage (see page 89). Even worse the writer says that he has travelled on such a train on a Sunday, mocking Sabbatarians. He suggests that his nearest neighbour, a shoemaker 'he blushed to believe', must be depraved, as not only was he travelling on a Sunday but he was also smoking, which was against the regulations and subject to a 40 shilling fine at the time. Here the open carriage was an advantage as generally it was impossible to police smoking on trains at this time, despite numerous complaints, and railway companies eventually had to allow it.[7]

A young gentleman in the corner had avoided talking to fellow passengers and so the writer imagined he would be of a higher class – possibly a lawyer's clerk, smoking cigars, and drinking brandy and water from a glass rather than a bottle. It was assumed that this young man was embarrassed to be seen in such company. Another gentleman seemed ill at ease, trying unsuccessfully to sleep and frowning. The writer suggests he was a businessman saving money by using an excursion fare, rather than seeking pleasure. (On the return journey he was surprised to see the businessman again, as he assumed he would have sold his return ticket on to someone wishing to get from Portsmouth to London cheaply.) He also describes a pale-faced boy singing and suggests satirically that the boy should not be singing on a Sunday, but then neither should the birds. The passengers were puzzled by another man, who seemed to be very knowledgeable about the railway – 'all the mysteries of railway signals, branch lines, sidings, switches, points' – and who explained that he took excursion trains very regularly, with his wife and child, to get out of the town. The point was well made that the excursion crowd was complex in profile and motivation. The writer finally takes a moral stance in common with many writers and reformers of the day, by suggesting that the passengers would all have been better fitted for work the following week because of their excursion.

Another anonymous account featured in the *Preston Chronicle* in 1857.[8] *A Sketch of my First Visit to London; By a Native of one of the Northern Counties* was written by an excursionist visiting London for the first time. He had travelled from Preston on a cheap three day trip offered by Mr Marcus in 1857.[9] In writing this account he wanted to offer his first impressions which he felt would be valuable to others because they are 'vivid and striking', compared to those from people who know London well. He is also prescriptive, full of advice, describing the many arrangements which helped to make the excursion a positive experience. There had been a savings bank to prepare for the trip, and lectures which primed excursionists with what they would see in London, especially at the Crystal Palace exhibition of arts and of machinery. A printed programme of 'objects to be seen and visited' was drawn up, on the back of which was a rough map of London with bridges, leading streets, places to visit, and cab and omnibus fares from stations. One of the people involved with the trip had prepared a list of places to see en route and passengers also had a railway map and timetable. The writer also offers advice on cheap lodgings.

The focus of this account was on both the journey and the destination, with a very detailed description of all the places he visited in London, but the novelty factor focuses on London itself and its buildings rather than the train journey. His background preparation appears to include much reading about London and its buildings in advance, with references to travel guides and published pictures of buildings. He was unprepared however for the 'unparalleled' impact of the Crystal Palace building, its 'boldness, magnitude, and magnificence', and felt it surpassed his expectations. He had read his Mayhew, and acknowledged at the end of the account that his experience did not include the scenes of misery which he knew were underlying London life.[10]

From his own perspective it was a significant experience in his life, worthy of a lengthy article in the press, but also a big event, shown by the fact that even though the journey started at 5.30am, 'hundreds of friends were present at the station to see our departure.' The excursionists visited St James's Park, where they waited to see Queen Victoria pass from Buckingham Palace 'to hold a drawing room at St James's', and the writer suggested that 'it is most difficult to persuade a fellow who has been "at London seeing the Queen", that he is not a person of extraordinary importance.' A subtle change was occurring as a result of excursion travel, as ordinary people might feel that they had enhanced their standing in the community by using the excursion train to visit London, impossible beforehand. Such activity might be seen, therefore, to create an aura of distinctiveness around a person, but as so many more people were visiting London now on excursion trains 'there is not such a halo of importance hovering around the London visitor as formerly.' The writer appeared to be an ordinary worker, securing himself against unnecessary expense by bringing his own refreshments for use en route. He complained about having to use 'bullock-truck' carriages to get to Crystal Palace and criticises the way that differential outfits were worn by waiters in the various classes of refreshment room at the Palace: while some wore black with white chokers, he had to be content with others in 'fustians or corduroys'.

There were many references to the differences in landscape, parks, housing and buildings, and even conversation, between Lancashire and London. He felt that the machinery on display at the Crystal Palace was inferior to that in the cotton mills of Lancashire, and not worthy of viewing. He was also disappointed by the workshop. He was frustrated in his view of the landscape outside the carriage window, complaining that it was not as remarkable as he might have hoped, as the speed of the train (40 miles an hour) prevented passengers from seeing much, as did the presence of cuttings and tunnels. Moreover he grumbled that 'you are continually whizzing past cottages, farmhouses and little villages or towns…you find a tiresome sameness.' He described the typical architectural features of cottages and houses, but was unhappy at not being able to see much of towns, where the approach was via a cutting or on ground level. This new opportunity to look at the landscape in a different way therefore failed to live up to his expectations.

An anonymous account in the *Daily News* in 1857 was written by a Clerkenwell excursionist from London, entitled *A Vacation of the Million; Being Notes by an Excursion-Trainer*. He referred to himself as 'but a hewer of wood and drawer of water', reflecting a labouring life, but admitted that he had some experience in writing articles for the press, although was not 'a professional scribe'.[11] The account described a day trip on the South Western Railway from London to Salisbury.[12]

The trip appears to have been an impulsive idea, motivated by posters on the walls and the idea of the 'wondrous stones on Salisbury Plain'. His descriptions of the buildings he passed however seem remarkably knowledgeable, so he must have been very well-read, despite his background. He reinforced his class early on however, by referring to 'we, who cling to the lower spokes of Fortune's ladder', as opposed to the 'upper ten thousand blazing away at the moorcock' at holiday time. In his case the novelty factor related to his destination, Salisbury and its Plain, rather than the journey, but the account focused on both, injecting humour and observations. He compared the hedgerows along the road to those which he knew in Regent's Park and remarked that it was the first time he had seen inside an ancient cathedral. He suggested that despite press criticism, excursionists normally favoured open carriages, because of the fresh air and open sunlight, and that these always filled up first, thus to some they were less uncomfortable than the closed carriages. However on this particular trip, the London & South Western open carriage became a disadvantage at one point, when the train stopped between two high embankments 'where they remained at the mercy of the juvenile population who took stock of the train from the railway bridge.'

The writer reflected on how these new travel spaces were very sociable, commenting that 'there is no place more favourable for forming acquaintances than an excursion train, and before we got well clear of the tiles and chimney pots we were all thick as oats in a bin,' and people were getting out their hampers and bottles. This extended to the sharing of desirable objects of consumption: 'my cheroots become public property, and everyone's glass is at my service – the golden age has come again, and we have all things in common.' On reaching Salisbury, he and a new companion walked around 10 miles to Stonehenge. Despite the solitary nature of this tourist destination they were not immune from modern-day tourist concerns, as they were approached by a guide who gave them information about the monument, selling them what they regarded as an expensive postcard. Somewhat surprisingly, after walking a further 10 miles back to Salisbury, they were in time to catch their return train.

Hand loom weaver and working-class writer Benjamin Brierley wrote his lyrical piece about a Whit Saturday trip in the *Manchester Times* in 1860.[13] In *Our "Cheap Trip" and How We Enjoyed It* he recalled what in many respects must have been a very uncomfortable experience. Brierley was well-read from an early age, later helping to set up a mechanics institution in his home town of Failsworth, near Manchester, so he was prepared for the geography of his trip.[14] By 1860 he was still working as a silkwarper, but had published his first articles three years previously.

This amusing and poetic piece recalled the emotions of his experience, painting a vivid and characterful picture of the excursion train, focusing on the journey and the destination. Brierley had walked to Ashton for a 6am start on the trip to Worksop on the Manchester, Sheffield & Lincolnshire Railway, with the aim of searching for evidence of Robin Hood.[15] The cost of his ticket was 1s 6d for the return trip across the Pennines. His emotional state suggests that he was apprehensive the night before the trip, with dramatic dreams about dangerous trains. The account reflects Brierley's thoughts about space and place; he referred to 'rushing betwixt two worlds that appear to be whirling round in counter motion', towards a richer, greener landscape full of promise.

On arriving at Ashton station, Brierley received several invitations from people to join them in their already swarming carriages, a 'seeming endless line of chattering humanity', but he is looking for some particular friends of his. He spotted them in what he refers to as a 'tripe stall, or "hot pea establishment" on wheels.' This was in fact a luggage wagon covered with canvas on poles and fitted out with seats. He was hauled on board and 'safely deposited betwixt two rough, unyielding benches' and 'surrounded by a lot of fellows in whose society I intend to pass a pleasant day', including an artist and a blacksmith. The 'box' was cold and draughty, the occupants had to lift up the canvas to see the landscape, and they were drenched on the way home, four hours in pouring rain. Brierley's description of the sounds of singing, whistling and swearing and 'the mad iron monster at the front' which enveloped him (see page 91) blended his personal experience with the technology of his transport. He is one of the few writers who refer to this new technology, with several worrying details, such as the discomforts of the impact of one carriage against another:

> 'Bang, bang, bang go all the carriages, one after another; each bumping into its neighbour like a battering ram; the bufferless 'tripe stalls' getting the heaviest shocks. Heads are brought into mutual contact without introduction.'

Music was an important part of Victorian working-class culture and informal singing was a common occurrence in accounts of excursions, both individual and group singing.[16] In Brierley's account it was sociability and music that were helpful in lifting spirits, used as a frequent defence against the dehumanising experiences in poorly managed trips. Brierley went on to recall travel habits which had been learned from the era before the new railway excursions: at Worksop the excursionists headed for Manor Park, where 'our excursion people have scattered themselves over the lawns as they would have done had they been at Dunham' (a canal boat destination for short trips from Manchester).

These working-class accounts paint a picture of what it was like to ride on a railway excursion at this time, rarely depicted in transport history. The novelty of such early journeys was demonstrated by the way that crowds lined the sides of the lines and the bridges to view the spectacle of the mass railway excursion. At times though, novelty was used as a moral weapon: the Bishop of London, in opposing Sunday railway excursions in 1835, compared steamboat excursions to those offered on the new railways, arguing that as the former were established and therefore no longer novel, then they were less likely to engender 'excitement' and 'impulses' arising from 'rapid assemblages'.[17] There were certainly concerns about whether the crowds generated from this novel experience might turn into an angry mob.

As railway excursions became more routine during this period, then novelty in a trip was more likely to feature a destination than the technology of the journey. Some people learned to express an appropriate amount of 'wonder' at the novelty of sights and sounds on their excursions, while others had not learned the 'proper' reaction.[18] In his autobiography, Coventry ribbon weaver Joseph Gutteridge records an excursion trip to the Great Exhibition in 1851, 'the longest journey I had ever undertaken,' and reflects on his unbounded delight and pleasure at seeing the Exhibition: '[the treasures] kept my mind in a state of continual excitement for some time.'[19] He gives no details of the journey, despite its novelty; the excitement about the exhibits arose from his own interests in craftsmanship and physical science. By contrast George Whitehead, a village wheelwright from West Yorkshire, displayed neither comment nor emotion when recording his first and only trip to London the same year in his diary, but then this was the style he adopted throughout his diary keeping: 'Robert Bell and George Whitehead went to London to see the Great Exhibition &c June 24th and came back July 3rd 1851.'[20] For Brierley, the aspect of the trip which represented novelty was visiting Worksop for the first time, although he also described the concern his fellow passengers felt at their first experience of crossing over a viaduct.

It was even possible for a person to change their sense of identity following an excursion experience, as discussed by the London excursionist on page 94, aware of the distinctiveness around a person who had visited London. In a further example, from a press report in August 1850, a 'rustic', a constable from a village near Mansfield, had been persuaded to take a cheap trip up to Hull, by rail and steamer. Inexperienced in seaports, when the time came to catch the steam packet from New Holland over the river Humber to Hull he was very nervous of entering the ship. He was astonished by what he saw but very happy to be back in Nottinghamshire again: 'getting to England again' he reportedly vowed not to go again.[21] Here the steamer had underlined his sense of a borderline between the known and the unknown, and reinforced his sense of Englishness. As he had not seen a seaport or a steam packet before, his journey was unhappy and bewildering, and his main concern was that his fire should not be out when he returned to his home.

Most modern writers focusing on the experience of railway travel offer a particularly middle-class perspective. In describing the experience of viewing landscape scenes through the window of an enclosed carriage this is not the typical crowded excursion cattle truck. They seem to present the third-class traveller as something 'other', almost a zoological specimen, to be disregarded when examining travel.[22] Where accounts have focused on the 'panoramic view' from the first or second-class carriage, this fails to reflect the experience of the masses travelling in third-class carriages, often with small highly placed windows, or indeed the open wagons which were frequently used on excursion trains, which offered a 360 degree view, similar to that from a cart.

Excursion agents and publishers realised at an early stage the importance of the market for travel guides, for example the Liverpool & Manchester Railway published guide books as soon as it opened, in 1830. In July 1835 the *Tourist's Companion: or, the History and Directory of the Scenes and Places on the Route by Railway and Steamer from Leeds and Selby to Hull'*, a neat pocket volume, was advertised by Edward Parsons of Leeds, although at 4s clearly for a middle-class market.[23] In 1846 Joseph Dearden produced a *Hand-book to the Cheap Trip*, selling for 3d, to support an excursion from Preston to Liverpool.[24] Importantly, the democratisation of the railway excursion encouraged Abel Heywood of Manchester to produce an extensive range of detailed penny guides in the 1860s, with around eighty towns covered by 1871, from Aberystwyth to York. Although cheap lithography had supported the production of many more texts and guidebooks to support the new travellers, these had almost all previously been aimed at a middle/upper-class market.[25]

The experience of participating in an excursion featured a distinctive kind of sociability in these new spaces, a sense of enjoying being in a crowd and taking pleasure in this new company, reinforced by much chattering and singing. The joys of sociability and intimacy arising from railway excursion crowds were highlighted in Edwin Waugh's diary entry about a trip to Blackpool in September 1849. Waugh was a journeyman printer and later clerk, who was to become famous for his dialect writings featuring Lancashire. The diary describes how Waugh:

> 'woke at five... walks to Salford Station... to his delight he is slowly joined by a throng of excursioners, working people, especially working girls. Being taken up by the throng of upwards of two thousand people at the station he exclaims, 'I felt that the world was one house, and all men and women in it dear relations.' ... He finds in his carriage there and back, the company of working women and an old teetotal reedmaker, also a 'modest-looking young man, seemingly of the clerk species.' ... From nature, from the sea, he derives pleasure, but most of all from the 'one house' of all the men and women of the world.'[26]

Interestingly, recent studies have suggested that activity such as spending long periods with others in close proximity can release oxytocin in the brain, and engender greater empathy towards others, promoting pro-social behaviours, and it might be argued that this was taking place in these situations.[27] Waugh was completely taken up with the excitement of the experience, with the sheer scale of the numbers of people involved within close proximity, in new public space at the station, and by the pleasurable social relations reinforced once he entered the travel space of the carriage. On another occasion, Waugh described a visit to Milnrow, near Rochdale, in 1850, when he took a seat on a train 'among a lot of hearty workmen and country folk coming back from cheap trips to Wales and the bathing places on the Lancashire coast.'[28] Waugh told how the people around him were 'communicative and comfortable' and how a collier lad started to sing a long 'country ditty'. It was very crowded, and latecomers squashed themselves into seats under protest from others who said they were 'too full o'ready'. He adopted a familiar phrase sometimes used in the press in recording that they were like a 'street on wheels', featuring the varied nature of the crowd, with people closely packed, forcing them to develop relationships.

Indeed the enclosed space of the carriage forced excursionists into interaction with a variety of strangers, often over a long journey, connecting to others in a very public way.[29] Participants may indeed have been forced into sociability by the lack of a view, with the closed space obliging them into intimacy. To some people however there were disadvantages in participating in this new adventure, namely the distinctive effects of an enforced sociability. In 1842 a writer to the press about the railways around Preston spoke of two types of traveller – 'those persons who have no regard to privacy on their journey – to whom the first person they meet is the most welcome companion', and another class, 'who go there as a party of their own, and to whom the motley assemblage, inseparable from motley intercourse, is an intolerable annoyance.'[30]

It was not only the railway carriage of course which offered people a sociable experience on excursions. As early as 1828, a personal account appeared in the press of a steamer trip to Boulogne and back for 20 shillings entitled 'A cheap trip to France' (thus the phrase 'cheap trip' commonly used to label railway excursions in the nineteenth century, did not start with the railway). The confines of the steamer and the experience of being on a joint adventure encouraged a very sociable crowd of some 250 people – mostly male, who formed themselves into groups 'with tongues wagging with a volubility which put all restraint at defiance', with some taking the opportunity to 'lie most confoundedly'.[31] As the railway confined excursionists to the constricted space of a single carriage or wagon, it enforced sociability, because of its constraints and the sheer scale of the numbers of participants travelling long distances.

The conditions experienced by these new working-class excursionists featured aspects such as darkness, discomfort and a fear for personal safety, and the rare personal accounts evoke a realism which contrasts strongly with the clichéd descriptions of press reporters. An animal theme was used frequently in describing the experience of a trip, implying that participants often felt dehumanised in the crowded and confined public space of the carriage. Chartist Julian Harney described the typical West Yorkshire third-class carriages in the early 1840s as 'detestable pig-pens on wheels', uncovered in all weathers and with no seating.[32] Such complaints appeared frequently in the press, alongside other complaints about lengthy delays, both problems caused by the severe overcrowding of trains. A letter writer signing herself 'an old woman' complained of conditions on board the charity railway trip from Preston to Fleetwood in July 1850, when she was overcome by the heat, crowds and delays. She wrote that 'the carriages were only adapted to convey half the number that really did go; and yet there we were, clustered together like so many cattle, some of us nearly exhausted with heat and thirst.'[33] Other animal comparisons were used: a correspondent complained about a trip from Leeds to Liverpool in August 1852 on the Lancashire & Yorkshire Railway, when on the return trip the crowd was too large for the train and people were 'bundled into the carriages and packed more like dogs than human beings, with no other alternative but to ride on top or be left behind.'[34] Observers sometimes took up this theme: a reporter described the Great Western Railway excursion trip in September 1850 from Oxford to Southampton as having second-class and open carriages or cattle trucks. Only 400 people travelled because of this and they were heard to ask for the 'drovers', whom they thought should be provided. Once in the carriages they started bleating and bellowing.[35]

There were arguments by those who were affronted by the casual treatment of working-class travellers by railway companies. An angry account of an excursion appeared in the *Northern Star* in 1844:

'…the bad arrangements for entering the carriages, such as they were; the disgusting manner in which thousands of males and females were indiscriminately packed and crammed into these carriages; the disappointment and unpleasantness caused by the long delays at Liverpool, Manchester and on the road; the keeping of hundreds of people for an hour and more together soaking in the rain; the treatment many of the females received at Liverpool, from those whose duty it was to have assisted them in re-entering the sheep-pens: all, all, was truly disgraceful to even this most *miserable* management… A number of poor men sacrificed the money they had paid for their tickets, rather than allow themselves and wives, to quote their own words, 'to be packed in dirty stinking sheep pens, like lucifer matches in a box.' … But then, what matters; they were *only the labouring classes.* They were only those who toil excessively through a weary life, to feed, clothe, and support the *daily* 'pleasure trips' of their *superiors,* the idle, the useless and the cumbersome. Sheep-pens and pig carriages were good enough for *them.* What would the *swinish* multitude have else!'[36]

This type of account was rare in the press in presenting a class viewpoint, but typical of the working-class perspective of the *Northern Star*. It articulates the feelings that the working class deserved a better and more pleasurable leisure experience after their hard labours, and implies that they had been taken advantage of by profit-seeking railway companies. For some of the masses on these trips this may have been their first exposure to the kind of industrial conditions and sounds already endured by many of their fellow citizens.

For those already used to crowded living conditions, the levels of overcrowding and mismanagement by railway companies must have been severe to merit such comments, and it was only natural that the experience produced feelings of being dehumanised. The travellers felt that they were ignored as individuals, their concerns about lack of air, for example, ignored.

The railway line itself provided an extra layer of potential discomfort; Brierley referred to darkness in his description of Woodhead Tunnel as 'gray, dun, black as Hades', with a thick and vaporous air, 'the mouth of what might be Pandemonium'.[37] A colleague compared it to 'penetrating the very marrow of the backbone of Old England' and after ten minutes, upon emerging from the tunnel, everyone's face was covered in soot. Darkness often occurred as a theme, with worries about the unknown, about morality and comparisons with Hell in the new public space of the railway carriage or truck. Tunnels could be especially uncomfortable when people were travelling in open carriages. A self-taught operative in a Leeds woollen mill, J. Bradshawe Walker, wrote a song about the tunnel, which was designed to reassure travellers, by pointing out the 'wondrous things' still there above and the 'hidden store' below, and the eventual 'bright day' reappearing:[38]

THE TUNNEL GLEE

Bright day, farewell
'Tis darkness all,
We're out of call;
And who can tell
Of the wondrous things,
On feet, or on wings,
That are overhead—
The living and the dead;
Or what hidden store,
From the floor or before,
Lies darkling around,
Deep, deep in the ground?
High hills above us
We pant for the night.
Away! away!
All hail bright day.

There is a certain irony that this song, written by a working-class operative, was used

Plate 1. Stockton & Darlington Railway excursion handbill, 1859. (*National Railway Museum/Science & Society Picture Library*)

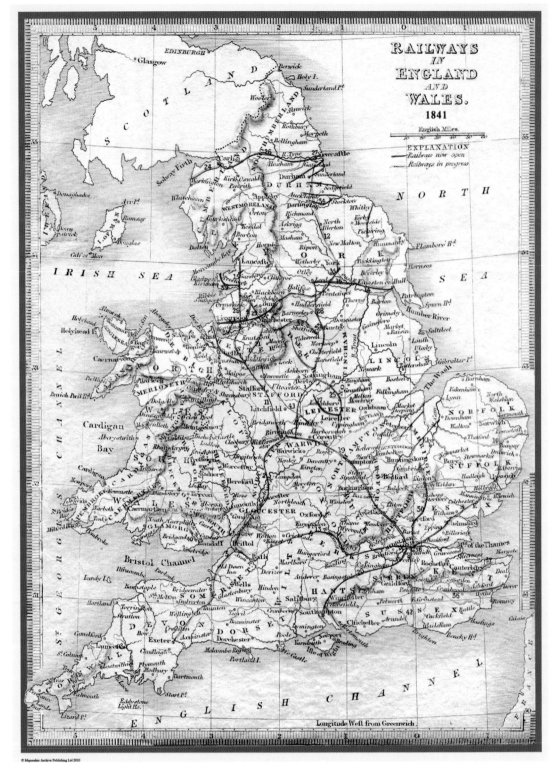

Plate 2. Bradshaw's Railway Map of England and Wales, 1841. (*Mary Evans Picture Library/Mapseeker Publishing*)

Plate 3. Crutchley's Railway Map of England and Wales, 1863. (*Mary Evans Picture Library/Mapseeker Publishing*)

Plate 4. Handbill for excursion trip to Leeds and Hull, on Good Friday, 9 April 1841 (*National Railway Museum/Science & Society Picture Library*)

Plate 5. Charles Rossiter, *To Brighton and Back for Three and Sixpence*. (© *Birmingham Museums Trust*)

THE SPIRITUAL RAILWAY.

THE UPWARD LINE.	THE DOWN LINE.

THE UPWARD LINE.

THE line to Heaven by Christ is made,
With Heavenly truth the rails are laid;
From Earth to Heaven the line extends,
And in eternal life it ends.

Repentance is the station, then,
Where passengers are taken in—
No fee for them is there to pay,
For Jesus is himself the way.

God 's word is the first Engineer,
It points the way to heaven so clear;
Through tunnels dark and dreary there,
It does the way to glory steer.

God's love the fire, his grace the steam,
Which drives the engine and the train,
All you who would to glory ride,
Must come to Chri t in him abide.

In first, second, and third class,—
Repentance, faith, and holiness,—
You must the way to glory gain,
Or you with Christ can never reign.

Come, then, poor sinner, now's the time,
At any station on the line,
If you'll repent turn from sin,
The train will stop and take you in.

If all these trains should by you pass,
And you are found in neither class—
When neither truth, or fire, or steam,
Can make you willing to get in:

Then, sinners, you will weep at last,
When Heaven is lost, and time is past,—
The Heavenly train are all gone by,
The Sinner must for ever die.

When all these trains at Heaven arrive
With all who did in Christ abide,
How sweet their voices, how the h
And praise their great eternal King.

The King eternal on his throne,
Announces that the trains are come;
There robes are ready to put on,
And Jesus says the words "Well done."

THE DOWN LINE.

THERE is a Railway downward laid,
Which God the Father never made,
But it was laid when Adam fell—
What numbers it conveys to Hell,

Six Thousand years are nearly gone
Since first this Railway was begun;
The road is wide, and smooth, and gay,
And there are stations on the way.

Appollyon is the Engineer,
His coat of arms his servants wear;
The steam his breath, which rivsh train
The fire is sin, which feeds the flame.

The first, second, and third train,
Are full of passengers within;
The steam is up, the flag enfurled,
How quick they move to yonder world.

Her fortune smiles, and pleasures gay,
At every station on the way;
Her dress and fashion you may find,
Of every sort and every kind.

The cheerful glass is drank with glee,
And cards and music you may see,—
Both old and young, rich and poor,
All standing near the station door.

Appollyon now begins to boast
Of numbers great—a mighty host,
Who are inclined their place to take,
To travel downward to the lake.

O! think on this while yet you may,
And stop your speed without delay;
O! leave the train that leads [to Hell,
If you with Christ would ever dwell.

Ladies and Gentlemen! it is true that some trades are flourishing, while others are in a state of starvation, the bearers are, and have been, out of employment a considerable time, and being destitute, and also strangers in this part of the country, they offer these few verses for sale (hoping that you will become
urchasers of us poor tradesmen).

RIAL & Co., Printers, 2 & 3 Monmouth Court, 7 Dials.

Plate 6.   The Spiritual Railway song sheet. (*Courtesy of the Lester S. Levy Collection of Sheet Music, The Sheridan Libraries, The Johns Hopkins University*)

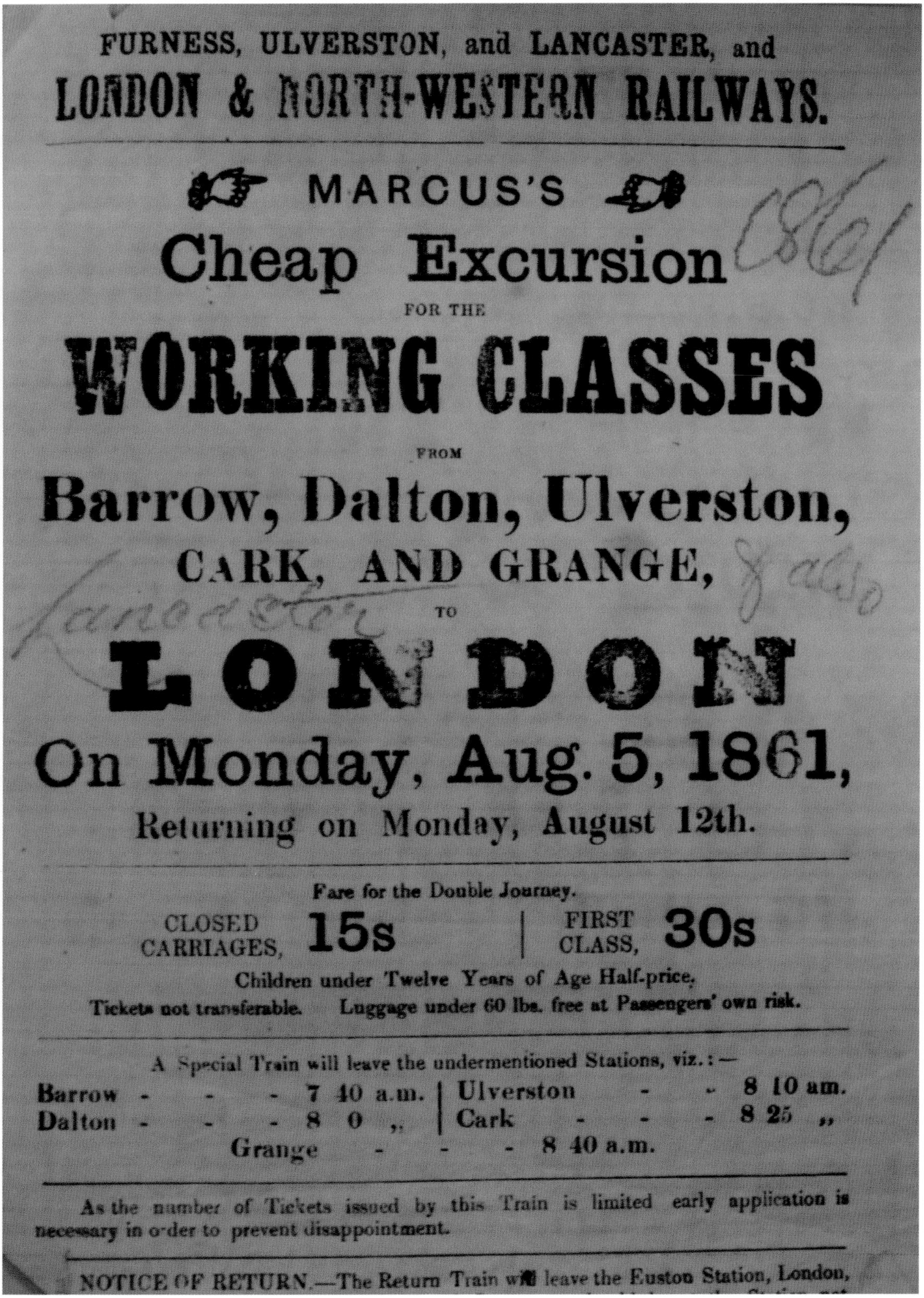

FURNESS, ULVERSTON, and LANCASTER, and LONDON & NORTH-WESTERN RAILWAYS.

☞ MARCUS'S ☜

Cheap Excursion

FOR THE

WORKING CLASSES

FROM

Barrow, Dalton, Ulverston,

CARK, AND GRANGE,

TO

LONDON

On Monday, Aug. 5, 1861,

Returning on Monday, August 12th.

Fare for the Double Journey.

CLOSED CARRIAGES,	15s	FIRST CLASS,	30s

Children under Twelve Years of Age Half-price.

Tickets not transferable.   Luggage under 60 lbs. free at Passengers' own risk.

A Special Train will leave the undermentioned Stations, viz.:—

Barrow	-	-	-	7 40 a.m.	Ulverston	-	-	8 10 am.
Dalton	-	-	-	8 0 ,,	Cark	-	-	8 25 ,,
		Grange	-	-	-	8 40 a.m.		

As the number of Tickets issued by this Train is limited early application is necessary in order to prevent disappointment.

NOTICE OF RETURN.—The Return Train will leave the Euston Station, London,

Plate 7. Marcus excursion handbill, 1861. (*National Railway Museum/ Science & Society Picture Library*)

Plate 8. The River Wall at Wylam Scars, Newcastle & Carlisle Railway, 1836. (*Science Museum/ Science & Society Picture Library*)

to help middle-class excursionists in one of Thomas Cook's first handbooks for a trip to Liverpool from Leicester in 1845, to reassure them that although they had left the open skies behind temporarily, these would return.[39]

Carriages were rarely lit at this time. A newspaper account in 1858 referred to the absence of lighting in crowded third-class carriages on the Lancaster, Preston & Carlisle lines, whereas first and second-class carriages were lit. This gave rise to moral concerns; the writer described the experience of a lady on a cheap trip to Leeds, where there was the 'huddling together [of] a mixed company of males and females in… carriages, all in darkness, to remain in this shameful, comfortless state till one o'clock in the morning', because of delays.[40] The darkness in the newly encountered space of the tunnel gave rise to confusing advice about how to behave. A correspondent to the *Daily News* in October 1853 referred to a previous complaint about the 'absurd principle of passengers keeping their places in railway carriages in the case of accidents' where it had been advocated that passengers would be better off getting out. He reflected on an excursion trip which he had undertaken, where the train came to a stop in the middle of a tunnel, and in his view it would have been very dangerous for passengers to have tried to find their way out safely. He highlighted the suggestibility of large crowds, where 'how soon a crowd of people lose their presence of mind and fly into the greatest danger,' and felt that if people were encouraged to leave their seats they would do this every time there was a stoppage.[41]

Excursions were often uncomfortable experiences, arising from factors such as dirty wagons, the use of open carriages, seating arrangements, the lack of refreshments and the sheer numbers in the crowds accommodated in a confined space. Such discomforts might however be compared to the steamer excursion, where problems arose from a different cause. For example, a steamer excursion from Preston to the Isle of Man and Dublin in July 1844, with 400 to 500 passengers, suffered from gale force winds: 'nearly every soul on board was sea sick…glasses were broken, furniture upset, and great numbers, powerless to help themselves, were stretched out at full length, moaning and retching on the dining table, forms, sofas and chairs, of the state room where they were tossed and rolled about with every motion of the vessel.'[42]

There are many descriptions of uncomfortable conditions on railway excursions from letter writers to the press in this early period. However there appeared to be few incentives for railway companies to consider the comfort of their passengers, to make technological changes and improve facilities, as demand was so high for excursions, but at the same time companies had not yet decided whether such activity was entirely profitable. The Preston & Longridge Railway used stone wagons for their excursion trains in 1842 (this line led to some quarries) and there were complaints that the sand and dirt was not removed from these before they were used on Sundays.[43] With regard to toilets, people had to manage as best they could, which would be difficult on a very long journey, as toilets on trains were not introduced until 1882, and then only on a few first-class services. There may have been gaps in the floor of some of the wagons, otherwise passengers would have to use the station urinals or trackside areas.[44]

In 1849 a writer to the *Daily News* who signed himself 'one of the million' complained of appalling conditions and company policy on a Sunday trip from London to Dover in May. Although he and a friend were in a third-class covered carriage on the way down, for the return trip these were locked, even though empty, and they were forced to use 'sheep cars'. The journey of 80 miles, after 7pm, left them 'begrimed and half suffocated by the soot, steam and smoke' to which they were exposed as a result. Fortunately a torrential rainstorm did not occur until after their arrival back in London.[45] Open carriages were frequently used, with varying opinions about the level of comfort afforded. It had been reported that the London & South Western Railway Company had stopped using open carriages for excursion trains in 1855, but it may be that these were still used later for excursion traffic. The North Eastern Railway was certainly using them in 1856, with travellers complaining of the conditions on an excursion train from York to Newcastle, a journey of 85 miles on a wet night.[46]

A writer in 1852 compared conditions in English railway carriages with those on the Continent and in America[47]:

'All railways are more or less infected with this vice [squalid economy]. They vie with each other in subjecting second and third-class passengers to insult and discomfort. An English second-class carriage would not be endured on the Continent or in America…in England you have to sit on wooden boards, guiltless of paint, with railway labourers, or criminals going to gaol, for your *vis-à-vis.*'

He went on to paint a vivid and amusing picture:

'the recent device of turning its interior into an advertising van… why, for two or three hundred miles, should his eyes be compelled to rest upon Eureka Shirts and Moses' Mart, and all the polychromatic typography, which announces paletots and pothouses?…A second or third-class carriage, conveying 120 persons in the month of July, with barred windows, and plastered over with pictorial shirts, siphonias, and tea shops, deserves a place in one of the circles of the *Inferno.*'

It appears from these comments that it was not only the barred windows of a congested third-class carriage but surprisingly the prevalence of numerous pictorial advertisements that offended him, a relatively minor component when compared to the other discomforts.

Refreshments were important to the excursionist on a long and tiring journey, where they might have no other means of getting food and drink cheaply. An account from Preston at Whitsun 1849 described the 'vast quantities of the "good things" of this life which the excursionists had provided themselves with; among which there must have been some of a savory and saucy nature, from the dropping of the gravy, &c, which oozed from the baskets as they passed along.'[48] Brough's account showed how numerous strategies were employed to conceal these. He described how some passengers brought out beer, and gin and water, and an old lady ate some bread and butter which she had smuggled in a basket under her shawl, despite the strict prohibition of luggage.[49] Sometimes passengers expected to use station facilities for their refreshment: a report on a Thomas Cook trip from the Midlands to Scotland in 1849 describes a thousand passengers arriving at Gateshead, having travelled about 200 miles: 'they appeared to be almost wholly absorbed by their corporeal wants' leading to an 'overwhelming rush to the refreshment-rooms', although in half an hour this was difficult as the train was longer than the station area. As a result the attendants were called on to serve bottled porter from the foot-boards of the carriages, some even after the train had started again. The third-class passengers on this train were in a sorry state as their carriages were uncovered and it had rained all the way from York, so the Midland Railway allowed them to wait at Gateshead until the next morning, for covered carriages.[50]

Accidents to excursion trains were widely publicised for several days afterwards in the regional and national press, but this did not appear to discourage the public from participating in such trips. There were many recorded instances of tragic circumstances on crowded trips, where dangerous practices led to injury and death. There is certainly evidence that the excursion train was more accident-prone than normal traffic during the 1850s and 1860s, getting worse towards 1860.[51] There was concern about the safety record of the huge excursion trains, such as a trip of 6,600 people in 1844 from Leeds to Hull, with 240 carriages and nine engines in a train consisting of four divisions.[52] In September 1844, on the North Midland line, 5,500 people took part in a trip from Sheffield to Hull in 170 carriages in three separate trains. On their return, some of the passengers climbed on the carriage roofs while the train was travelling slowly, despite advice to the contrary by the railway attendants. A collision between two of the trains, caused by a connecting chain breaking, led to passengers being thrown off the roofs and one was killed.[53] On a cheap excursion from Manchester to Alderley Edge, on the Manchester & Birmingham Railway, in September 1844 large crowds had turned up and forty-three carriages and wagons were needed for the 3,000 passengers. The wagons had no doors at the sides and no steps, and whereas at Manchester stepladders had been provided for passengers to climb in through the ends, there were no such ladders available at Alderley. A man was helping a 'respectable female' to jump out onto the buffers when the engine suddenly jerked and she fell between the rails with her son. The train went over her head, killing her instantly. The company later sought to blame this accident on a passenger who had apparently re-attached a chain.[54]

A trip in August 1850 from Scarborough, Bridlington and Driffield to Hull resulted in considerable discomfort for the passengers (although no death or injury). It ran into problems because it was completely overloaded on its return journey, with 48 carriages, 'literally crammed so full that porters could scarcely enter them to collect the tickets.'[55] It was reported that one of the problems was that 870 passengers had joined the trip at Driffield: 'On the arrival of the train a desperate rush was made, and a scramble for places ensued, many females being rather indelicately thrown down. The carriages were literally packed, and many were glad to gain a place even on top of the carriages.' It set off back from Hull at 9.30pm, at around 10 miles an hour and the engine finally broke down 2 miles north of Bridlington, at around 1am. A replacement engine was telegraphed for and eventually arrived at 4.30am. The passengers had been confined to their carriages until 3am, at which time they were given the choice of walking along the line to Bridlington or waiting for the engine to arrive. Those from Scarborough (2,500 excursionists) did not get back there until 6am.

Some excursion trains used huge third-class carriages which were very wide, leaving little space between the open side and the structures alongside on the line, and at the station. To add to the danger there were no protective bars over the apertures. A press correspondent noted in 1852 that South Eastern carriages were too wide for the line, especially as 'when men are boxed up 120 strong, in a single carriage, they will, if they can, put their heads out of the window,' putting them in danger of decapitation by lineside fixtures. A Bethnal Green silk weaver on a trip to Ramsgate that year had the misfortune to put his head out of the window as it passed through Ashford Station without stopping, and it was smashed to pieces against an iron pillar.[56]

A large number of reports described the accidents, both minor and serious, which befell excursion trains, as these had dramatic impact which attracted readers. It was especially so at this time because of the extensive amount of carriages overfilled with passengers and the minimal levels of staff available to take proper care of outings. Reports would be duplicated across a wide range of provincial press in other areas, as well as the London-based press, and often included gory details such as people left decapitated or limbless by trains running over them after they fell out of crowded carriages. There would occasionally be conflicting versions of such occurrences, with local publications doing their best to protect the reputation of a local company when a London-based correspondent over-egged the seriousness of an accident. In 1850 a fatal accident occurred on the South Western Railway, involving two heavily overcrowded excursion trains from London to Southampton. The first had difficulty climbing an incline and, as a result, the second train was used to push it up, causing a huge jolt, with passengers thrown around. Descriptions of the accident noted a fatality due to a passenger reportedly sitting on the edge of a carriage. However, in the same newspaper, in an article reprinted from the *Spectator*, a correspondent complained that traditionally such accounts were softened and falsified in favour of the company, that it was really reckless driving, and many passengers were injured from the jolting. As a result, the paper went on to suggest cynically that, as it seemed that the engine drivers were keen on colliding with each other, they should set up some 'jousting competitions', without passengers, with the prize being the chairman's daughter.[57]

There was a widespread acknowledgement that excursion trains could be dangerous; the *Times* suggested in 1852 that 'an excursion train is somewhat in the nature of a cannon ball, which sweeps along the surface of the line at uncertain intervals, and which does not invariably share the destruction it scatters around it in its progress.' As a result the writer suggested that the best place to travel was in the middle, to avoid collisions at the front and the rear. This report followed a serious accident at Bolton and the writer blamed the railway companies for allowing systems of cheap trains with little extra staffing, causing delays, and which were unsafe to ordinary traffic on the line.[58] A writer in the *Standard* in 1860, in the context of a proposed excursion of Volunteers to Paris, commented:[59]

> 'An excursion is a very dangerous thing; it is rather vulgar too. It fits well enough with those jobs which enterprising railway companies or speculators out at elbows are wont to get up to replenish their coffers. We involuntarily associate it with hurraing multitudes, too much good cheer, a certain unsteadiness of position, followed by breaking coupling-chains or running down inclines, collisions, smashed carriages, harrowing wounds, and violent deaths. These are things which sober men do not covet.'

In 1854 the *Morning Post* questioned how it was that passengers were so accustomed by now to the dangers of excursion travelling that insurance was necessary against the chances of death and mutilation: 'excursion trains, with passengers of boisterous mirth, roll over the wrecks of yesterday's mortality, no one present heeding or caring.'[60] Sometimes unsubstantiated rumours spread widely, for example in 1857 in a report which was copied to the provincial press throughout the country, it was stated in the *Hull Packet* that a young child had been smothered in a densely packed excursion train of ninety-six carriages (including cattle wagons) taking 3,600 passengers on a trip from Leeds to Hull. The *Leeds Mercury* later refuted this claim, although the *Hull Packet* did not.[61]

Sometimes passengers had to take their own actions to protect themselves from serious harm, as when a Great Northern Railway trip to London from Hull in September 1851 suffered a collision just north of London. A passenger explained how the train was stopped at Hornsey Station because of a luggage train ahead and that excursionists had got out of the train to stretch their legs. The guard ushered them into the train again and tried to lock him and his family into their carriage, but he refused. When he heard another train coming up behind and saw people behind jumping out, he dragged his wife and daughter out quickly and they all fell down the bank, together with his son who also jumped out. The other train, an excursion train from York, collided with theirs, lifting two carriages off the track and causing a large number of serious injuries.[62]

On occasions young people travelled by themselves. A young lad of eight was badly injured on an excursion trip from Huddersfield to York in August 1848. He had been in a cattle truck, and, when the train stopped near York station, he climbed onto the railing at the top of the van and fell off as an engine was passing. He lost an arm.[63] There were other vulnerable travellers, for whom excursion crowds were dangerous. A young man, deaf and dumb, took a trip to Liverpool from Colne in August 1850, on the East Lancashire Railway. Unfortunately, because of the confusion in the large crowd of 4,000 passengers, he was separated from his friends. His mother, several months later, advertised for news of his whereabouts, as he had not been seen again.[64]

Railway companies were often unprepared to meet the requirements of the sheer mass of participants. In 1860, on a Sunday school trip from Lancaster to Grange-over-Sands, despite the organisers having booked 500 places, the London & North Western Railway had no carriages available on the day and eventually provided 'two or three' assorted carriages in which to cram 400 passengers.

Surprisingly it does appear that most people actively enjoyed their excursion experiences, and were ready to accept all the potential problems and discomforts in order to achieve a level of exciting and memorable leisure mobility. Although railway excursion travel was dangerous at times, there are comparable examples of the danger of steamer excursions. A correspondent in the *Liverpool Mercury* described his alarming experiences with the *Snowdon* steamer on an August excursion from Liverpool to Rhyl in 1846, which ran aground at one point. The shore boats were not seaworthy, the steamer was not safely equipped and it was claimed that large quantities of liquor were drunk by the sailors aboard.[65]

It was possible for ordinary working people to use strategies involving cheap trip trains to look for work. Hannah Cullwick was a domestic servant who had a long term secret relationship with a gentleman, Arthur Munby, whom she eventually married. Helpfully she was encouraged to keep a diary of her activities by Arthur.[66] Although she was born and died in Shifnal in Shropshire, much of her working life was spent in London, Margate and other places in service. She recorded in 1864 taking a cheap train to Margate to look for work, using the Register Office for this, a widely used employment agency for domestic service at the time. In October 1867 she left work in Margate and took advantage of the last excursion from Margate to Crystal Palace, as the return fare was cheaper than a single to London. The train went to Penge and she walked with the rest of the 'excursionists' to Sydenham, around a couple of miles. She went in the Palace and then continued her journey to London, including an omnibus ride from London Bridge. People went to great lengths to use the once-in-a-lifetime opportunity offered by the extremely cheap excursions available. In July 1851, a labourer was reported to have taken a cheap trip to London from Huddersfield to see the Great Exhibition.[67] He paid 5s for his ticket and left on Tuesday evening after work with a few sandwiches in his pocket and 1s in his purse to pay for his entry. After seeing the exhibition the next day he ate his 'grub', drank from the crystal fountain and returned home that night, returning to work the following morning, without having to pay for accommodation or food while in London.

There are numerous examples recorded in the press of adventures on excursions. A tripper of 'humble circumstances', travelling from Blackburn to the Lake District for the day, wandered in the Lakes too far and missed his return train. As he had no money left he walked back 63 miles, arriving the next day.[68] Two servant maids from Durham were sent out by their mistress to the public washhouses with three weeks' dirty linen. When they arrived there they changed into their Sunday best, paid a washerwoman to do their washing, and set off to meet young men to take the train to Tynemouth for a day at the seaside.[69] Occasionally it all went wrong for the excursionist. John Topham from Bradford went on a trip to Liverpool in 1859. He complained bitterly about his experience on arrival in Liverpool, when he was charged with being disorderly. He had his pocket picked, was set upon by 'blackguards' in a public house; when he asked for directions to the docks his guide ran away with his hat, and finally, when he complained of short measure in a snuff shop, he was arrested and hauled off to the Bridewell.[70]

Ticket problems were numerous and, on at least one occasion, the crowd tried to use its mass to force a solution. Conditions published for a Great Northern Railway trip from York to the Great Exhibition in 1851 had allowed return within twenty-one days. A complainant to the press arrived at King's Cross in the morning (after nineteen days had elapsed) with other excursionists to catch the 7am excursion train, but they were prevented from getting a seat because of the large crowds. Further trains were promised but not delivered. Around 11am a placard was hoisted, announcing that no more excursions trains would leave until at least 9.30pm. At this point the crowd tried to use its power to gain entry to an ordinary train, but policemen prevented this. As a result the writer paid a further £1 9s for a fresh ticket on an ordinary train. Despite later letters to the company he received no compensation.[71] A similar problem occurred with an excursion train from Bristol to London in September 1851, when a writer and others could not get the return train as it was full, but they were denied access to later trains because of misleading information. One poor woman had only 4d and nowhere to go for the night, but she was taken pity on by another female.[72] Some problems occurred at the departing station: a correspondent to the *Daily News* in August 1852 complained that railway policemen prevented him from accompanying his wife and daughters on to the platform for a London & North Western Railway excursion trip from Euston Square. This caused great concern when one of the children became separated in the dense crowd. There was a further dispute about half fares which, although advertised, were not available.[73]

Railway companies sometimes took advantage of regular passengers by adding problematic excursion carriages to normal trains. A report of a court case at Preston in August 1852 described how a local dentist was accused by the East Lancashire Railway of avoiding paying the correct fare. He had tried to pay a 1s fare on a train, alleging it was an excursion train, but was told he was not in the correct section and in that case he should have already bought an excursion ticket. Evidence was presented that the excursionists were only in the third-class compartments at the front of the train (a trip from Preston to Liverpool), and the dentist was in a first-class carriage and refused to pay the 5s fare. He went on to state that he was unhappy that the company ran excursion trains which delayed the regular trains that he normally used, and that was the grievance he was trying to highlight. He was intending to pay the 5s for his normal return train back to Preston, but as it had turned into a cheap excursion train, crowded with many delays, he did not see why he should. He felt that the fraud was by the railway company on the public. His case was found guilty, but the magistrates agreed that the practice was common but highly improper.[74]

Sometimes unhelpful action by railway companies had the potential for disaster. A correspondent referred to a trip to the Isle of Man from Manchester in 1853 with his wife.[75] The return had been advertised as a 5pm special from Fleetwood, but the time had changed when they arrived there and they were put on the normal government train at 6.10pm. Excursionists were then removed from this train at Oldfield Road Station (Salford), half a mile from their Victoria destination, on a dark wet night at 10.30pm, with no platform. Passengers then had to cross the other railway line with their luggage in the dark and find their way to the station office. These weather conditions were very uncomfortable, as at this time it was usual for the working classes in Manchester to wear clothes made of fustian or cotton, which was not warm and absorbed the damp, whereas middle classes benefited from woollen cloth, flannel vests, scarves and shirts.[76]

Complaints by a writer to the *Manchester Times* in September 1854, about cheap trips to destinations such as London and Oxford, highlighted the need for a return date to be specified, the fact that luggage was limited and had to be stowed in their carriage rather than in a luggage van, and that tickets were not transferable.[77] A Liverpool man described his experience in April 1856 on a trip from Birkenhead to Manchester on the Birkenhead & Chester Railway, persuaded to do this 'by flaming placards posted on the walls in Liverpool.' Firstly, in order to catch the train from the Birkenhead side of the Mersey, he had to pay double the normal railway boat fare – increased from 1d to 2d. Secondly, the passengers had to disembark at Ordsall Station, 2 miles from the city. Thirdly, when he tried to catch a return train the following day, as advertised, he had to wait until 8.30pm, as the 5pm was not available, and so the excursionists did not arrive back in Birkenhead until 11.30pm, when there was no railway boat to take them back across the river. Finally a boat was arranged for 12.30am, but they were charged 6d for the fare.[78]

A writer described a cheap trip undertaken from Manchester to Blackpool and adopted a slightly more serious and snobbish attitude to the excursion crowd, but acknowledged the impact of this new leisure activity. He highlighted the differentiating role of ticket costs, explaining that the fare was 'half-a-crown, so that we are tolerably select.'[79] The passengers included teachers and scholars from various schools, and as the tide was out when they arrived 'the multitudes that had come by the various trains were spread far and wide along the beach.' He suggested that this excursion had brought various groups of visitors who had clearly not seen the seaside before, as they could not understand what was happening with the tides; he estimated that there were 10,000 excursionists in Blackpool at that point, with many factory workers, mechanics and dressmakers. At the same time he suggested that fashionable visitors already at the resort were contemptuous of the trippers. His friend reflected on the ground-breaking activity of the railway excursion, contemplating that their grandfathers would have been astonished to think that operatives might be able to travel for 50 miles to the seaside for a day's recreation, returning home for supper the same evening, and this might be compared with a man being known previously as a great traveller for travelling 10 miles from his fireside. The writer suggests that Watt and his fellow inventors were thus more influential on people's lives than philosophers and great writers.

These accounts help to show the conditions experienced by the new excursionists, but they had to meet another challenge. The size of the crowds, the places they visited and the day on which they travelled were to have an impact on the way that their behaviour was reported.

Chapter Eight

Men Behaving Badly?

'These cattle waggons had been fitted up with seats nailed across them, without backs, and with a light roof, which supported a stout linen sheet, attached by ropes to their sides. During the progress of the train, the excursionists cut the ropes…clambered up the sides of the waggon, in disobedience to the injunctions of the guard, and indulged in all sorts of gambols and tricks upon each other. One, more daring than the rest, ventured even to sit astride on the roof of the waggon, in spite of the remonstrances of the guard of the train, and some of his fellow passengers; and in that position he stooped his head as he passed under the bridges…at length, as the train approached a bridge 100 yards from the Cockerbar Station, and 6 miles to the south of Preston, he turned his back on the engine, and, not seeing the bridge in time to stoop out of its way, he received a cut across the back of his head, which caused his brains to protrude.'[1] *(Accident on Whit excursion to Liverpool on the East Lancashire Railway, 1857)*

The crowded excursion train offered many ways in which young men could assert their sense of playfulness. Twenty-two-year-old John Beckett, from Blackburn in Lancashire, and reported to be 'quite sober', was enjoying a summer trip to Liverpool in 1857 on an excursion train organised by the East Lancashire Railway, when he climbed on the roof, caught his head on a bridge and fractured his skull severely.[2] Surprisingly he seemed to have survived the immediate aftermath, as it was reported that he was taken to hospital where 'the operation of trepanning was successfully performed.' On this occasion the railway company was found to be at fault, responsible for heedlessly forming an ill-housed crowd and causing danger to excursionists. The accident report by Captain Tyler, Inspector of Railways, notes that the company had borrowed eight cattle wagons from the Lancashire & Yorkshire Railway to provide accommodation for extra passengers when the estimated crowd had swelled from 1,000 to 2,500. He commented that 'of all passengers, excursionists are the most difficult to control', and recommended that risks due to their imprudence and misconduct be lessened by railway companies providing safer carriages, and these must share some blame.

Third party evidence from observers and inspectors poses a number of questions. How did this sort of behaviour arise? How far did it represent general conduct? What was the role of the railway companies and other observers in shaping reports of behaviour? In searching for evidence to answer these questions, some reports of surprising consequences can be found. The press account of John Beckett's accident appears alongside that of another tragic event, this time when the pressure of a Liverpool excursion crowd caused a painter to tumble from his tall ladder when painting some lofty premises, breaking his thigh; he was a widower with two very young children who were dependent on him.[3]

Discomfort and danger proved insufficient disincentives against travel when balanced against the potential for new ways for ordinary people to enjoy themselves at leisure. There are many descriptions in the contemporary press of the behaviour of the travelling masses in the mid-nineteenth century, sometimes crowds who appeared to be 'behaving badly', although these descriptions are heavily outnumbered by the kind of traditional reporting about behaviour where all were decorous and the crowd was well received, with a safe return home. Concerns about incendiary crowd unrest feature rarely, for example 'a few very large mobs' on pleasure trips referred to by a railway shareholder in Sheffield in 1849.[4]

Behaviour in the crowded carriage of the excursion train was influenced by the physical structure of the carriage, as well as other factors, such as the type of group being carried, the efficiency of the organisation of the trip and staffing rules, with ensuing repercussions for the health and safety of passengers. Travel space inside the train, in the carriage, underwent some crucial changes during the mid-nineteenth century, as a result of the growing crowds of working-class excursionists. However, although some writers have claimed that after the 1840s the British masses no longer travelled in open freight wagons, a fresh examination of sources shows that these were often used for excursion trains throughout the 1850s. In his 1855 article, satirist Robert Brough compared travelling in an open excursion train to the problems of the closed carriage:[5]

'Travel in an open carriage by an excursion train? We know the thing is horribly plebeian – low...the open carriages themselves – although it is true they are not called the "third-class," and are not fitted with a *stifling* low roof, with wooden shutters that keep the light out, and louvre boards that let the draught in... are always looked upon as being the third-class – if not the fourth. No, on the whole, the thing is so disgraceful.'

Travel space for the excursionist could be very simple and bleak compared to the traditional railway carriage. The illustration from 1847 (Figure 16) demonstrates the basic nature of third-class travel space in open wagons at times, with a mingling of excited classes crammed together, some people standing, some sitting, some perched dangerously on the edge of the wagon. There are no women in this illustration (it was a race excursion), and their presence might have influenced behaviour in favour of a more civilised conduct.

Figure 16. Illustration showing a third-class carriage transporting people to the Epsom Races in 1847. (© *Illustrated London News Ltd/Mary Evans Picture Library*)

Open carriages could, however, be dangerous for otherwise well-behaved passengers and sometimes quite innocent behaviour led to disaster. In Walsall in 1860 an open carriage was being filled by children on a trip, and as the carriage was being shunted, the children all moved to one side, at which point the carriage overturned. It was reported that no-one was hurt.[6]

While the 1844 Railway Act had specified that Parliamentary trains must be covered to escape passenger duty, there was nothing to stop a company using other types of carriage for an excursion, as long as it still offered at least one Parliamentary train a day. The disadvantage was that they would have then incurred passenger duty on all the excursion receipts, not just first and second-class receipts where these were generated. A report on the passenger duty in 1876 suggests that, following the 1844 Act, it became at times the norm for excursion trains to be given entire exemption from duty by the Board of Trade, despite a lack of conformity to the standards laid down in the Act, as a result of the discretionary powers given to them, and sometimes the government approved exemption of duty on open carriages.[7]

Behaviour inside the crowded excursion carriage or wagon often related to the type of group being carried. Powerful figures were able to use their status to enforce conformity to rules of behaviour in certain organisations, such as a mechanics institute or Sunday school, or on trips organised by an employer, such as a mill owner. This kind of paternalist influence reflected those which had shaped behaviour on the earlier steamboat excursions. A report from the Factory Inspectors in 1845 referred to a large Liverpool cotton mill organising a July Sunday school anniversary annual steamboat excursion across the Mersey, which only allowed children to participate if they showed good general conduct and were 'in the habit of attending some place of instruction, or of public worship on the Sunday.'[8] By contrast other trips were more of a free for all, such as the excursions where all tickets were sold to the general public for trips to large towns, race meetings and prize fights.

Sometimes behaviour was shaped by the way that staff carried out their duties, as railway workers might interpret the rules of the company in a particular way. Railway staff were sometimes described as colluding with their passengers in misbehaviour, appearing occasionally to have placed profitable sales ahead of safety in the management of ensuing crowds. Accident inspectors took this view in reporting on a tragedy in August 1858, at the time 'the worst railway accident that has ever occurred in this country', when 14 passengers were killed and 220 others injured, many seriously. Couplings had broken on an excursion train returning from Worcester to Wolverhampton on the Oxford, Worcester & Wolverhampton Railway, leading to part of the train sliding back down a gradient and hitting a following train. The inspector reported that one of the guards had allowed excursion passengers to join him in his brake van, smoking and drinking with them, and even to work the brake with him. Furthermore, staff appear to have exceeded their authority in allowing large numbers of people on the trip. Although the handbills had ordered that only teachers and children of the Sunday schools would be allowed to go, this was clearly not the case, with an equal number of adults and children in the 1,500 passengers booked.[9]

Sometimes behaviour might be influenced by a particularly well organised and planned excursion, where the excursion crowd was managed effectively. There are three remarkably similar accounts of trips from the north west to London in the summer of 1857 which refer to well-managed crowds organised along military lines.[10] These accounts refer to the crowds being organised into 'companies' of thirty people aligned to their carriage number, each headed by a 'captain', with 'party-coloured ribbons' to be worn in buttonholes to identify 'sections'. Two of the accounts describe a trip organised by the Rector of Warrington, Rev. William Quekett with a colleague, Rev. R.A. Mould, the other a trip from the Preston area commissioned from the London and North Western excursion agent Mr. H.R. Marcus. It may well be that these were in fact the same excursion, as many of the details coincide, however significantly the successful organisation of the crowd was not left to the railway company or to its staff. The writer does, however, comment on the tight control of the excursionists when the train halted, with guards and porters preventing them from alighting, apart from a brief ten minute stop for refreshments at Wolverton. Carriages were used for this excursion, with windows which enabled the traveller to view the changing landscape, although on arrival at Fenchurch Street station in London, they were hurried across London Bridge and were herded into open carriages to take them to Crystal Palace. It appears from the lack of comment in accounts that behaviour was good, presumably because of the level of organisation.

A striking feature of passenger behaviour in the crowded carriage, attracting little notice to date in railway history, was the prevalence of roof travel. Significantly in the 1840s it was quite common for these new passengers to break out of the enclosed space of the carriage and clamber over the sides and roofs, a characteristic of train travel still occurring in places in modern day India, despite prohibition.[11] Roof travel was exceedingly dangerous. When 2,700 Lancashire manufacturing workers were conveyed on a Whit trip to Liverpool in 1858 by the East Lancashire Railway, the excitement of their day, the broiling sun on the return journey and the heavily overcrowded train encouraged several passengers to climb on the roofs of the carriages. A young factory operative, Joseph Ainsworth, decided to walk along the roof and look inside the lamp-holes at his comrades inside. Unfortunately he was struck by a bridge near Burscough, but as the train was slackening its speed, he was not killed on the spot. The accident report pointed out that some bridges were only three feet higher than the top of the carriages, thus regardless of behaviour it was unsafe for anyone to travel on top of a carriage. However seats for the guards were positioned on the roofs for braking purposes. The report recommended that existing outside seats on top of some of the carriages should be removed and that the use of only two guards on a train was insufficient to work the brakes and keep control of a large train of excursionists.[12]

Why did some young men in particular seek to travel on the roof of the excursion train? Often this arose from a sense of excitement and anti-authoritarian attitudes. In the 1840s and 1850s this behaviour was often generated by the design of the carriage, which limited the views available from the interior, and by the sociability of the experience. It could be argued that it was a way in which these young men were able to claim 'superior' space for themselves. Third class covered carriages in 1845 had only tiny windows high up in the sides, with little or no ventilation, therefore a wish to climb on top might be seen as understandable.[13] Excursionists were bursting out of the enclosed space to show off their prowess up above. Some early observers seemed to accept roof travel behaviour. In his practical treatise on railways in 1839, Lecount recognised that people 'may chuse to ride on the roof of the carriage' and recommended therefore that netting be hooked between each carriage, to catch people from falling under the wheels.[14] It is not clear why this appeared to be acceptable, but possibly it reflected the practice of stagecoach passengers riding on top of their vehicle, as a cheaper option.[15]

Another major factor encouraging roof travel was the mismanagement of excursions by railway companies, when passengers climbed to the roof because of severe overcrowding and overheating, a regular problem. A report of an early trip in 1843 involving teetotallers from Glasgow refers to their 'clustering outside [the carriages] like bees' because the crowd was too great to fit inside.[16] Again a press account of an inquest before a jury, following a fatal accident in September 1844, also demonstrates how this kind of behaviour occurred. It was on the North Midland line, when 5,500 people took part in a Monday trip from Sheffield to Hull in 170 carriages in three separate trains.[17] It appears that tickets had been sold by a promoter, Mr Thomas Wiley, a spirit merchant, who, after selling 4,111 third-class and 249 second-class tickets, had to stop selling tickets, as the Sheffield station superintendent told him there was not enough accommodation for passengers.[18] On their return some of the passengers climbed on the carriage roof while the train was travelling slowly, despite advice to the contrary by the railway attendants. A coupling chain on the first train broke, causing it to stop, and a second train collided with it at low speed. The jolt was enough to throw passengers off the roofs and one young man, a table knife cutler, was killed. His colleagues gave evidence that they had been placed in an open cattle truck, and then moved into a carriage where they could neither sit nor stand comfortably because of the crowds. They were then tempted on to the top of an adjacent second-class carriage because of the empty seat at the top. It was reported that railway officials told passengers riding on top of the carriages several times to get down, but excursionists insisted on staying on top, giving 'saucy answers'. This seat was presumably intended for the guard. But there is certainly evidence of passengers being allowed to sit in great numbers on the roofs of carriages on early trains, such as in 1836, with the Newcastle & Carlisle Railway (see Plate 8).[19] Grand Junction Railway first and second-class carriages also had roof seats in 1837 for passengers preferring to travel outside.[20]

People were viewing excursion crowd behaviour from different perspectives: the railway company, the journalist, the accident inspector and the passenger. Each had particular concerns which shaped their views of behaviour and their judgement of it. Sometimes comments encouraged stereotypical perspectives. In the account of the North Midland accident in 1844, Superintendent Peter Clarke complained that 'he never saw people so unruly as those from Sheffield,' but argued that he had allowed greater sales of tickets because of representations made to him, and it was reported that a 'strong body of police' were involved at Sheffield to keep order.[21] Clarke agreed he should not have used cattle trucks, but was following the practice of other lines. The press account records evidence before the jury, constructed from statements made either by railway managers and staff, by other passengers or by the coroner. The press observer was shamed by the comments made, and their aspersions on the local community. Additional editorial remarks regretted that 'our townsmen' should have acquired this reputation, but expressed the view that this should encourage the company to limit their ticket sales and local people to change their conduct, in the hope of displaying more 'self-respect and propriety of behaviour'. The coroner expressed the view that while excursions should be encouraged as they promoted advantages to the public and profit to the railway company, he recommended that the selling of tickets should match the accommodation available, and that passengers should not be permitted to ride on top of the carriages.

Roof travel sometimes occurred with the collusion of staff. Although railway company employees often tried unsuccessfully to persuade excursionists back into the carriage, staff sometimes conspired with the public in placing them in dangerous situations when large crowds were being accommodated, as in the case of Newcastle Races in June 1844. When a cheap trip was organised to the meeting by the Great North of England and the Newcastle & Darlington Junction Railway, it was noted that at Hartlepool there were so many people waiting for the train that 'they were compelled…to go outside, and were, therefore, placed on the top of the different carriages; so that they were exposed to the pelting of the pitiless storm.'[22]

Women have traditionally been hidden in the history of leisure, shunted into the background behind developments in male culture, for example in racing, football, working men's clubs and brass bands. In the Victorian period it was assumed that women's leisure opportunities were focused on the home rather than public space.[23] However the presence or absence of women might be seen to influence the behaviour of crowds in the excursion carriage, especially as it could often involve the mixing of classes. In America it was suggested that it was the presence of 'respectable' women on nineteenth-century trains that enforced a need for social order.[24] Ladies' cars were used on 1840s American railroads, and these could also be used by their male escorts, although the conduct of these men would be closely monitored 'to ensure that women were not exposed to smoking or rough conduct or language.'[25] The British excursion carriage could not be policed in the same way, as each carriage was enclosed, inaccessible from other carriages and only reachable from the platform.[26] A writer suggested that 'at times of departure and arrival, importunities may be practised, and impertinences offered to unguarded female passengers.'[27] Ladies' carriages were made available at times, generally only in first class, although it appears that the Midland Railway offered a ladies' carriage on their 'penny-a-mile' service in 1846.[28] There is a rare example of a 'ladies cheap trip' to Blackpool from Salford Station in 1855, offered by Mr Stanley, agent for the Lancashire & Yorkshire Railway.[29] Generally, however, ladies' carriages seemed to be a source of much concern to women, who feared being closeted away without access to help from the guard or male travellers.

Sexual attacks on women were often described in court reports and in the press in the nineteenth century. The new leisure activities offered by railway excursions gave women the chance to participate in great numbers, increasing the potential for sexual encounters in the enclosed public space of the excursion carriage. Women were generally not protected from offensive behaviour arising out of the close proximity of men and women in this new space. In May 1851 a 14-year-old girl, Ann Ebdon, had completed a post in service, and was on a day out in the country with her family. A court report described how, on her return in a crowded South Eastern excursion train, an elderly surgeon was accused of indecently assaulting her. Standing near the surgeon, who was seated, the court heard from her that he started to assault her, by trying to put his hand up her petticoats. Although she objected to his behaviour she was unable to prevent him, and her family were some distance away in the carriage. When they arrived at their destination she complained to them and they had him arrested. Although she had tried to complain to her aunt and to nearby passengers at the time, she was too ashamed to explain exactly what was happening.[30]

It may be that anonymity in the railway carriage presented opportunities for welcome and unwelcome erotic behaviour, and there were several cases reported where men assumed that the presence of women in a confined shared space made them 'fair game'.[31] In 1850, a Wesleyan Sunday school teacher, a warehouseman, was accused with his colleague of annoying female passengers from Catholic schools when sharing a carriage with them on a May trip to Fleetwood by the Wesleyan Sunday school and the Catholic schools, resulting in a court case at Bolton. Despite many requests from the railway servants the two men had refused to move, and eventually they were both forcibly put off the train at Preston and left to walk 22 miles home in the rain.[32] In October 1855 a court case described how a man had amused himself by kissing females as they passed through a tunnel on a Bristol trip and, when a fellow passenger remonstrated with him, he assaulted him.[33] A similar case at Southwark in 1859 arose from arguments about insulting behaviour by two men against a woman in a tunnel on a Brighton trip, leading to an assault.[34] In 1859 a man was found guilty of assaulting a woman in a tunnel on their return from a cheap trip to Liverpool from Huddersfield, when the lack of lights in the carriage compounded the dangers, and the bench declared that it was important to put down assaults of this kind in cheap trips.[35] Thus male behaviour in the enclosed travel space of the excursion caused particular problems for women, arising from the frequency of dark interludes in tunnels and the absence of observation, which might have encouraged better conduct.

Such misbehaviour on cheap trips had not been confined to the crowded railway carriage. An 1846 report of a court case concerned behaviour on a steamship excursion, when a man on the *Waverley* trip to Grimsby was convicted of assault. After talking 'beastly language in the presence of females', he had struck someone who remonstrated with him about his improper conduct.[36] Again, during a rail/steamer trip from Kirkintilloch to Arrochar in 1856, a 'large number of excursionists conducted themselves in a most disorderly manner, quarrelling and fighting with each other on board the steamer, both in going and returning.' As a result a young woman was alarmed, became seriously unwell as a result, and died later that day.[37]

A significant development in the new travel space was reported however in 1851, when observers were amazed that a group consisting only of female members of a labouring family were able to take a trip from Huddersfield to London for the Great Exhibition, 'unaccompanied'.[38] The fact that this was reported indicates how unusual it was. It may well be of course that this group felt more secure as an all female group and the crowd enabled this group to feel comfortable. Thus despite the risks of offensive behaviour by men, arising from the constrained and often dark conditions of the carriage or wagon, it might be argued that the combination of the attraction of destinations such as the Great Exhibition, together with cheap mobility for the masses, opened the doors to female emancipation, certainly in allowing women to take unaccompanied leisure trips.

There are instances of defensive strategies being adopted by excursion passengers to protect their travel space inside the carriage and to defend themselves against the crowd. The aim was to make their own conditions more comfortable or to ensure that the space was restricted to passengers who they believed to be of their own social group, such as the family, or work colleagues. Excursion agent Stanley commented in 1853 that delays were caused to trips to North Wales from Manchester because some passengers had refused to let further excursionists into their carriages, when in his opinion these had not been full.[39] On a works trip from Brymbo, near Wrexham, to Liverpool in 1858, three burly workers succeeded in protecting their carriage space from further entrants.[40] On an 1858 excursion by the Great Western Railway from Paddington to Swindon, to view a total eclipse of the sun (accompanied by an astronomical expert to deliver a lecture), a writer describes how his colleague looked out of the window, filling it with his broad shoulders to prevent others entering, until some interesting colleagues arrived with astronomical equipment and attractive females, at which point he invited them to enter.[41]

Such behaviour added to the potentially explosive situation inside the crowded carriage, with each group feeling the need to mark out and define their space, a kind of tribal behaviour. This was particularly prevalent with religious groupings, and in some cases abusive behaviour against other groups was involved. In 1855 a Lancashire court case arose from a cheap trip to Liverpool by two groups of children, one from the Church of England Sunday schools and the other from the Dissenters.[42] This was a Monday trip designed to take scholars away from the dangers of Darwen Fair on that day. After heated discussions between the different Sunday school managers about the need for clearly delineated space, they travelled out in separate trains because of their reputation for rivalry, but on the return journey a group of Church people had to use the Dissenters' train. A Church of England clergyman took over a first-class carriage on this with a few people but then refused to allow a woman to enter, striking her over the head and mouth to stop her. She succeeded in her case for assault, with damages of 10 shillings against the clergyman.

There is only rare evidence that excursionists attempted to use their mass to take possession of the travel space of the carriage when they were unhappy about conditions. While the lack of communication between carriages prevented railway companies from policing behaviour in the train, this enclosure gave them the balance of power in policing traffic movement generally, enabling them to control the possession of a carriage by simply detaching it. It would have been more effective for a disgruntled crowd to use its mass to stand on the lines or block the station space, preventing all trains from moving or other passengers embarking or disembarking. A Mr Scott and Mr Redfern organised an excursion by rail and steam in 1843 from Leeds and West Yorkshire, to Manchester, Liverpool and North Wales, liaising with relevant railway and steamship companies. Unfortunately, on the train's arrival at Manchester, one of the speculators went missing with the proceeds and the excursionists were asked to pay the fare again from Manchester to Liverpool as well as the steamer journey. The party tried to take group action: 'the pleasure-seekers took possession of the carriages, and refused to pay anything, the locomotive was detached, and the party left on the line, without any means of progressing a single yard,' but after three hours the group had to give in.[43] Thus those attempting to take possession of travel space against the will of company staff were usually unsuccessful, because of the railway company's ability to detach carriages if necessary and render them stationary. It appears that excursion crowds were unable to find ways of harnessing their behaviour effectively in space controlled by railway company management. Furthermore there was no consumer organisation to represent their complaints. The power of consumerism developed only in the later nineteenth century, and so at this time their only weapon was individual letters to the newspapers.[44]

Drink and drunkenness played a part in behaviour in travel space. There was much debate about drink and the working classes in the mid-nineteenth century, especially after the appearance of unregulated beershops. These encouraged cheap beer in working-class areas after 1830, which eventually provoked a growing temperance movement. Social drinking was of great importance in working-class popular culture, but the demands of industrialisation were incompatible with levels of drunkenness which had been acceptable in the past, and this became a major social problem. Although the middle classes condemned the drinking habits of the working classes, some people defended them, saying that drink for the masses was 'a right, a custom and a necessity'.[45] There were, however, differential class perspectives on drunkenness during the nineteenth century, with the working man penalised for drunken behaviour which might be ignored when observed of the middle and upper classes. While it might be assumed that there was a level of drunkenness on excursions, encouraging unconstrained rowdy behaviour, a commentator in the *Saturday Review* in 1859 (when railway excursions had been running for twenty years) suggested that 'railway excursionists are noisy, vulgar, and disagreeable to come across but seldom drunk.' It appears that the railway companies had somehow forced the poor excursionist towards sobriety, because his family were with him and also because of the level of respect and fear shown by him to railway officials, making 'travellers behave well and remain sober.'[46]

At times however, reported excursion crowds featured an unruly and disreputable drunken element, taking advantage of the cheap ride. A case in September 1856 referred to a trip on the Lancashire & Yorkshire line from Sowerby Bridge to Blackpool, when, on the return journey, two men were found drunk on the floor of their carriage, which had been kept locked as usual on special trains. They accused railway staff of joining them in a drinking session and the case was dismissed.[47] On the same line, Railway Superintendent Normington described the very well patronised Sowerby Bridge Annual Temperance Society excursion to Liverpool, which used three or four crowded trains in the late 1850s. On their return, 'a large number of the passengers were found laid in the bottom of the carriages helplessly drunk, and had to be taken away from the station on platform trucks.'[48] Such occasions demonstrate how a so-called 'respectable' working-class trip might be misleading, as it could feature disreputable behaviour, especially when tickets might be sold to the general public. Drunken episodes could escalate crowd behaviour: an excursion train leaving from Edinburgh was the scene of a riot in 1858, when a drunken man tried to jump onto a carriage and was stopped by a porter and the station master, who had to call for police help when he assaulted them. A crowd of around 400 other people at the station then joined in against the station master and the police in a serious disturbance. Some men were later found guilty of assault against the police.[49]

Occasionally the press would deliberately counterpoint reports of the scenes of drunken excursionists with excursionists who were seen to be rather more well behaved. A report of excursions on the Dundee & Perth Railway in 1847 contrasted the 'inebriety' of some of the operatives on their arrival at their destination with the 'decorous' behaviour of a procession of children from the charity and ragged schools, each carrying a tin bowl with some bread and meat, on a cheap trip.[50] In the main, however, the effect of drink on behaviour in the crowded carriage depended on the type of group being carried and the views of the observer. It appears that it was rarely a problem with excursions. It might be concluded that the new excursions gave the working classes an alternative outlet for enjoyment, which, because it might be shared with the family rather than with workmates, reduced the incentive to drink heavily.

Behaviour at the station itself was shaped by a number of factors: the inherent characteristics of the crowd, the physical attributes of station space, and the way that railway companies handled the excursion. Reports of excursionists' behaviour sometimes reflected the supposed characteristics of a crowd such as destructiveness and suggestibility in certain situations, and this was especially noticeable at stations.[51] On Whit Sunday May 1845, when there were cheap trips between Sheffield and Rotherham for Rotherham Fair, the railway company underestimated demand and huge crowds were left in Rotherham after the last train had left in the evening.[52] Some had to find accommodation, others, including the old and the young, had to walk 6 miles home at a late hour, and some gathered around the station in the hope of another train. The press correspondent expressed great concerns about the 'tremendous pressure' of the crowd around the station doors, the dangerous confusion and the way that as soon as an extra carriage was provided, there was 'a general rush and scramble to get into it while still moving', suggesting that his informant would see the need to insure his life if he took another trip. Again, in August 1845, a report described a cheap trip for the poor by the Preston Temperance Excursion Committee from Preston to Fleetwood, when 'thousands have availed themselves … to escape for a day at least from the pent-up alleys and the noise and tumult of the town, into the pure fresh air of the country, and the invigorating breeze of the sea shore.' The reporter complained of the 'press of numbers' and being 'nearly elbowed to death in the crowd', and was thus fighting the crowd as an outsider rather than flowing with it and surrendering to it.[53] So, for reporters unused to this kind of incident, it was a terrifying and potentially deadly experience. It may well be that many reporters were not used to the close mingling which reflected the daily experience of the poor in their housing and streets.

These crowds could be destructive, arising out of a loss of personal inhibition and attacks on boundaries, although evidence is scarce, possibly because the railway companies and the urban elite owners of the press were keen to represent excursion activity in a good light. In 1838, when the newly opened London & Southampton Railway organised trips for Derby Day at Epsom from Nine Elms Station in London, the excursion crowd, eager to depart, stormed the railway station by force.[54] The high level of demand, stimulated by the efficiency of linking transport modes – steamboats and London & Southampton Railway omnibuses – which brought hopeful rail passengers to a single transport hub at Nine Elms Station, led to great crowds massing as early as 6am. The railway filled its carriages, running trips to Epsom continuously, carrying an estimated 3,000–4,000 passengers. However, by 10am, there was still a large crowd of impatient racegoers, including 'many respectably dressed ladies'. The crowd's destructive force lifted the station door off its hinges, despite the presence of railway police control, and the crowd rushed into the main hall. An account suggests that 'the shrieks of the women were dreadful' until they were removed from danger, but several of the men jumped over the counters and entered a waiting train. Unfortunately the railway company foiled their activities by detaching them from the carriages containing passengers who had paid and leaving the interlopers at the station. At this point the railway police force had to be supplemented by the Lambeth and Vauxhall police division, headed by an inspector, to clear the area, but apparently 'no great mischief was done'. Notices were then displayed to say that no more trains would run that morning, but some passengers reverted to travelling by cab to the race. This was spectacularly described in the press as a 'tumult' involving a 'mob', later becoming an iconic story from the early days of excursions, possibly reflecting the drama of the event.[55] It shows how mixed crowds, including presumably 'respectable' men and women, can suddenly take on a life force of their own, leading to destructiveness.

A further example makes it even more obvious that delays and lock-outs by a railway company, here on a trip from Southampton to London for the Great Exhibition in September 1851, could evoke serious problems and destructiveness.[56] A crowd of 3,000 passengers had arrived at the station at 6am but were kept out until the train came at 7am. When the doors finally opened, the rush was so great that 'the windows of the station were broken, several persons were injured, and a great number of hats, shawls, bonnets, caps and shoes were lost. Numbers of women fainted or were taken ill, and children were nearly crushed to death.' An account tells how many local tradesmen had paid for their servants to take this trip and 'a large posse of "maids of all work" … dressed respectably, each with a little basket of provisions for the day, were, with the crowd, congregated early before the station.' Many of these had their clothes torn in the rush and were frightened, and it was reported that it was impossible for the railway staff to retain control of the situation, for example third-class passengers ended up in first-class compartments, without paying. Such evidence shows that even the 'respectable' working classes could become a mob under certain conditions, often triggered by the organisation managing the excursion and by the space in which they were confined.

The nineteenth-century railway station has been portrayed as a gateway between two kinds of travel space, the city and the railway, creating a 'liminal' space between the two, a way of cushioning the shock between the city and the industrialised space of the railway.[57] However, while the waiting room has been traditionally seen as a public space used as a holding area until the trains arrived, in the case of British excursions the stations were often completely closed to the new travellers until the staff were ready, causing huge problems outside the station doors. Stations were typically crowded by the very nature of large numbers of people funnelling into a departure, and excursion crowds were created inside and outside the railway station, both at the point of origin and at the destination, by the practices of the railway company. The locking of the doors at stations, when railway companies were expecting excursions to embark, created a point where a large crowd was generated. In 1846, a correspondent complained in the *Manchester Guardian* that he had hopes of a trip to Alderley with his wife, three children and servant. Arriving early, they suffered a long wait with hundreds of others in the hot sun as the door was closed until shortly before the trip was due to depart. After getting their tickets they could not find a seat in second or third class, and the company promised more carriages. Open carriages were placed on the line but the train went off without them. A crowd of 'most respectable ladies and gentlemen' amassed at the superintendent's office to find out what was going on, but no-one would come out until a gentleman used a piece of wood to break the window at the booking office. At this a young man looked out and told them his job was just to take the money and that 'we could go where we chose'. Disappointingly they were refused a refund on their tickets.[58] Thus, once again, 'unruly' behaviour by a 'respectable' element of the excursion crowd was shaped by the conditions experienced. Again, a correspondent to the *Wrexham Advertiser* in 1859 complained of the practice at Birkenhead Station of closing the station door when excursionists were due to arrive. Several thousand had to wait on a steep hill, pressing down towards the three foot wide door. When it finally opened, the crush was great, with at least one woman fainting under the feet of the mass of people. Railway officials reacted in panic by beating the crowd over their heads with sticks.[59] It may be that they used this approach to prevent further trampling of vulnerable passengers underfoot, or alternatively they were concerned to keep this large mass of people out of their station.

The design of the station space – the booking office and the platforms – frequently prevented an orderly progression. A reporter described the crowds of passengers getting on excursion trains at the London Bridge terminus on the London Brighton & South Coast Railway for a special military musical fete at Crystal Palace in 1854.[60] Although there was a separate entrance at the station for excursionists who had already bought tickets, this entrance took them into:

'the same over-crowded room, in which, from a dozen pigeon holes, there was a ceaseless cry for tickets…and a gradually increasing crush and pressure, which it required all the tact and management of the officials to contend with…then came the headlong rush for the trains. Luckily the railway company had anticipated [this] …and laid on extra trains, and of extra length, which the moment they were drawn upon the platform were filled and moved off at intervals of around ten minutes. Unfortunately, however, there were generally about three times as many assembled on the platform as the train would accommodate, and the rush and the scrambling, and struggling that took place among the excited crowd, may be imagined. All distinction of classes, and we may add, of castes, was lost in the scramble, and soldiers and sailors, ladies of title in silks and satins, and working people with babies, baskets, and bundles, looking as hot and thirsty as if they had meditated a halt at the refreshment room at the foot of the staircase, before entering the palace, were all mixed up together and glad to get a seat in any carriage and in any company.'

Thus the demand for the new excursions completely overwhelmed the constraints of the physical space available. There were attempts at organising functional space for excursion crowds by using a special door for excursionists, but this was ineffective as it led to the same crowded area as the normal doors. Platform space could not accommodate these large numbers either, despite the availability of extra long trains to siphon off the travellers, thus the ensuing behaviour was seen to be a complete scramble and struggle, shaped from a melting pot of class, gender and age groups, which might not have been in close quarters together previously.

It was not only the compact space of the railway station which led to crowds breaking out, but the inadequate handling of excursion crowds by the railway companies. The management of the excursion should be set in the context of the level of normal railway traffic, which in the 1840s was developing at a fast rate. Nineteenth-century novelist Wilkie Collins described passenger mobs and traveller's riots in his novel *No Name,* set in the 1840s. He wrote a satirical diatribe on the failure of railway companies to manage crowds at railway stations, using York as an example, even when these were not necessarily complicated by excursion trains, using incendiary language such as 'mobs' and 'riot'[61]:

'He reached the platform a few minutes after the train had arrived. That entire incapability of devising administrative measures for the management of large crowds, which is one of the characteristics of Englishmen in authority, is nowhere more strikingly exemplified than at York. Three different lines of railway assemble three passenger mobs, from morning to night, under one roof; and leave them to raise a travellers' riot, with all the assistance which the bewildered servants of the company can render to increase the confusion…Dozens of different people were trying to attain dozens of different objects, in dozens of different directions, all starting from the same common point and all equally deprived of the means of information.'

This clearly shows how station space was particularly difficult to manage, because even in normal conditions a busy station servicing several companies might have to handle large groups of travellers needing guidance, information and help with luggage. The addition of an excursion crowd, lacking experience of the station and its practices, could tip the balance into complete chaos.

As we have already seen in many examples of overselling excursions, the railway companies seemed unable to predict accurately the level of potential demand for a new excursion service. This may of course have arisen from their ineffective management structures and a constant growing demand, but it might be argued that the use of a multitude of ticket sellers and excursion agents caused such problems. One of the major shortcomings in handling crowds was understaffing. An observer commented in 1858, 'one peculiarity of railway management being that there are only the same number of officials employed when 2,000 people are about to take their departure as there are when there are only two dozen to be stowed away.'[62] A press report in 1857 described the lack of staffing at London Bridge Station for excursions on the South Eastern Railway on Sunday morning trips to Margate and Ramsgate. When the excursionists had bought their tickets they were then subjected to having their packages and parcels searched, because these were charged extra, but there was only a short time to do this, around fifteen minutes. There were only two members of staff, a porter to weigh the packages and a clerk to register these, for a crowd of 200–300 people. The clerk was soon besieged by an angry crowd who were fearful of missing their train, leading to a 'disgraceful scene of riot and confusion'. Apparently, 'men's coats were torn off their backs, women's bonnets smashed, and a few crinolined…females…came out of it flattened like pancakes, and bruised like oats…'[63] Thus the railway managers' lack of foresight led directly to behavioural problems with the crowd. Too few people to help often led to tremendous problems, with people waiting, becoming impatient and bursting out of the space allocated to them.

However there are rare examples of careful planning by railway companies. Detailed accounts of these are hard to find, presumably under the principle that a good system disappears from view, only the bad systems are newsworthy, because they inspire anger and dissatisfaction. On the Manchester & Leeds Railway, the *Manchester Times* estimated 12,000 scholars in a total of 140,000 people conveyed on the line during Whit week 1846. This railway seems to have taken steps to manage crowds rather more safely than other companies, as Sunday school carriages were attached to regular trains to prevent accidents. Furthermore, the press commended its management of crowds at Victoria Station for the Jubilee conference of the Methodist New Connection, with a new line of rails for cheap trip trains and a surprisingly well organised reception of these:

'Whenever a cheap train arrived at the station, the passengers got out at the right
hand side of the carriages, and passed through a line of officers, stationed there for
their guide and protection, to a separate gate on the off side of the station. Through
this gate they also entered when about to return; and if it happened that the train
was not in readiness, they had an opportunity of resting themselves on seats fitted
up for their use. A band of music was also placed on a temporary platform and they
played various airs for the waiting travellers. Ginger beer was also served out to
those whose throats were parched with the terrible heat.'[64]

Crowd management was facilitated at times by the way that Sunday schoolchildren were
marshalled. On a Sunday school trip from Sheffield to Hull in September 1844, members
of the public, who had also been able to buy tickets, arrived early and besieged the station,
later occupying some of the carriages, but the strict discipline of the children and their
managers apparently prevented further confusion when they arrived, and a report also
suggested that the railway companies handled the situation well.[65] In this case the power
exercised by the Sunday school managers over their charges led to conformity and careful
order, presumably with walking in procession.

An anecdote about French excursions from 1850 highlights two points of difference
between the French and British systems in managing the pressures of excursion crowds
in station space.[66] Paris was experiencing a high demand for excursion trains at that time,
with cheap trips to Dieppe. A large crowd of people had gathered to buy tickets for an
excursion to Dieppe and, as the crowd was impatient at not being processed fast enough,
a 'clever fellow' started to issue 'regulation numbers' rather than tickets, to be presented
some minutes before the departure of each train, at 50 cents a time, achieving a total
revenue of around 700 francs on these transactions. It is not clear if he was a member of
staff offering a level of flexibility unheard of in Britain at that time, or a hoaxer, from this
report, but when the train was due to depart, these people, around 1,200 in number,
demanded their places and, on being refused by staff, the angry crowd 'broke open the
doors and rushed to the train'. As a result the officials called in the infantry to force them
out of the wagons, a response which does not appear to have been used by British railway
companies against excursion crowds. The military response indicated the seriousness
with which the French railway company treated these transgressions.

Some excursionists tried to use the new excursion opportunities to maximise their
advantage. A party of fifty-three Irish labourers was reported to have hired a cattle wagon
for a trip from Liverpool to Birmingham in August 1844, at a cost of 2s a head. When a
further group attempted to do the same, the railway directors raised the price to 4s, which
was too high. (The cost of hiring the wagon for cattle was £2 10s and for pigs £2 15s.)[67]

The large and busy crowds concentrated in constrained areas on the platform, in the carriage and around the station attracted the efforts of unscrupulous people. The very act of massing people in one spot facilitated and inspired the pickpockets to make use of their skills, and criminals found ingenious ways to take advantage of the excursion crowd. However, in 1854, Sir Richard Mayne, Metropolitan Police Commissioner, claimed in evidence to the government that the advent of cheap excursion trains had reduced crime levels in London (presumably by transferring this to destinations elsewhere).[68] Some commentators at popular destinations remarked on the effects of cheap mobility on increasing crime:

'…the opportunities afforded to adventurers of all classes by the improvement in our means of locomotion. Excursion trips, cheap trains… have the effect of bringing strangers together to an extent unknown and impossible in former times. People bent on pleasure are likely to be recklessly social; the intercourse of a railway carriage serves admirably for purposes of introduction.'[69]

The implication was that adventurers were able to use the opportunities to take advantage of friendships developed among 'strangers' en route to use at the destination, thus painting the excursion crowd in a negative light. While some of this criminal activity was of a type that was not new to leisure mobility, there were two other types of illegal activity which took advantage of the crowds involved in cheap excursion travel, the procurement of prostitutes and excursion ticket fraud.

Firstly there were people at the destination who saw the potential of the excursion crowd in the procurement of prostitution amongst innocent girls, a substantial problem in Victorian England. The recruitment of prostitutes was primarily from the poor. Magistrates in Southampton in 1860 highlighted how cheap excursion trains were used by procuresses travelling to the provinces, on this occasion appearing as well-dressed women calling at the house of three attractive young orphaned girls, to decoy them with the promise of situations in London households, but brought them to brothels instead. Most such girls were around 14 years old, and similar incidents were described in the 1850s.[70]

Secondly, certain destinations attracted a huge market in excursion ticket fraud, with unscrupulous dealers responding to the new crowds around destination stations. Those found guilty of using illegally bought tickets came from a wide range of classes, from people on 'the tramp' to 'highly respectable' tradesmen. They had bought excursion tickets from dealers waiting at the stations, who in turn had bought them from travellers on their outward excursion journey. These travellers, having reached their destination, either sold their ticket or gave it away to the dealer, despite the railway companies specifying that tickets were not transferable. This arose from the fact that often excursion return tickets were cheaper than a normal single ticket. The unlucky traveller who tried to use the cheap ticket to travel one way from the destination was sometimes found out by the inspectors and taken into custody. Reports of prosecutions arising from this activity appear in the press in the early 1850s, for example at the South Western Railway station at Southampton in 1851 and 1852, and the Great Western Station at Bristol in 1852.[71] These incurred large fines and occasionally the threat of up to two years' imprisonment, as the railway companies were concerned about the likely effects on their income if the practices were not effectively policed. Brighton was also a significant location for ticket dealers, one of the most notorious here was known as 'Punch'.[72]

The railway companies used a number of strategies to detect this fraud, including numbering tickets and adopting different colours for different days/weeks. Both the buyer and seller were culpable, but it was usually the buyer who was detected. Some reports described how ticket dealers held on to tickets for a period to accommodate the rotation of colours, but they were usually caught out by the numbering, as the altering of this could be easily detected. By 1859 there was serious concern over the traffic in excursion tickets, and it was considered that many of the 'roughs' living in large towns were able to make a living out of this trade. As a result the Railway Tickets Transfer Bill was brought before Parliament, to give railway companies a general power to stop this ticket abuse. Unfortunately it was pointed out that the drafting of the Bill gave wide powers, not only to the railway company, but 'all other persons', potentially allowing them 'to seize, apprehend and detain' suspects. As a result it was suggested that anyone 'innocently' giving away their excursion ticket, or even having his pocket picked of it, might be caught under this clause and detained unfairly. A suggestion that tickets should be named with the person who bought them was discarded as unworkable. The Bill was withdrawn and this illegal practice was still being carried out towards the end of the century.[73]

It is clear that reports about behaviour on excursion trains were influenced by physical conditions and overcrowding. When the new excursionists reached their destinations, however, there were more difficulties, arising from factors such as class and religion.

Chapter Nine

Claiming Leisure Space

'The North Staffordshire Railway Company thought proper to make up their then dividends by advertising in flaming handbills a series of cheap excursions along their line to the Rudyard Lake, a regatta to be held on Easter Monday, with sport of all kinds, music, steamboats, firing of guns, &c. Miss Bostock and several of the neighbouring landowners expostulated, but without avail. The regatta took place, and with an invasion of 6,000 people of all kinds from the manufacturing districts the jury might imagine how little the privacy and comfort of the plaintiff could be consulted. The vast crowd came, the quiet reservoir became a scene of tumult, amid the hissing of the steamboats, the firing of guns, and the shouts of people. Miss Bostock's park was unreservedly trespassed upon, crowds scaled the walls and fences of the park, broke down the trees, and, last though not least, openly insulted, by obscene and abusive language, Miss Bostock and her friends.'[1] (Court report in press, August 1851)

In the twenty-first century we may take leisure space for granted, but such space has been fought over in many ways over hundreds of years, with ordinary people desperate to find destinations for pleasure trips for the few hours when they were released from work. The above court report, from the *Morning Chronicle* in 1851, lifts the curtain tantalisingly on excursion crowds at Rudyard Lake, Staffordshire. It displays a more colourful scenario when compared to the kind of stock phrases often used in press reporting. Presented from the point of view of the complainant, Miss Bostock, against the North Staffordshire Railway, it clearly demonstrates the potential for large leisure crowds to cause all sorts of problems when gathering. It also shows how it was possible for ordinary working people to gain control over a significant amount of new space as a result of their fresh mobility, something they desperately needed because of the lack of open space available to those living and working in many industrialised towns and cities in the 1840s. Correspondingly, the middle and upper classes sometimes felt threatened by the new excursions and the loosening of their control over space.

In the Bostock case, crowd behaviour was reported from a number of perspectives. We have an account from the landowner as participant, but other accounts come from press observers. In this court action Miss Bostock's representative has deliberately chosen striking words to paint a picture of what might be seen as a provocative action against her by the excursion crowd: 'invasion', 'a scene of tumult', the 'firing of guns' (a celebratory artillery salute) and the 'hissing of steamboats'. The report sought craftily to stoke up concerns among the upper classes during the mid-nineteenth century, following the riots and demonstrations in 1842 and 1848 which had spread across the country. The language used in court to describe the publicity for this excursion as 'flaming handbills' suggests that the event might be seen by some observers as a kind of uprising or riot. There was clearly an underlying element of class tension in this narrative, for the court report emphasised Miss Bostock's status as a 'lady of rank and family', living on the country estate, Cliffe Park, adjoining Rudyard Lake, in comparison to the excursionists, who were 'people of all kinds from the manufacturing districts'.

Closely linked to the disapproving perception of the crowds, and the deliberate attempt to stigmatise them as rioters, are the efforts of social elites to protect their appropriated spaces against these crowds. Miss Bostock took this action to try to stop the North Staffordshire Railway (who had taken over the Trent and Mersey Canal Company) from running cheap trips to the lake, which the company owned, for regattas. These had been advertised for Easter Monday and Whit Monday in 1851, shortly after their station had opened there. The basis for her court action was that the lake was only meant to be used as a 'reservoir', rather than for leisure, and that in addition people had trespassed from the lake onto her property.[2] By contrast, in their contemporary accounts of the event, the provincial press used the kind of positive language which was more usual in their support for rational recreation initiatives. The *Manchester Guardian* painted a pastoral idyll, describing how numerous long excursion trains filled with holidaymakers 'poured forth from large manufacturing towns to this centre of rural festivity', some carriages even carrying race-boats on their roofs. Passengers came from Manchester, Stockport, Macclesfield, Staffordshire, Stone, Newcastle-under-Lyme and the Potteries. The reporter suggested that it was a rare occasion which brought together a number of working-class artisan groups for pleasure, expressed almost as tribal groups: 'the silk workers and dyers of Leek and those of Macclesfield, with the cotton spinners and weavers of Lancashire and Cheshire, and the potters, colliers and pitmen of Staffordshire.'[3] Surprisingly there were no reported conflicts either between upper-class residents and the crowds, nor between such different visitor groups, despite the tensions between groups of workers being clearly reported, with each having their own cultures and practices. The *Manchester Times* suggested that as many as 10,000 people were present, with company both 'gentle and simple' but 'not the slightest accident or contretems occurred to mar the pleasures of the day.'[4] Further national press accounts were also very positive, such as *The Era,* which reported on the 'praiseworthy arrangements' resulting in 'things going off in apple-pie order' and *Bell's Life in London and Sporting Chronicle,* which mentioned 'highly respectable' regatta festivities.[5] In general, therefore, the press appeared to be supporting the masses rather than the gentry in focusing on the benefits of this enterprise.

Rudyard Lake demonstrates how the railway companies themselves helped to tip the balance in helping the masses to use leisure areas successfully at destinations, by putting profits ahead of legal threats. Although Miss Bostock instigated a series of hearings against the railway over the next five years, leading to the grant of a perpetual injunction in 1856 to stop the lake being used for regattas, the hiring of boats or other public amusements, the North Staffordshire Railway ignored the injunction (Miss Bostock was still complaining in 1860). The railway continued to run excursions to the lake, for example with the London & North Western Railway at Whitsun 1864 from Manchester. Finally, in 1903, long after Miss Bostock's death in 1875, the North Staffordshire Railway were able to buy Cliffe Parke to develop it as a holiday resort, although they were unable to overturn the injunction until 1904.[6]

Several factors constricted leisure space for working people in towns and cities in the Victorian period: the movement away from rough urban street culture, the development of police forces, and the pressures on previously open spaces for new houses for the middle classes. These encouraged supporters of 'rational recreation' for the working classes to create new public parks, although these were still controlled by powerful groups such as local politicians and traders. At Boggart Hole Clough in Manchester, for example, public space for the masses was challenged in the 1890s, when crowds of working people were prevented from listening to socialist speakers in public parks.[7]

Excursions extended the potential for ordinary people to use leisure space at a variety of destinations, often in attractive settings. The influx of large numbers of excursionists exerted a powerful force; certainly seaside resorts rapidly changed their nature and character once excursions started pouring thousands of cheap day trippers on to their shores. Excursionists arriving in Blackpool from industrial towns in Lancashire and Yorkshire in the 1840s and 1850s, especially at Whitsun, had a marked effect. Here it was the local authority, which played an important role by the mid-1850s in shaping excursionist behaviour, using bylaws to control, for example, bathing, cabs, boats and donkeys.[8] Favourite destinations included London and other large towns and cities, exhibitions and other events, and occasionally military musters and encampments. The handbill at Figure 17 promotes a cheap trip on the Lancashire & Yorkshire Railway from Colne to Blackburn Park at Whitsun 1863, for a 'Grand Review of the Artillery and Rifle Volunteers'. 'Respectability' was a key feature of life at this time, and some excursion destinations might be characterised as rough rather than respectable, including trips to hangings and to the races, although the latter would include a range of class participation. A trip arranged to see the results of the Holmfirth flood in 1852 might be viewed in two

Figure 17. Handbill for excursion to Blackburn Park. (*Tony Mercer collection*)

ways, either a less respectable outing by people looking for enjoyment in viewing a freak situation, or a more respectable trip for people wishing to assess the extent of the damage, possibly with a view to providing support for those people made destitute.[9] Trips to seaside resorts might also feature a mixture of groups of rowdy excursionists, together with families and couples, seeking a pleasant day or few days away. Excursions to country estates, pleasure gardens, exhibitions, historic locations and natural features might be included at the more respectable end of the spectrum. Temperance trips might be regarded as respectable, but at the same time they might feature drunken excursionists taking advantage of a cheap trip. Rather more unusually trips to structures such as the Britannia Tubular Bridge attracted the masses as a spectacle of technological innovation, a new modernity. The Britannia Bridge was almost the Disneyland of its day, providing the excursionist with a 'novel sensation', which disturbed his/her everyday view of the landscape, but at the same time celebrating the designer and builder, Robert Stephenson. Most of these destinations had not been visited in great numbers by ordinary people until excursions made them possible.

Upon arriving at a destination, the masses on occasion took steps to claim space, usually as a result of their large numbers, and often surprisingly successfully. The press were indeed very surprised at the good behaviour of the unusually large excursion crowds generated by the Great Exhibition of 1851. A report wonders at the way that 100,000 people at the Exhibition 'can remain in crushing contiguity to each other during nine hours…without a single violation of the rules', in daily 'monster meetings'.[10] At times however the excursionist was characterised as a stranger, with all its connotations of 'otherness'. When a cheap trip was taken by 3,200 people on the Manchester & Leeds Railway from Hebden Bridge to Hull in 1844, the press report noted 'our town has again and again…been thronged with wondering and delighted strangers, in search of cheap and rational enjoyment; and to use the expression of the dramatist, "the cry is still they come!"'[11] For the residents, these excursionists were people who had not been observed before, they were seen as unfamiliar with the locality, and easily identified as non-resident. The strangeness of the new arrivals was not due to something individual, but to their origin, and strangers arriving at a destination were viewed by their hosts as a particular type of group with 'foreign' characteristics. It is easy to see how a small community where residents knew each other intimately might describe the visitors as strangers, but reports about 'strangers' also feature in the case of large towns, where residents would not necessarily know all their fellow residents by face. There, excursion crowds were recognised as visitors from another place, possibly by type of clothing, by accents or by behaviour, or because they were accumulated into a large gathering. 'Stranger' was commonly used as a neutral description for visitors to a place of touristic interest during the nineteenth century, for instance there are *Stranger's Guides* to towns published in the 1840s. Grundy's *Stranger's Guide to Hampton Court Palace and Gardens* was only 3d, for example, and therefore aimed at a mass market.[12] The reporting of 'strangers' arriving lasted for the whole period between 1840 and 1860, and is particularly noticeable in Yorkshire. Initially the response to the crowds was surprise, as this was an unexpected and unexplained mystery. For example, in 1840, an excursion crowd of 1,250 Leeds operatives arrived in Hull, flocking in 'such numbers, that the inhabitants were quite at a loss to tell what such an influx of strangers portended', and their later departure was watched by a 'great number of spectators, assembled to witness the novel sight.'[13] In August 1848 the streets of York were said to be 'completely inundated with a vast concourse of strangers' on excursion trips from Huddersfield and neighbourhood, arriving on cheap pleasure trains.[14] At Whitsun in 1855 excursion trains brought many people from the West Riding of Yorkshire to York and a local reporter notes that 'a citizen could not fail to be struck with the crowds of strange faces continually passing before him.' The grounds of the Yorkshire Philosophical Society were thrown open to 'the million', to be 'besieged, possessed, and praised', in a setting 'usually appropriated by our more patrician citizens'.[15] Sensitivities about strangers arriving on steamer excursions were also expressed in April 1851 in a report of an excursion trip from Belfast to Bangor on a steamer by the Young Men's Total Abstinence Society. It describes the deck being completely filled with well-dressed tradesmen and their wives and daughters, decked in their holiday finery and the females carrying provision baskets.[16] A band was playing and there was utmost hilarity, jokes, laughter and merriment. Young lads and lasses from Bangor were on the lookout for company when they arrived, but jealousy was sensed and Bangor boys asserted that their 'toon was a place whar nae insults wad be taken frae strangers'. The general outlook of the local commentator on massed strangers however seemed to be that of a novelty, allied to a pleasure in educating their minds, and helping them to avoid moral temptations, rather than any sense that they were blocking normal thoroughfares.

Stereotyping was sometimes a feature in reports. An account about excursionists attending the Great Exhibition in 1851 used racial stereotypes in describing the crowd. It referred to 'the Anglo-Saxon element', the 'eager Hiberno-Celt', the 'peppery Cymbrian', the 'earnest and thoughtful Scot', the 'vivacious Frenchman', the 'phlegmatic German', and 'the proud and reserved Spaniard', who subsided into 'one great amalgam of sobriety and decorum'.[17] It was felt that it was perfectly acceptable to represent visitors from another region or country by an artificial stereotypical characteristic, which emphasised their difference. A large crowd of teetotal excursionists, 20,000 out of 68,000 visitors that day, attended the Exhibition on an August Tuesday, following temperance demonstrations in London. The Chartist *Northern Star* claimed that it was apparently 'the largest "teetotal army" which the cause of temperance has ever yet collected together in this country,' and that these were working-class families with 'orderly habits'.[18] However, it was reported in the press that a large group of them sang a *Welsh song* which 'produced a sensation entirely novel in this place', and apparently excited and disturbed the listeners so much that one made 'a violent attack on three women' and knocked them down. As a result singing was then prohibited. The press reporters treated the occasion with some amusement, commenting on the fact that the fountains stopped functioning as the teetotallers entered, preventing them from taking their usual beverage.[19]

In a few cases the element of 'strangeness' might relate to strange accents and clothing, but most reports of strangers do not discuss these characteristics. In 1850, however, at a time when people might have felt they were used to large crowds of working-class visitors to London, a new phenomenon arrived, an extra layer of 'strangeness'. The London correspondent of the *Nottinghamshire Guardian* described a 'Gallic cheap trip' to London, with 'hundreds of "forreners" in monstrous moustaches, enormous hats, mysterious blouses, and incomprehensible continuations' (a form of trouser). The *Morning Post* reported that there were 1,400 Parisians on this trip, brought to London by the South Eastern Railway, and commented on how the lengthy cavalcade and unusual appearance, 'the majority being of the working-class, *en blouse*, and wearing beards, attracted much curiosity.'[20] Again this novel experience was viewed by local people as a spectacle, as opposed to an unwelcome invasion, and therefore excursionists were allowed to occupy space.

There was generally little negative response to the potential nuisance value of excursion crowds of strangers, and none of the reports from the hosting towns complain of the crowd levels in this respect. It may well be that the 'strangers' were seen as a welcome economic opportunity for spending with local traders. Some commentators recognised this aspect, even if the visitors were working class, coming only for the day. In May 1846, Hudson offered the first York and North Midland cheap trip of the season on the new line to Scarborough, which had opened the previous year. The *Hull Packet* wrote excitedly about the opportunity for 'a ride of nearly 200 miles – a portion of it through the most beautiful scenery in Yorkshire – and a visit to the "Queen of the northern watering places".' It appears that it was assumed that this excursion would be attractive to the middle classes, but at the same time the report emphasised the liberality of the railway directors and hoped that this initiative will encourage 'the million' to take part. In the event only around 200 people rode on the train, in twelve carriages, giving rise to much disappointment amongst the people of Scarborough. It seems that the commercial interests in Scarborough thought they were going to benefit more from spending at their resort. Clearly behaviour was good and the press report refers to the need to allow for a slightly longer stay next time 'for a little rest and recuperation'.[21]

Thomas Cook had recognised the public relations value of highlighting the economic benefits of tourism, although his market was mainly middle class. At a public meeting in Edinburgh in 1858, he claimed that he had brought an average of 3,000 visitors to Scotland on his tours each season for twelve years, generating around £360,000 in benefit to the Scottish economy.[22] During the mid-nineteenth century there are a number of examples of local reporters calculating the spending power of working-class excursionists at destinations. The value of excursion tourism to Hull was calculated in August 1844, in a report estimating that around 20,000 pleasure seekers had visited the city on cheap trips over the previous twenty-three days, each spending around 2 shillings there and worth a total of £2,000, as well as profits to the railway company.[23] A note in the *Preston Chronicle* in October 1844 calculated that as much as £10,000 would have been spent on a recent cheap staying trip from the north to London.[24] Business opportunities worked both ways however. A press report of cheap trips from Blackburn to Blackpool and other seaside resorts in August 1851 commented on how money spent at the destination would have reduced expenditure with traders in the sending towns. It calculated that 12,000 visitors to Blackpool on an August Saturday might have spent £1,800 otherwise in their home towns, a substantial loss to the local economy.[25] Spending potential was used for other purposes too: a report in the *Liverpool Mercury* in June 1857 estimated that as a result of the Whit week trips on the Lancashire & Yorkshire line involving over 53,000 working people, at least £15,000 would be spent in three days, counting loss of time, railway fares and personal expenses, at 6s a head. It used this calculation to suggest that at this time there was little evidence of economic distress in the manufacturing districts, as otherwise these people would not have had the money to spend on leisure activities.[26]

Sometimes, however, hosts might be presented as taking advantage. In 1849 it was reported in the *Preston Chronicle* that a visitor to the Lakes on a cheap trip complained that the price of porter was *'two-pence halfpenny'* a glass.[27] The same year there were also complaints that, during a cheap trip by Sunday schoolchildren from Lancaster to Windermere, local people demanded payment in advance from the children for a glass of water, a response described as 'the grasping propensities of the inhabitants of Bowness.'[28]

There might be subtle codes of behaviour which were not always apparent to the excursion crowds. These were sometimes transgressed in the eyes of the destination hosts, putting the crowds at a disadvantage. A cheap trip by Leeds Sunday School Union (Dissenters) to Ripon in July 1849 had apparently been given permission by the Dean to visit the Cathedral 'to do just what they liked'. Consequently there were complaints in the press that they 'sang and played and *ate their dinner*, in the nave of the cathedral.'[29] Some rules of behaviour were devised as a protective mechanism to 'defend' excursionists against unwelcome advances from local residents when arriving at a destination. A glimpse of this might be seen in a report of a canal trip, when a party of 400 children from Swinton went on a boat trip on the Worsley Canal to the Art Treasures Exhibition at Manchester in 1857, landing at Knott Mill (later to be Deansgate Station, in the city centre).[30] The press report describes how the children had been briefed the day before, with a catechism about rules of behaviour, the kindness of the guardians in paying for the trip, and how they should be obedient and not be led astray by the attentions of the children in the area they were visiting. The writer describes how the minute the trippers landed they were surrounded by a 'swarm of non-descripts, all in rags and tatters'. One of the participants recalls the experience as like 'sailing through ink' because the local faces were so blackened. It was reported that many 'bribes' were offered to the visitors to move out of their prescribed ranks, but they resisted. Adopting a moralistic tone, the commentator noted:

'on one side upwards of 400 strong, hearty, blooming girls and boys, intelligent, neat, clean, and comfortably clad; and on the other side, ignorance, wretchedness and misery, from the puny infant to the decrepit grey head, bowed down with age.'

This must have been a very arresting visual reminder of the contrast between certain urban and rural working-class groups in Lancashire, with behaviour arising from circumstance.

Excursionists were sometimes seen as invaders, arising from concerns that these new arrivals were 'outsiders', who were planning to 'mark' or control space in some way, disrupting activity and introducing a break from order and normality. It may also have been that the sheer numbers involved evoked a threatening power, arising from their mass rather than class. Sometimes local communities viewed large excursion crowds in this way, especially if crowd behaviour was reported to be poor. The power of these leisure crowds to use space at a destination to mark their presence, and excite and concern observers and commentators, was illustrated by many newspapers, and could achieve either a positive or negative effect. On a trip in July 1846 of 180 boys from Herriot's Hospital in Edinburgh to Berwick on the North British Railway, 'the visitors excited a great sensation among the inhabitants, and were everywhere followed by a large and admiring crowd.' They marched around Tweedmouth in an 'interesting procession'.[31] Marching through a new space became a spectacle to be marvelled at, as the press repeatedly reported that resident crowds followed them and cheered. Such a noisy taking over of space did not please everyone. In July 1849, 600 people arrived in Grimsby on a works trip from Sheffield on the new Manchester, Sheffield & Lincolnshire line. They visited Grimsby Church and, 'wishing to make the natives aware of their arrival, "banged the bells about as though they had taken the town by storm, and a new order of things was about to be adopted". Although the "burgesses" were amused, not so the old clerk, who complained that "these sparks of the anvil" should have become "cocks of his middin", in such an abrupt and unceremonious a manner.'[32]

At times, excursionists might be seen to bring about unwelcome changes, when the need to maintain a social tone was an important consideration for some destinations. An advertisement for a hotel in Hornsea in the East Riding of Yorkshire in 1859 showed that it was trying to protect itself from such 'invasions' by attempting to position itself as a place 'without the bustle and annoyance occasioned by crowds of excursionists so frequently conveyed by Railways to other Watering Places.'[33]

It appears that at times, fear of diseases such as cholera were used as a weapon, when local residents might take steps to prevent excursionists from visiting destinations. Cholera epidemics in the early and mid-nineteenth century generated much debate about how this distressing disease was transmitted.[34] Contagionists held that the disease spread from person to person or through microbes in contaminated water, whereas the miasma theorists believed that cholera was spread by 'emanations' or vapours in the air arising from filth in streets and houses. While the former had dominated debate until 1800, during the nineteenth century the miasmists began to prevail, leading to pressures for sanitary reform. Contagionists had previously tended to belong to the 'ruling classes', whereas miasmists were often lower status physicians, but also commercial men anxious about the implications of the quarantine measures adopted by the contagionists. In 1849 a Manchester writer suggested that 'publicans of one large town… spread exaggerated reports about cholera in Liverpool, with a view to deterring passengers from visiting that town', as the business was damaging their trade.[35] Two reports in 1854 highlighted the role of the railway excursion in this concern, with varying stances reflecting both sides of the debate on the causes of this disease. While the role of 'contagion' in the spread of cholera was much argued publicly, by this time it was generally acknowledged that the causes of cholera arose from poor drainage and unhygienic sewerage practices rather than straightforward direct infection.[36] The *Sheffield & Rotherham Independent* reported that a severe outbreak of cholera had occurred at Cleethorpes, an east coast resort near Grimsby, much visited by Yorkshire operatives and their families on excursions. Two large trips arrived, from Sheffield and Beverley, but four of the visitors died during the night.[37] The report tells of great consternation in the town, and, as a result, the town leaders and railway companies made great attempts to assist the excursionists to return to their home towns as soon as possible, mobilising vehicles and issuing free railway tickets. Over the next few days between forty and fifty people developed cholera and fifteen died, thus the threat was a very real one, rather than a pretext. The Sheffield reporter attributed the outbreak to poor drainage and sanitary practices in Cleethorpes, and thus the evacuation of excursionists appeared to be carried out to protect them from developing the disease in the local area. Although there were great concerns about this disease, these did not seem to be about excursionists as active carriers on this occasion. However, when an excursion trip from Yorkshire to Poulton-le-Sands, north of Preston, led to three fatalities among the excursionists, on that occasion the *Lancaster Gazette* reporter did attribute the outbreak to the excursionists, but admitted that sewerage at Poulton needed improvements and that shellfish refuse was left to rot on the streets for manure. A later Board of Health meeting attributed the outbreak to an ill-managed cesspool.[38] The local press took the view that this was a severe blow to the local economy, as the report complained that 'Poulton is now almost destitute of Yorkshire visitors.' It appears that the spread of potentially fatal diseases involving excursion travellers may have been of great concern to people at the destinations, either because it impacted upon the reputation of the resort, or because they believed the excursionists were carriers, and access was sometimes prevented.

Powerful groups such as Sabbatarians, the aristocracy and the press all played a part in preventing the masses from visiting their destination, by using the law, money and voting powers. These groups had underlying class motives, for example Sabbatarian actions tended to focus on the working classes rather than the upper classes, who were able to continue their Sunday leisure activities unimpeded behind the closed doors of their country houses and carriages. The Sabbatarians controlled the availability of Sunday excursions and also limited access to leisure spaces such as parks. They represented Sunday behaviour as either 'acceptable' or 'unacceptable', in the street, in the church and in other public spaces. Even at the seaside, which could be defined as a democratic space, dependent on who owned the foreshore, as the beach and the sea have few limits, Sabbatarian influences could prevail, castigating excursion crowds as disturbing hordes.[39] The arrival of an excursion train at a small seaside resort was often viewed as an invasion. The occupation of destination space by Sunday excursion trippers led to criticism of their loud and joyful behaviour by Sabbatarians, who felt that Sundays should be quiet and dutiful. A correspondent to the *Manchester Times* in July 1849 on a visit to Fleetwood from Manchester noted the daily arrival of thousands of working-class visitors on the Lancashire & Yorkshire Railway.[40] He was particularly concerned about Sunday trips:

'for the last four Sabbaths nearly two thousand people, from different parts of the country, have each day been turned loose on the shore, sandhills and streets of this place, to the great annoyance of the quiet, orderly, and religious portion of the community…thousands of people…assemble at the railway station amidst levity, noise, and confusion; they pursue their journey with laughter and merriment… they are followed by numbers of the lower class, who offer them shelter and boiling water 'for a penny a head'…after their rambling around the town, sailing and bathing, with little regard to decency.'

He felt that excursion parties were a magnet for the local poor, who were easily influenced by these new visitors and their behaviour. He complained that local people were not attending church and Sunday school so much, because 'the working and poorer classes…are all watching the arrival and movements of the strangers, or engaged in turning their visit to advantage.' The writer felt that as the trippers only visited once in the season, then a Saturday would be better, and used the example of a Saturday trip from the Paley works, which was apparently very well behaved and organised, to support his Sabbatarian motives.

A correspondent to the *Ipswich Journal* in August 1851 complained about crowd problems when the Eastern Counties/Eastern Union Railway ran cheap excursion trains on Sundays from London to Ipswich. He complained of disturbances on the Sabbath, with crowds of local people waiting for these trains to arrive, sometimes fighting and drunk, and hoping to take money off the excursionists.[41] Sunday excursionists descending on the small Welsh town of Llangollen in August 1858 were attacked by powerful Sabbatarian groups, who made sure that their voices were heard in attacking this 'invasion' in the press.[42] A report of a Sunday school trip from Sheffield to Worksop Manor Park in September 1849 compared their excellent behaviour to that of a previous day school trip from Sheffield, which had resulted in some broken trees and shrubs, with poor behaviour blamed on lack of supervision by the managers. The commentator suggested that if this happened again then 'the noble owner of the estate will feel compelled, however reluctantly, to close the park gates to our new-made neighbours of large and populous towns, such as Sheffield, Manchester etc.' It appears that there were underlying religious tensions behind such reports, as in September 1851 the closure of the park on Sundays was announced, following reported 'depredations' and Sabbatarian pressures from the town against 'a large influx of strangers (brought by the railway every Sunday), who do not seem to have any regard for that sacred day.'[43]

Sabbatarian views would affect the reception of excursionist 'invasions'. When the Eastern Counties Railway opened their line to the small seaport of Harwich in Essex in August 1854, a key link to north European ports, they ran Sunday excursion trains. However the *Essex Standard* denounced these in a Sabbatarian polemic, reporting that 2,000 people had arrived in Harwich and 'the nuisance and disturbance to the residents of that little town, we are told, was inexpressible.' A month later though a press report refers to visiting excursionists 'by land and water', frequently 200 people deposited 'to roam and frolic to their hearts' content until the evening', but it is not clear which day of the week this was. Large-scale outings of Eastern Counties employees to Harwich were reported in 1855 and 1856, but whereas the 1855 Saturday trip was reported favourably, the 1856 Sunday trip was criticised, with a letter alongside from an outraged Sabbatarian.[44]

Sabbatarian pressures succeeded in introducing a piece of legislation during the 1850s which resulted in the working-class excursionist becoming subject to a particular class-based distinction, when their status as 'real' travellers came into question following the Sale of Beer Act 1854.[45] Key groups (in particular magistrates, the police and publicans) responded to the arrival of excursion crowds into public houses at their destination with particularly nuanced views. There were a number of interpretations of the status of the excursionist, dependent on the perspective of the observer. The Act was an emphatic example of class discrimination, which applied to the public house frequented by the working man, rather than to the hotel visited by the rich. It restricted the sale of beer in public houses on Sundays and public holidays in England and Wales, to the hours between 1pm and 2.30pm and between 6pm and 10pm, which meant that someone arriving after 10pm, following a long journey, would not be able to get a drink. Whereas the ordinary man might have thought he had achieving a worthy ambition in travelling hundreds of miles to the metropolis, powerful groups were once again winning the contest over leisure space, by keeping the working classes out, relegating the excursionist to a lower grade of participant in the consumption of leisure, as an exemption from the 10pm limit only covered '*bona fide* travellers'.[46]

Magistrates played a key role in ruling on this issue, and their decisions were dependent on the level of liberalism in their outlook. The term *bona fide* had been added to the previous legal terminology in an attempt to encourage magistrates to be careful whom they acknowledged as a 'real' traveller, implying that a mere excursionist was not a *genuine* traveller. Refusing to view an excursionist as a '*bona fide* traveller' would prevent him/her from accessing welcome refreshment at his destination. (By contrast steamboat excursionists had their refreshments on board, although they were unlikely to be travelling late at night.[47])The new legislation proved challenging, as excursionists were likely to arrive in towns in desperate need of a drink at this time. There were particular problems in public houses around the terminus of the South Western Railway at Waterloo and the Eastern Counties at Shoreditch, leading to riots among angry excursionists when the Act came into force on Sunday, 13 August 1854.[48]

In the case of the magistrates it appeared, therefore, that because the excursionist was perceived to be in a large group, likely to be working class, and had arrived very *speedily*, then all these factors counted against him in assessing his status as a *real* traveller arriving at his destination. Magistrates tied themselves in knots to interpret this exemption when the police hauled in publicans who were serving excursionists after 10 pm on Sundays. Some magistrates were favourable. In the report of a case at Southwark in October 1854, a publican stated that he asked to see excursion tickets before admitting excursionists and that in his view most had come up 'a hundred miles from town' therefore he regarded them as *bona fide* travellers. The report noted that the police had said 'the persons in the house looked like country people... but it was difficult...to discover who were travellers and who were not.' The magistrate decided they were travellers. The terminology of the 'traveller' was hotly debated and there was much diversity of opinion by magistrates.[49] Most interpretations discriminated against the person on a cheap trip, as the example of a Select Committee witness shows, who made clear that *bona fide* meant 'more than pleasure'. Trips for pleasure for the masses were often not regarded as 'proper', although of course the middle and upper classes had been doing this for years without discrimination. Edward Yardley, a Thames magistrate, seems to deny any value to the cheap trip, when he said to the Committee: 'I cannot bring my mind to the conviction that excursionists are travellers because they are going for an "excursion or a promenade".' Such debates clearly show how difficult it was to reach an agreement about the importance of this new kind of mobility, within the existing social structure. A London magistrate found it impossible to define the term 'traveller' and felt disposed to award it a liberal (but gender-biased) interpretation: 'a man who went for recreation or business to such a distance that he required refreshment.' In his view however the addition of *bona fide* to travellers excluded the excursionist, as it implied something more substantial or worthy than pleasure. Some magistrates said the legislation *included* all excursionists, some said it *excluded* all excursionists, some suggested it depended on the distance travelled.

The police were also engaged by the issue. They were reported to have said that 'passengers who arrive in London by railway are not travellers within the meaning of the act.' There were numerous difficulties involved in proving status as a working-class traveller, both to the publicans and to the police when they became involved, because this depended on their word and showing a relevant ticket, which the excursionist might have already given up.[50] Publicans also had difficulties, as their defence organisations had conceded constraints on their operation, by agreeing to the restrictions without contesting them, to ensure that they could maintain their profitable business.[51] Thus, although they had been keen to recognise the excursionist as a traveller and allow him/her in, at the same time benefiting substantially from a profitable and growing market, their concerns about their legal obligations constrained their ability to act until the law changed again.

By December 1854 there was a growing campaign focusing on the oppressive effect of the new legislation on excursionists and their rights, led by unhappy publicans who had seceded from the original trade organisations, and their champion, the Liberal MP Henry Berkeley, an 'arch-enemy of Evangelicalism'.[52] A Select Committee was appointed to investigate, chaired by Berkeley and packed with his supporters.[53] Berkeley recognised the need to support the needs of the working classes, painting a rosy picture of their desire to occupy new space at their destinations, both inside and outside the public house, at the same time claiming that Sunday trippers from his area (Bristol) frequently attended church during their excursions. He welcomed the new opportunities for the masses to visit the seaside and expand their minds.[54] Berkeley quickly used a brief recommendation from his Select Committee to push through a repealing Act in 1855, which extended the Sunday closing time to 11pm and removed the term *bona fide* from traveller exemption. This still meant of course that a term was used without a functional legal definition.[55] The speedy means by which the Act was repealed owed much to public concern about Sunday trading riots in 1855 however, as well as Berkeley's clever manoeuvres.[56]

The press was a powerful player in shaping how local people viewed the arrival of excursionists at a destination. However, views and perceptions of the new excursion crowds by the host destinations and by reporters feature rarely in press coverage of the period beyond stylised narratives covering a few facts and reports of good behaviour. Each publication had a political stance, and the views and forces of Sabbatarians, commercial interests and railway stockholders influenced the comments and reports appearing in these publications. Correspondence columns included material selected, edited and/or censored as with all reporting, according to editorial preference. The provincial press was very focused on its local base, and in the Victorian period local people began to feel a sense of pride and affection for their own cities, reflecting public buildings, monuments and civic pageantry. Some excursion accounts demonstrate how the experience of welcoming a crowd of visitors generated a curious mixture of pride and cynicism amongst residents at a destination, especially one unused to tourist attention. Reporting on excursions often appeared in the provincial press under 'Local Intelligence', with information secured from local reporters based in towns and villages surrounding the newspaper base.[57] Their perspective tended, therefore, to highlight the wonders of their localities, and they were normally very proud to report that large numbers of people had visited their area. Very rarely were reporters negative about a trip, unless the circumstances were out of control, as with a visit to Whitby from York which was 'greatly marred by the incessant rain which set in, and they acquired but an indifferent impression of the town and neighbourhood.'[58] Pride in and loyalty to one's own locality was a value typically held in rural areas, spreading throughout the Victorian era into the towns and cities, reinforced by the new groupings such as clubs, bands and sporting teams, even developing a form of tribalism.[59] Occasionally it was the spectacle which impressed, despite a seeming inconvenience to local residents and businesses; in Rhyl in 1857, a trip of working people, mainly miners and colliers, arrived from Wrexham, and a reporter described the excursion crowd on Rhyl's single main street: 'into this street the whole of the excursionists poured until it was almost filled from the top to the bottom – one dense, solid black mass of pleasure-seeking human beings.'[60]

Views about excursionists from a particular region sometimes reflected certain perceived characteristics of that region. A press report from 1858 on West Riding excursionists coming into Liverpool in a 'vast influx' reassures the writer on the state of prosperity in the West Riding manufacturing districts, as well as their conduct, although 'uncouth in manners and speech'.[61] In 1845 and 1846, visitors to Sheffield on cheap trips were given the opportunity to inspect manufacturing processes in some local firms, an interesting fore-runner of elements of industrial tourism which developed in the twentieth century in the 1980s and 1990s.[62] A local commentator was very scathing about these factory visits in 1845, suggesting that the 'concocter' of the placard was 'uncommonly clever at dressing up a case', and inviting local townsmen to 'a perception of our grandeur'. At this time Sheffield lacked the urban elites, the political leaders who might foster a sense of civic pride, as it was not so much a city as a group of distinct working-class communities, despite being one of the seven largest towns in England by 1851.[63] However, by 1846, this activity was being more proudly mentioned: 'others, through the kind permission of some of our townsmen, were favoured with an inspection of the different processes of the stable manufactures in several of the principal establishments in the town.' There is the possibility that excursions were helping to develop a sense of pride in a town's achievements.

Bradford was a rapidly growing town, which became incorporated in 1847, but it had a Radical reputation, with a reputation for riots after anti-Poor Law, Orange and Chartist uprisings there in the 1830s and 1840s.[64] An 1850 directory was uncomplimentary about its public buildings so it is not surprising to find that in that year a *Bradford Observer* reporter commented that an excursion *to* Bradford was 'rather a novel idea'.[65] His report described a small trip of Sheffield people on a very rainy day, suggesting concern that the visitors would not have been impressed by a town 'ankle deep in mud', but hoped that such trips might become more frequent, as Bradford was proud of its industry and commerce.[66] In Nottingham in 1857 journalists, evoking civic pride, complained that they were not on the line for excursionists and that Bradshaw's railway guide treated Nottingham very poorly and inaccurately in its descriptions as a travel destination.[67]

Sometimes the press suggested that the new railway excursions would have an effect on relationships between towns in a region. The press report of the Sheffield excursion to Leeds in 1840 commented that 'no amusement can be more harmless, or more calculated to produce kind and social feelings between the inhabitants of neighbouring towns.'[68] It is not clear how far this was an aspiration of the reporter rather than a reality, but it was certainly a theme running through activities by mechanics institutes in relation to visiting each other on excursions. Occasionally an excursion led to a return visit from the destination town, as in the case of the visit from York to Whitby in 1850.[69]

The term 'tripper' has been used as a product of the railway age, referring to working-class tourists with a limited amount of time to visit one place cheaply.[70] It appears to have been first used regularly in the early 1850s in the provincial press in relation to railway excursions. In 1852 some 8,000 to 10,000 people were visiting York in 'vast assemblages' at Whitsun, making use of excursion fares, and it was reported that these included 800 'trippers' from Todmorden.[71] However the term had been used in the press at least as early as 1813 in relation to general holidaymakers, with a reference to 'trippers to the seaside for a week' at Margate.[72] In 1851 the poet and journalist Eliza Cook cemented the term by writing an article on *The Cheap Tripper* for her *Journal*, describing:

'a new character that has sprung up within the last few years in the manufacturing districts. The Tripper is the growth of railways and monster trains. Before they were, he was not.'[73]

This suggests the growing importance of this new phenomenon, proclaiming the appearance of a new 'tribe' of leisure tourist.

At the same time the press could paint excursion crowds in much more negative tones to suit its own agenda. The working classes had been engaged in sea-bathing over many years, usually naked and unsegregated, so it could not necessarily be said that the working classes were following the lead of the upper and middle classes in taking advantage of seaside destinations.[74] The 'Padjamers' had visited Blackpool on carts, bathing naked and drinking hard, but spending very little, thus not benefiting the local traders.[75] With the new railway crowds the problem was made worse by the nuisance of local hawkers following them around. The press could be critical of behaviour at seaside resorts.[76] In 1856 a report on an excursion crowd painted a riotous picture of an invasion of people, arriving in Weston-super-Mare from Bristol. It suggested that the local population had been much disturbed, although frustratingly this report appears to be uncorroborated by other evidence:

'A horde of savages making an excursion on a civilised settlement is the only figure we can imagine as fitting to express the general feeling held by our townspeople in regard to them. A mass of boys and girls, and young men and women, comprising the lowest dregs of the more disreputable neighbourhoods of Bristol, who swarmed every avenue and invaded every nook; the songs of the birds were hushed by the oaths of blasphemy, the ears of innocence shocked by the accents of obscenity; the air was polluted with the smoke of the noxious pipe, puffed forth by almost infant lips; gardens were robbed; drunken boys were to be seen staggering through every thoroughfare, fights were of frequent occurrence in the streets of the town, and scenes of lewdness met the eye of day. It was of course out of the question to expect our two policemen, aided by three special constables, to be able to watch over the movements of some 5,000 or 6,000 persons, roving at will over town and suburbs.'[77]

This account is surprisingly vehement in its description of how the visitors were seen by their hosts, contrasting the 'horde of savages' who were 'the lowest dregs' with our 'civilised settlement'. The large number of visitors involved, 5,000–6,000 people, would inevitably have overrun a small community of around 9,000 people at that time, and therefore it is perhaps understandable that local residents were shocked by this event.[78] The sheer mass of this urban crowd arriving in great numbers and the underlying rivalry between the 'civilised' watering place of Weston-super-Mare and the 'disreputable neighbourhoods' of Bristol contributed to a projection by the press of this type of activity as completely unacceptable. It is not clear of course how far the underlying values of the commentator shaped the press perception of this behaviour. It may well have been written in a bid to defend Weston from future invasions by trippers.

In May 1849 the *Times* attempted to dampen down enthusiasm for developing mass mobility over the English Channel, discouraging the idea that the masses might wish to explore new horizons. It expressed great alarm that parties of excursionists were about to visit Paris, with concerns that 'the quality of these migratory hordes will deteriorate' with further excursions.[79] The writer suggested that the cheapness of the excursion would militate against participants conducting themselves on the streets of Paris 'with becoming decency and propriety', being part of a 'bacchanalian excursion party' in the face of the 'mocking and fiery spirit of the Parisian mob'. He criticised the excursion agents as mere speculators and noted that these parties were not official 'deputations', therefore if there were misbehaviour on either side they could expect no special consideration. Thus, by implication, the behaviour of excursion masses could not be trusted, because they were not from the upper classes. The working-class excursionists in groups should not therefore be allowed to travel overseas in such groups, as the writer makes an assumption that behaviour would be poor and reflect badly on the 'British reputation'. In this manner the press attacked the entrepreneurial spirit of excursion agents who held the key to excursionists' access to new spaces for leisure, although there is no suggestion that this would apply to workers emigrating for work purposes.

Such press criticism attempted to exercise a powerful restraint on the working classes extending their ambitions to travel overseas; possibly their comments influenced excursion organisers to shape their trips with constraints not imposed on middle and upper-class travellers. In 1860 a Working Men's Excursion to Paris was proposed, which eventually took place in May 1861. Excursion trains carried 1,700 people from Liverpool, Manchester, Leeds, Sheffield, Bradford, York, Bristol and Bath as well as London, coordinating with trains and steamers between London, Folkestone, Boulogne and Paris. The projectors took great pains to emphasise that this trip had no political motives, implying that the working-class traveller could not be trusted to refrain from attempting to unbalance the social order, but was said to be planned to encourage fellow feeling between English and French workmen, and to share manufacturing techniques.[80] Such attitudes possibly arose partly from the history of this excursion, which had originally been proposed by a Frenchman, Klotz Rowsell, who had written to the French Emperor suggesting that he organise a 'Volunteer's excursion' to Paris. Understandably this had not mustered support from either the British or the French, in view of its military connotations.[81]

New destinations for excursionists took a variety of forms, for example cities, historic buildings, the seaside and countryside. The aristocracy sold land to railway companies for lines, and the pattern of their landholding at some seaside resorts influenced the development of such resorts and access by the masses. Aristocratic spaces such as the country estate proved to be very popular with excursionists in the mid-nineteenth century.[82] Country house visiting had been popular as early as the second half of the eighteenth century: Horace Walpole complained in 1783 that he was 'tormented all day and every day' by people coming to see his house in London, with records showing around 300 people visiting each summer.[83] But until the mid-nineteenth century it was the gentry and professional classes who were involved in the 'relaxed pastime of country house visiting' as 'polite tourists', aspiring to get closer to the aristocracy.

The democratisation of country house visiting was achieved by the railway. When the Manchester, Buxton, Matlock & Midland Junction Railway opened its line from Ambergate, north of Derby, in June 1849 it only extended as far as Rowsley, but helpfully that was a mere 3 miles from the great house at Chatsworth.[84] With the arrival of working-class masses at these country estates, large crowds were reported, without causing particular concerns from landowners. Some aristocrats recognised that the working classes would not necessarily be a threat against their attractive estates. At Chatsworth there had always been a spirit of allowing all to visit. The Duchess of Devonshire described a notice from 1844, which actually dates back at least as early as 1831, when it was noted by J.C. Loudon in his account of a gardening tour of the country:

'The Duke of Devonshire allows all persons whatever to see Chatsworth, the house as well as the grounds, every day in the year, from ten in the morning till five... The humblest individual is not only shown the whole, but the duke has expressly ordered the waterworks to be played for everyone without exception.'[85]

Unusually in this instance there is an emphasis on a possible mix of classes, 'the humblest individual', although before 1849, Chatsworth's location would have made it difficult for anyone without suitable transport to visit. Loudon praised the Duke's approach and made the usual positive claims about behaviour:

'this is acting in the true spirit of great wealth and enlightened liberality...in the spirit of wisdom... We have never heard of any injury being done to any object at Chatsworth; every party or person always being accompanied by an attendant.'

It was suggested that the new railway led to 80,000 people visiting Chatsworth each summer during this period. It may well be that Head Gardener Joseph Paxton's energy and drive, and his rise from humble beginnings, mentored by the Duke of Devonshire, encouraged them both to allow many more ordinary people to see the estate. The first mass excursion of 400 people from Derby took place in June 1849, but the fare at 3s

6d second-class return appears quite expensive for a journey of around 11 miles each way, although it would have included admittance to the house and grounds (the Duke had expressly instructed his staff not to accept tips from the visitors), and also enabled people to see Haddon Hall and Matlock Bath if they wished.[86] A further 'pleasure trip and temperance gathering' was described from Sheffield in July 1849, and although omnibuses and other vehicles were available to meet the trains, allowed by Paxton to take the shorter route through the park, these were soon filled, but many people were happy to walk the 3 miles to the house. Around 4,000 to 5,000 people arrived in one day, 'the great park and grounds in front of the house being one complete mass of people all arrayed in their holiday attire.'[87] This suggests that at times working-class excursion crowds were able to make successful use of new leisure space, supported by aristocratic power and the approbation of the press.

In some cases it appears that the aristocracy welcomed approval and admiration of their magnificent works by as many people as possible, and this might have influenced their views on the behaviour of their visitors. It may be that the aristocracy agreed to open their houses to the masses as a kind of compromise to defend against radicalism following concerns about Reform and Chartism.[88] They were under pressure from the middle classes to host visits from organised excursions, as a form of noblesse oblige, a way of acting in keeping with their status, but in the case of Chatsworth it seems that the Duke and Paxton were genuinely keen to ensure that the masses were able to appreciate the spectacular works undertaken there, of which they were very proud. In 1854 Paxton claimed that the working-class visitors to Chatsworth were always quiet and orderly, referring to one occasion when a group started to eat a picnic in the grounds rather than the Park, which was not allowed, and their own fellow group members admonished them.[89]

In 1847, when Leeds Mechanics Institution paid a visit to Castle Howard with colleagues from other Yorkshire MIs and members of the public, there were thousands visiting the estate and the 'noble owner' threw open the doors of his house to the multitude, albeit thirty people at a time.[90] Writing in her diary in 1853, Countess Granville was visiting her sister at Castle Howard and remarked that 'the cheap excursion trains enchant me… They sit about with their baskets of provisions as if it were the Bois de Boulogne, and the Methodist schools sing hymns beautifully.'[91] Sir Thomas Hesketh of Rufford in Lancashire hosted several visits to his estate by cheap trip participants on the newly opened East Lancashire Railway between Liverpool and Preston, in 1850, 1851 and 1852. Large crowds ranging from several hundred to several thousand working-class teetotallers from Liverpool and Preston travelled to a 'temperance fête' in his grounds. The press noted their behaviour, highlighting the good conduct and enjoyable time, and the way that the local villagers joined in with the activities, with the National Anthem being sung at the end.[92] The owner adopted a somewhat paternalist approach to encouraging the middle and working classes to mingle. Some excursions had temperance themes, and processions were formed, shaping order. Although the masses were able to visit, it was on Hesketh's terms, and he retained control over his estate. Similarly, following a Sunday school excursion to Kirklees Park in West Yorkshire in May 1849, the children were collected into an obligatory procession to thank the owners 'for their kindness' during the visit.[93]

There are other examples: in 1852 Lord Londesborough welcomed 600 excursionists from neighbouring towns to his country house and it was reported that he 'appeared to take a lively interest in the recreation of his numerous visitors', despite a reputation for being highly strung and unwilling even to see his servants.[94] Some members of the aristocracy took a proactive approach to offering excursionists access to new public spaces. The Earl of Yarborough (who was also Chairman of the Manchester, Sheffield & Lincolnshire Railway) hosted excursion visits to his Lincolnshire estate, Brocklesbury Park, in 1849, to raise funds for the Lincoln Penitent Female Society, when 10,000 people arrived. He also hosted large-scale temperance excursions to nearby Thornton Abbey, for example 25,000 people one August Monday in 1849.[95] In 1856 Lord Lyttelton published a letter in the press urging employers to consider his country estate at Hagley as a suitable venue for works trips, with no restriction on numbers or frequency, apart from 'simple rules' to be followed.[96] These show how huge excursion crowds in aristocratic space could be regarded as acceptable rather than threatening, and although large numbers of the working classes were involved, such events projected an atmosphere of respectability, enhancing the reputation of large groups of operatives.

However it appears that at times the aristocracy did feel threatened by the masses accessing their space. Cheap trips to the grounds and gardens of Alton Towers in Staffordshire attracted over 4,000 visitors from Manchester on a September Monday in 1850. The reported plucking of flowers from the garden, accompanied by 'gross misconduct' and 'violence' by some drunken individuals, led to the head gardener closing these to visitors.[97] In Cheshire, the Stanleys, who lived at Alderley, objected to the invasion of their estate by excursionists on a new line (the Alderley station on the Manchester & Birmingham Railway had opened in May 1842).[98] Lady Stanley seemed to grudgingly accept large parties of Sunday school boys, possibly because their teachers seemed appropriately appreciative of 'the indulgence', although she expressed a concern about opportunities for political debate when predicting that there would be 'no polemical discussions amongst them', despite the family's Liberal views. At this time the Stanleys appeared to be more concerned about the 'Cottontots', the prosperous inhabitants living to the south of Manchester. Waddington, Deputy Chairman of the Manchester & Birmingham, came personally to persuade the Stanleys that they should allow the

'Cottontot grandees' to visit on days when the masses were not allowed, i.e. 'private days'. It was argued by Lord Stanley to his daughter-in-law that these would be 'respectable people', but Lady Stanley remarked that they were particularly offensive: 'you would be discomforted…if…lying reading or sketching or thinking…all of a sudden an uproarious party of Cottontots came upon you.' Lady Stanley recognised that the Cottontots had a power which ordinary people lacked; she amusingly found the 'Cottontot grandees' more annoying than the operatives, 'as one can neither hand cuff nor great dog them if they are intrusive or offensive.' By implication this owner felt able to use powers of restraint against the masses who were perceived to be misbehaving. But Lady Stanley was fighting a losing battle and by 1844, the Edge had been laid out with walks and seats. However the masses suffered some privations in accessing this beauty spot. On a cheap trip from Manchester to Alderley in 1844, when around 3,000 people descended on this small village, it was reported that the Manchester & Birmingham directors had entirely overlooked the 'commissariat department', and there was a complete lack of food and refreshments unless passengers had brought these with them.[99]

Most press accounts of railway excursions in the mid-nineteenth century used a familiar formula of stock phrases in their narratives, which emphasised the good behaviour of the crowds, the beneficial moral effects on the masses and finally a safe return home without the merest accident. This style of language appears to have resulted from a conspiracy between provincial newspaper editors in collusion with their colleagues among urban elites to present a positive picture of their towns and cities, a kind of intense localism while confronting the need for social reform.[100] It was seen to be essential that they portrayed, as far as possible, a well-ordered impression to outsiders, to avoid a reputation for rioting which might have a negative impact on their local economies. The *Manchester Guardian* for example, although initially radical, later came to represent the manufacturing and commercial interests of the city, while still supporting local improvements such as public parks and rational recreation, and therefore tended to be positive about excursions.[101]

While press reporting and commentary adopted a particular tone in covering excursions, it is clear that these might not represent underlying 'realities'. It is possible to find evidence from different perspectives of how space was claimed by the new excursions. For example, in 1850, it was reported in some newspapers that what was intended to be a small party of well-behaved Dissenting Sunday school teachers on an excursion visit to Exeter Cathedral turned into a large crowd of 3,000 Dissenters rampaging around the Cathedral. There were complaints in the Conservative and Church of England supporting press that these excursionists clambered into the Bishop's throne, took possession of the pulpit, drank from a bottle of water in the piscina, and tried on the canon's vestments. By contrast the liberal *Manchester Times* did not mention such behaviour in its report, merely that the clerical dignitaries had extended special courtesy to them, suggesting that the reported outrage might be more due to an anti-Dissenter press perspective which embellished the story.[102] A further example of a reported invasion occurred in the Scottish Borders in 1851, when around 900 operatives on a trip from the Stephenson engine works of Newcastle to Kelso, were reported to have become drunk. The observer complained that some were staggering about *without hats or coats*, a 'complete riot developed' and, 'the railway station was almost taken possession of by the drunken rabble.' Eventually two men were taken into custody. The account appeared in the *Bristol Temperance Herald*, and thus has a particular perspective critical of drink rather than excursions generally.[103] The criticism of the taking off of hats and coats reflected a key feature of behaviour which was no longer 'respectable', as it indicated a state of undress.

Hampton Court Palace opened to the masses in 1838, and this was praised by radical writer William Howitt in 1840, who also noted the impact of steam, in that many ordinary people were able to take cheap trips there on the newly opened London & Southampton Railway, whose station was at Kingston, not too far from the Palace.[104] A station at Hampton Court itself was eventually opened by the renamed London & South Western Railway in 1849, although a Palace historian claimed that the new station made little difference to the attendance figures, which averaged around 200,000 visitors a year between 1850 and 1870, in his view because of the other attractions available at that time. William Howitt had praised the occupation of this new destination space by the masses, saying 'the very people have taken possession' (of those parts not housing the aristocracy).[105] He commented that 'the average number of visitors on Sunday or Monday is now two thousand five hundred, and the amount of them for the month of August was thirty two thousand!' His comments and those of his critics, about the reported behaviour of the excursionists, became a cause célèbre in 1840, with typically opposing views. Howitt asked, 'and how have these swarms of Londoners of all classes behaved?' Apart from a few scratches on the stairs he avowed there had been 'not the slightest exhibition of …the English love of demolition' and that he had never seen a 'more orderly or well-pleased throng of people'. His reference to demolition appears to be a sideswipe at powerful groups who sought to pull down old buildings, and claims that it was the elites in these groups who were more damaging to the landscape than the working classes. Howitt noted that on Whit Monday there were thousands of poor people at Hampton Court with decorous behaviour, some travelling in spring vans as an alternative to the cheap railway trips. He made striking claims about the importance of this new mobility, influenced by his political and social reform background, in introducing the masses to culture, confirming the advantages of education for the masses, and demonstrating the benefits of rational recreation for the million.

On the other hand, an anonymous reviewer in the *Gentleman's Magazine* was offended by Howitt's favourable views of the visitors and suggested that 'demolition' is 'perpetually going on'. He claimed to have 'repeatedly seen offenders…fined for the damage which in wanton acts of mischief they had committed…flowers gathered and stolen.' He claimed that the people involved 'have not ceased to be the most intolerable nuisance that any town was infested with…ladies cannot walk out unprotected', and hinted at the conduct by using an Italian word *immondezza,* meaning filthiness.[106] There were, therefore, often two points of view about behaviour, depending on the background of the observer, and an apparent view that there were some public spaces that were suitable for the working classes and others from which they should be excluded.

It becomes apparent that observers had different views, when the issue of the behaviour of excursionists at Hampton Court Palace blew up again in *The Times* in 1852. Initially a leader article had criticised religious opposition to the proposed opening of the Crystal Palace on Sunday afternoons, suggesting that the poor were not attending church anyway so keeping Crystal Palace open would not make them go to church. This highlighted the class impact, as Sunday was the only day when the working classes had leisure time, unlike the middle and upper classes, and the lack of nearby green fields as an alternative. A few days later an anonymous correspondent responded to the article, highlighting contentious views about the behaviour of the masses in these new spaces, complaining that a Sabbatarian minister, Reverend Daniel Wilson of Islington, had suggested of the visitors to Hampton Court Palace (which had already been open unofficially on Sundays for quite some time) that 'people come intoxicated, and the scenes in these gardens on the afternoon of the Lord's day are beyond description…creating a hell upon earth.' The correspondent wrote that this was all untrue and suggested people check with the police as he had not seen any drunkenness. His claims were subsequently supported by the Palace Chapel organist, Dr Selle, who agreed that, despite his being at the palace every Sunday for seven years and seeing the conduct of the masses there, it was 'orderly, quiet and respectful', and he had never seen anyone drunk. He seems to be an authoritative source about behaviour, as he was a regular eye-witness in a respected position. Wilson wrote himself claiming to have talked again to the persons from whom he got his information and repeating it. He then reveals his underlying motives and class prejudice, by saying 'there is a marked difference between the respectability and good conduct of those who visit the Palace on weekdays compared to Sundays.' Finally a German correspondent wrote that as a regular Sunday visitor he had never seen any 'badly behaved or drunken person… often struck with the good and quiet behaviour of the multitude, of whom many were humble and… respectable persons.' He claimed that this contradicted 'the assertion, that the poorer classes did not know how to behave themselves.'[107] The Palace historian, writing in 1891, noted that Wilson had no personal experience of the matter, that he was using Sabbatarian 'sweeping, second-hand imputations' and when asked for his evidence he 'evaded the issue, reiterated his assertions, and took refuge in vague generalities.'[108] In falling back on unsubstantiated and general claims of 'bad behaviour', the prejudices of religious groups such as Sabbatarians and other commentators, who might be reformers and journalists, could distort accounts of excursionists' behaviour. In general however, there is no reason to believe that the working classes did not behave themselves in their new mobility.

The excursionist could be reported as an invader or occupier of space, as illustrated by accounts of a 'disturbance' at Bangor in North Wales in September 1854, but again viewable from a number of perspectives. A large group of Birkenhead workmen had enjoyed a Saturday railway excursion to Bangor, paid for by their employer, Brassey, Peto & Co, at the Canada Works, which was built to construct components for the Grand Trunk Railway of Canada.[109] The first press report, in the *Liverpool Mercury*, merely stated that the trip had taken place, noting that 800 workmen were involved, and highlighted the beneficence of the manager, George Harrison, Brassey's brother-in-law, in awarding each man his day's wages for the trip, as well as the costs. The second report appeared in the *North Wales Chronicle* (also syndicated to a range of other papers in the country) and features the characteristics of an invasion, the driving out of the hosts from their own spaces. It described disreputable disturbances in Bangor as a result of the trip and thundered that cheap trips were 'injurious to watering places' as they brought a 'rabble', which drove out respectable people from their neighbourhood. It suggested that 1,100 people were involved:[110]

'Large numbers of them were in a state of intoxication, and made an irruption into the Britannia Bridge Refreshment Rooms, taking and destroying everything in their way. Then they set to, fighting all the way along the Menai Bridge Road, and entered Bangor in a most riotous and disorderly manner. Some of them went into the inns and seized upon the porter and spirits, and others began again fighting. The whole city, from the Station to the Market Place, was scandalised, and the tradespeople were obliged to close their shops, such a scene of riot and confusion occurring. The ruffians who so disgraced themselves were not content with inflicting violence on each other, but beat and ill-treated women and children. The police at length interfered, and three of the fellows were captured and kept in the lock-ups till Monday, when they were brought before the Magistrates and fined. We hope we shall have no more excursionists of this description, or decent people will be afraid to come amongst us and reside here.'[111]

A police report in the *Chronicle* the same day covered the conviction of three men for drunken and disorderly conduct, and added a further perspective. It described a riotous and disorderly scene near the Market Place, when the men were fighting: 'hundreds of people were congregated, and the women were shouting "murder" from the windows of the upper room.' At the court hearing it was reported that one of the Brassey foremen spoke up for the men and expressed his regret, and suggested that these were the black sheep of a very large flock of a thousand men.[112] The significance of these reports can be placed in context when a further account appeared from an alternative viewpoint, two weeks later. The *North Wales Chronicle* published a letter from the organising committee of this trip, aggrieved by the reporting of this behaviour and concerned that it might affect future trips. It stated that most men were not intoxicated, and that the Refreshment Room was the only place available to eat and therefore most had picnics elsewhere. They later assembled on the 'green sward' to dance to a band, after which they marched back to Bangor headed by a band, keeping together to avoid missing the return train. The committee denied any fighting at this point, but accepted that, on their return to Bangor, not more than five or six were fighting, witnessed by their manager. The primary concern of the writers was, however, that such reports were likely to 'inflict a serious injury on all large bodies of working men.' The editor of the *Chronicle* could not resist a response published with this letter, claiming that it was 'impudent and untrue', referring to the excursionists as 'blackguards' and 'ruffians' with a contempt for 'sobriety and good order' and suggesting that the writers were trying to bully the press.[113]

The two accounts reflect opposing perspectives, with the use of words such as 'rabble', for example by the press, to paint a picture of ill-behaved visitors trying to claim space in a 'respectable' watering place by supposedly taking and destroying. The press describes its own residents as respectable and decent, whereas the excursionists were seen as riotous, disorderly, drunk and fighting. On the other hand, the visitors controlled their use of the new space by marching back to the station in a procession headed by a band. Even so this was seen as a provocative move by the local press, who then accused the organising committee of bullying them when it tried to defend the actions of the men. There was a clash here between the perspective of the residents, who wanted to retain an orderly image amid fears of invasion, and the concerns of the working classes that in large crowds they were misrepresented as featuring violent disorder, and maligned in their attempts to occupy space. While it is difficult to make a judgement about the truth of the statements in this case, the balance of press reporting about behaviour was negative, with a report by their observer and an account of court proceedings (both of which were critical), matched against a response from the men themselves, which although awarded a fair amount of press space, was followed by a rebuff from the editor.

The Lake District proved to be a regular class battleground, with varying views on who might be seen as 'good tourists' and 'bad tourists' in the occupation of tourist space, following the arrival of excursion crowds. After the railway line to Windermere opened in 1847, the newly organised cheap trips to the Lake District generated a high level of participation by the masses.[114] Large crowds gathered in popular places, some attracted by the celebrity of local residents such as the poet Wordsworth at Rydal Mount. This 'invasion' was debated hotly in the press at the time by reporters and in the correspondence columns, leading to discussions about who might be seen as fit and proper persons to take up such space and linking to the hierarchy of participants in the new tourism. Press accounts highlighted how 'invasions' of the masses might be treated differently to the 'tourist' activity involving the middle and upper classes, who presumably accessed these spaces by a kind of osmosis. When the Kendal & Windermere Railway was proposed in 1844, Wordsworth infamously expressed concern that his own area should be 'safe from the molestation of cheap trains pouring out their hundreds at a time along the margin of Windermere.'[115] It is not clear from this which apparent feature of molestation was worse, the impact of technology or of excursion crowds. He argued from a view of morality, suggesting that the lower classes would bring low habits to local residents: 'the injury which would thus be done to morals, both among this influx of strangers and the lower class of inhabitants, is obvious.' At the same time he used another weapon, invoking Sabbatarian views to argue against this activity, as it was likely to take place on a Sunday when the masses were free from work. Then tellingly he referred to 'summer TOURISTS (and the very word precludes the notion of a railway)', again emphasising a class-based hierarchy of which the excursionist was definitely in the lower reaches, not just on the basis of class, but because he arrived quickly on a train. At this time Wordsworth seemed to be awarding the 'tourist' a higher status involving private transport, although soon the tourist became an inferior category compared to the traveller. Wordsworth's elitist views, concerned that 'surely…good is not to be obtained by transferring at once uneducated persons in large bodies to particular spots', suggested that it was mobility itself that was the problem. He also suggested that 'the perception… of picturesque and romantic scenery…can be produced only by a slow and gradual process of culture', giving great advantage to those with the time and money to spend on this, as opposed to those who had little money and only one day in the week for leisure.[116] In his view it must be 'gradually developed…in individuals' and that 'imperfectly educated classes are not likely to draw much good from rare visits to the Lakes'… 'the humbler ranks of society are not, and cannot be, in a state to gain material benefit from more speedy access than they now have to this beautiful region.' Thus his motivations in attacking the excursion crowds arose from an outlook which was elitist, class-based and Sabbatarian. He accused the masses of 'molestation' in invading what he perceived as his own space and felt it could only be enjoyed by those he saw as respectable, presumably because they did not arrive in great numbers, speedily.

After the railway opened in 1847 there were excursions which tested out these views. An excursion from Preston to the Lakes in August 1848 was organised by Wesleyan, Independent and other dissenting Sunday schools – 'one of the main objects of the promoters was to keep their pupils from the race ground.' It also included parents and friends.[117] Seven trains of 148 carriages went to Windermere. Many had not been 'so far north' before, although this beautiful scenery was almost on their doorstep. The train passed through Lancaster and Kendal, boats and steamers were available for water excursions on Windermere and the trippers visited a number of other places around the lake. A few went to Rydal, where it was reported that apparently 'one party were rude and vulgar enough to obtrude themselves into the grounds of the venerable poet Wordsworth, and even to stare in at the windows of his residence.' The Lancashire & Yorkshire Railway had hired out refreshment tents to be pitched at Bowness. The press report made reference to the hospitality of the 'dalesmen and mountaineers', thus it appears that despite their large numbers the crowds were welcomed by the community they were visiting, an important point in the light of the controversial debate. The following week a letter appeared in the *Preston Chronicle* complaining about 'an impropriety of conduct' on the trip.[118] The writer said that it had been predicted that the railway to Windermere would bring 'crowds of vulgar people, by cheap trains, who would have no respect for the privacy, and no regard for the feelings, of those who had fixed their residences in that beautiful region, mainly for the enjoyment of seclusion, study and meditation.' He recalls that Charles Knight, in his guide to the Lake District, had suggested that the visitors who were more of a nuisance to local residents were in fact the gentry, who visited before the railway came:

> 'people who prowl about the residences of the celebrated persons who live here for the sake of quietness, knocking at the door to ask for autographs, staring in at the windows, taking possession of the gardens, thrusting themselves into the houses with complimentary speeches, and then sending to the newspapers an account of all they saw and heard, and much that they merely imagined.'

The writer complained that this behaviour was similar to that reportedly described in another paper: 'various parties had visited Rydale Mount…the poet was from home but the parties had the pleasure of a ramble in his garden…many ladies sat in his garden chair…' By contrast *The Times* later that month took the view that it was the gentry who were chiefly responsible for these invasions, referring to the Lakes being 'thronged with tourists, amongst whom are foreign and native nobility, divines, gentry, poets, painters and others' and that 'the homage paid to the poet Wordsworth at Rydal Mount by the greatest, the most noble and learned of this and other lands, is astonishing, the Laureate being literally almost daily overwhelmed by the influx of visitors, anxious to see the greatest poet and patriot of the day.'[119] The press took a proactive role in encouraging the invasion of the Lakes by the masses: the following year the *Preston Chronicle,* in advance of a Whitsun trip for working people, offered its readers a tourist guide to the Lakes in its columns, which highlighted the residence of Wordsworth and the way in which it was hidden from view by trees, but encouraged visitors to examine the beautiful view from the front of his house. Certainly later that year, during the August Sunday school trip to the Lakes, it was reported that some visitors obtained permission to walk through his grounds.[120] In claiming this leisure space therefore the working classes found surprising allies to support their wish to be accepted as visitors. However, frequently the presence of large crowds of excursionists led to a shortage of accommodation at a destination, for example in Bowness on Windermere in August 1856, when lodging houses had to offer sitting room floors for emergency bedrooms.[121] Clearly there were differences in the perceptions of working-class behaviour in these areas, with sometimes contrary views about the level of nuisance caused. The arrival of the masses could tip the balance from an annoying but low level of nuisance to residents to a much greater level of perceived nuisance. Influential commentators such as Wordsworth helped to shape the debate about the acceptability of the masses as tourists, although his views were not supported by many at the time and it was inevitable that the tide of tourism into the Lakes could not be prevented.[122]

There was much public debate about the suitability of another attraction for the working classes. The Manchester Art Treasures Exhibition of 1857 was generally regarded as a great success, with over a million visitors travelling to the Old Trafford site between May and October 1857 by road or rail. It gave rise to considerable discussion in the press, both during and after the event, about how many working-class visitors came on excursions, and how they behaved themselves. The expanding railway network had made it possible for visitors from the North and the Midlands to travel to the exhibition easily and cheaply, and the galleries were connected to the station by a covered walkway.[123] The railway companies went to some trouble to make the event accessible: the Manchester, South Junction and Altrincham Railway constructed new stations at Oxford Road and London Road in Manchester for traffic to the Exhibition, with ticket offices on the street rather than on the platform. At Old Trafford a special large excursion platform was built next to the Exhibition grounds, covered to protect passengers from rain. Employers, Sunday schools and temperance societies arranged tours, with transport and lunch provided; for example in September 1857, 450 workers from Winkworth, Proctor and Company in Macclesfield travelled to the exhibition.[124] To attract the working classes, tickets to the exhibition were priced at sixpence on some Saturday afternoons, against the regular price of one shilling. As a result, on the last day of the sixpenny admission, a fine gala day in September, there were around 20,000 visitors inside the exhibition, with a large proportion working class.

Many companies and agents ran trips to the Exhibition, including the London & North Western Railway (with Henry Marcus too) and the Great Northern Railway.[125] However, amid mounting concerns about attendance from a wider area than the north of England, Thomas Cook was appointed agent at a late stage in August 1857, to drum up business from Scotland and Ireland, using his extensive contacts.[126] One initiative of Thomas Cook in respect of this attraction which might be said to target the working classes was his 'moonlight trips', which left Newcastle at midnight on Monday arriving in Manchester at 7am, to return the next evening, although the day of the week and the price, at 6s 6d, seem to indicate against this.[127] A report on the results of the Exhibition was published in 1859, accusing the railway companies of lacking enthusiasm in promoting excursions direct to the Exhibition in the earlier stages.[128] An appendix to this report helpfully lists special excursion trains to the Exhibition, with the origin and approximate number of passengers. In total 349 trains were listed over the period from June to mid-October, sixteen of which brought over a thousand excursionists, mostly from the north of England and the Midlands, including some works trips and those by mechanics institutes. As none were listed from Newcastle or from London, there are likely to be many omissions in this record.

One report suggested that working men might be more interested in looking at works made from marble, wood and metals rather than paintings, reflecting a patronising view that the cultural interests of the working class might be limited to those linked to the manufacturing process.[129] It was true, however, that when 2,000 workers from Whitaker's cotton mill near Ashton in Lancashire were given a choice between a trip to the exhibition and a trip to New Brighton, they opted for the latter on the banks of the Mersey, especially as it included a steamer trip.[130] A contemporary commentator suggested that the Lancashire artisan preferred the fresh air for his holiday, and that many went because 'they were told they ought to go', and that it needed more 'preparatory introduction' among the lower classes.[131] There was, however, a penny guide published for this purpose: *What to See and Where to see it: An Operative's Guide to the Art Treasures Exhibition*.[132] Charles Dickens's sub-editor on *Household Words*, W.H. Wills, wrote that the so called 'destructive propensities of the English mob' were not displayed at the Exhibition, despite slanderous predictions to the contrary, but he agreed that the numbers of the working-class attending had been disappointing.[133]

The development of infrastructure at a destination to meet the needs of excursion crowds slowly grew, as attractions eventually found ways of meeting some needs. In January 1854, in order to better accommodate the massive temperance and mechanics institute crowds arriving on excursion trains, Sheffield Botanical Gardens decided to replace their refreshment tent with a large permanent building which would house 2,000 people standing and which could be used in the winter as a greenhouse. It was funded by advance payments from trip organisers and completed ready for the Whitsun events in 1854, when it was described as the new 'Crystal Palace'.[134] Other needs however remained unmet, as it was not until the Great Exhibition of 1851 that public conveniences were featured for the first time, built by sanitary engineer George Jennings, later followed by public toilets in London in Fleet Street and the Strand.[135] While a large mass of day excursionists would not have generated a need for lodgings at the destination in the same manner as staying middle-class visitors, it was still necessary to consider crowd management systems where excursions generated 'pinch points'. There are a number of examples of railway companies designing changes to their facilities to accommodate the massive crowds generated by excursions (and to prevent them from offending the regular traffic). For the 1851 St Leger race meeting a special temporary platform was constructed for excursion visitors arriving from Sheffield, to keep the noisy crowd away from the regular station, and trains were sent off at frequent intervals after the race meeting, assisted by a large police presence.[136] In 1852, the Great Western Railway constructed separate accommodation at their Paddington terminus for excursion traffic.[137] In 1853, the London, Brighton & South Coast Railway also created separate excursion accommodation at their London Bridge terminus, with an eye on the development of the Crystal Palace traffic.[138]

A Different View

Traditionally histories of railway travel have focused on the middle-class traveller, consulting his *Bradshaw* and gazing at the panoramic view from the window of a tidy compartment. Such histories have neglected the third-class traveller as another species, mainly through lack of evidence. Many working-class travellers were hanging on to the roof of a crowded carriage, endangering their lives, or enduring hours of travel in an open wagon in heavy rain. Although transport histories proclaim the end of open carriages with the introduction of the Parliamentary train in 1844, this new research has shown how open carriages and goods wagons were frequently used for excursions throughout the period, extending even as late as 1872. Again, traditional views of the waiting room at the station are based on the middle-class experience. When large excursion crowds were expected at the station, the doors would be locked, leading to a dangerous chain of events. Station space was designed for small groups of middle-class travellers to pass through in an orderly manner. This was often not suitable for the crowds on excursions and it was rare that railway companies made special changes to the physical space during this period to meet the needs of excursionists.

It is clear that Thomas Cook only played a very minor role in mass mobility in this period, when compared to other agents such as Henry Marcus, railway companies and organising groups. This book has introduced other little-known people such as Joseph Brown and Charles Melly into the history of working-class transport.

The railway excursion in the mid-nineteenth century did much to change society's views about the working classes *en masse*, generally in a positive direction. It also enabled ordinary people to experience new landscapes and cultures, far from home. Perceptions of class and behaviour by both participants and observers were seen to be modified as a result of the new excursions. The brief press report in 1851, observing the small group of working-class females travelling unaccompanied on a cheap trip from Huddersfield to visit the Great Exhibition in London, might be seen as particularly significant.[1] The nature of these observations, highlighting practices which would be considered by modern eyes as quite unremarkable, but which were regarded as astonishing at the time, viewed with contemporary perspectives of class and gender, demonstrates how the railway excursion was beginning to change society.

Notes

Chapter One

1. *York Herald*, 27 September 1856.
2. J. Armstrong and D.M. Williams, 'The steamship as an agent of modernisation 1812–1840', *International Journal of Maritime History,* XIX (2007), p. 154.
3. James Walvin, *Beside the Seaside: a Social History of the Popular Seaside Holiday* (London, 1978), p. 31; Gary Cross and John K. Walton, *The Playful Crowd: Pleasure Places in the Twentieth Century* (New York, 2005), pp. 12–13.
4. Augustus Bozzi Granville, *Spas of England and Principal Sea-Bathing Places, 1: The North* (Bath, 1971 orig 1841), pp. 344–347.
5. *The Era*, 22 May 1853. 'The Million' was a phrase commonly used at the time for the mass of ordinary people.
6. *Preston Chronicle,* 6 June 1846.
7. *London Chronicle*, 13 May 1775.
8. J. Clarke and C. Critcher, *The Devil makes Work: Leisure in Capitalist Britain* (Basingstoke, 1985), p. 58.
9. In 1846 the Corn Laws were repealed, following lengthy campaigns (C. Cook, *Britain in the Nineteenth Century 1815–1914* (London, 1999), p. 128.
10. D.A. Reid, 'Playing and Praying', in M. Daunton (ed.) *Cambridge Urban History of Britain Vol. III 1840–1950* (Cambridge, 2000), pp. 754, 769; J.K. Walton, 'The Demand for Working-Class Seaside Holidays in Victorian England', *Economic History Review,* 34 New Series (May 1981), pp. 249–265; *Manchester Guardian*, 25 May 1850.
11. Alan J. Kidd, *Manchester* (3rd edn., Edinburgh, 2002), p. 45.
12. Granville, *Spas of England*, p. 411, 415.
13. P. Bailey, *Leisure and Class in Victorian England: Rational Recreation and the Contest for Control, 1830–1885* (London, 1978), pp. 14–15.
14. Patrick Joyce, *Visions of the People* (Cambridge, 1991), p. 10; John Benson, *The Working Class in Britain, 1850–1939* (London, 1989), pp. 3–4. It is recognised that a definition by occupation is fraught with complexities.
15. *The Yorkshireman,* 29 August 1840. This inspired Thomas Cook one year later to embark upon his tours (Susan Barton, *Working Class Organisations and Popular Tourism 1840–1970* (Manchester, 2005), p. 29.
16. *The Yorkshireman,* 10 October 1840; *Sheffield & Rotherham Independent*, 3 October 1840.
17. *The Times*, 1 September 1841.
18. *Caledonian Mercury*, 6 July 1846.
19. *Yorkshire Gazette*, 21 July 1849.
20. *Yorkshire Gazette,* 30 Aug 1851.
21. *Yorkshire Gazette*, 15 June 1850.
22. *Yorkshire Gazette*, 13 July 1850.
23. *Hull Packet,* 17 July 1835.
24. *The Yorkshireman,* 10 October 1840.
25. *Leeds Mercury,* 12 June 1847; *Yorkshire Gazette,* 25 August 1849.
26. *Yorkshire Gazette,* 11 May 1850.
27. *Yorkshire Gazette,* 28 July 1849.

28. There is evidence of groups participating on steamers in the early 1840s, although possibly not commissioning the vessel for their own use. For example Oddfellows from Middlesbrough, Stockton and Sunderland travelled on a steamer excursion to Whitby in 1842, and the same year a group from Stockton Mechanics Institute took a steamer excursion to Tynemouth (*The Yorkshireman*, 30 April 1842, 21 May 1842, 28 May 1842).

29. J. Simmons, *The Railway in Town and Country 1830–1914* (Newton Abbot, 1986), p. 202.

30. J. Simmons, *The Victorian Railway* (London, 1991), pp. 295–6.

31. *Manchester Guardian*, 20 June 1835; *Preston Chronicle*, 25 July 1835 (taken from the *Liverpool Mercury*).

32. Jack Simmons and Gordon Biddle, *The Oxford Companion to British Railway History from 1603 to the 1990s* (Oxford, 1991), p. 150.

33. *Leicester Chronicle*, 16 May 1846.

34. T. Gourvish, *Mark Huish and the London & North Western Railway: a Study of Management* (Leicester, 1972), p. 69.

35. J.A. Thomas, *A Regional History of the Railways of Great Britain Vol VI: Scotland and the Lower Borders* (Newton Abbot, 1971), p. 45.

36. W.W. Tomlinson, *The North Eastern Railway: its Rise and Development* (London, 1915), p. 374.

37. *Cornwall Royal Gazette*, 10 June 1836.

38. Joss Marsh, 'Spectacle' in Herbert F. Tucker (ed.), *A Companion to Victorian Literature and Culture.* (Oxford, 1999), pp. 276–288; G.F.A. Best, *Mid-Victorian Britain, 1851–75* (London, 1979), pp. 218–21.

39. J. K. Walton, 'The demand for working-class seaside holidays in Victorian England', *The Economic History Review*, New Series 34 (1981) p. 249–265.

40. Ibid., p. 249.

41. *The Yorkshireman*, 21 May 1842, 4 June 1842, 9 July 1842.

42. *Yorkshire Gazette*, 9 June 1849.

43. J. Armstrong and D.M. Williams, 'The steamboat and popular tourism', *Journal of Transport History*, 26 (2005), pp. 61–77.

44. *Yorkshire Gazette*, 30 October 1852.

45. Valerie E. Chancellor, *Master and Artisan in Victorian England* (London, 1969), pp. 16–17.

46. *Nottinghamshire Guardian*, 9 September 1852.

47. D. Brumhead and T. Wyke, 'Moving Manchester', *Transactions of the Lancashire and Cheshire Antiquarian Society* 100 (2004), p. 20.

48. *Manchester Guardian*, 24 September 1845.

49. S. Barton, 'The Mechanics Institutes: Pioneers of Leisure and Excursion Travel', *Transactions of the Leicestershire Archaeological and Historical Society* 67 (1993), p. 51.

50. *Manchester Times*, 21 June 1851.

51. The stations at Oxford Road and London Road for the Art Treasures Exhibition were built for the Manchester South Junction & Altrincham Railway, and opened between May and October 1857 (*Lancaster Gazette*, 2 May 1857).

52. *Manchester Guardian*, 8 August 1859; *Nottinghamshire Guardian*, 11 August 1859.

53. *Bury and Norwich Post*, 4 July 1849.

54. *Yorkshire Gazette*, 27 March 1852.

55. *Blackburn Standard*, 23 March 1853.

56. *Hampshire Advertiser*, 27 October 1860.

57. *Sheffield & Rotherham Independent*, 10 June 1854.

58. Ian Carter, *Railways and Culture in Britain: The Epitome of Modernity* (Manchester, 2001), p. 8; M.J. Daunton and B. Rieger (eds.), *Meanings of Modernity: Britain from the late-Victorian era to World War II* (Oxford, 2001), p. 2.

59. *Morning Post*, 12 October 1859.

60. *Yorkshire Gazette,* 5 July 1851, 26 May 1849.

61. *Lancaster Gazette,* 13 April 1850; *Yorkshire Gazette,* 22 May 1852, 31 July 1852.

62. See for example *Morning Chronicle*, 15 December 1860.

63. *Leeds Mercury,* 29 August 1846.

64. *Nottinghamshire Guardian*, 31 May 1860.

65. *Manchester Guardian,* 10 June, 1840.

66. *Manchester Guardian,* 2 June 1860.

67. *Wrexham and Denbighshire Weekly Advertiser*, 18 July 1857.

68. *Huddersfield Chronicle*, 10 August 1850.

69. *Nottinghamshire Guardian*, 6 June 1850.

70. *Nottinghamshire Guardian*, 31 May 1860.

71. T. Nevett, *Advertising in Britain, A History* (London, 1982), p. 53.

72. Barton, *Working Class Organisations and Popular Tourism 1840–1970*, p. 37.

73. *Manchester Guardian*, 19 April 1845, 3 May 1845, 10 May 1845.

74. *Manchester Times,* 26 May 1849.

75. *Huddersfield Chronicle*, 1 September 1855.

76. *Preston Chronicle*, 16 June 1849.

Chapter Two

1. *Manchester Times*, 26 July 1845.

2. T.R. Gourvish, *Railways and the British Economy, 1830–1914* (London, 1980), pp. 26–27.

3. See for example: North Midland Railway (*Sheffield & Rotherham Independent*, 26 September 1840), Hull & Selby Railway (*Hull Packet*, 28 May 1841), Great North of England Railway (*Yorkshireman*, 21 May 1842), Midland Counties Railway (*Derby Mercury*, 24 May 1843), York & North Midland Railway (*Yorkshireman*, 19 March 1842; *York Herald*, 25 May 1844). Occasionally it is unclear whether an agent is involved but not mentioned in the advertisement, for example the trips promoted by the Manchester & Leeds Railway in conjunction with other lines, in May 1843 (*Railway Times*, 13 May 1843). Passenger duty was a particular problem for companies during this period, see page 86.

4. Tomlinson, *The North Eastern Railway: its Rise and Development*, p. 372.

5. *Derby Mercury*, 21 July 1841.

6. G.O. Holt, *A Regional History of the Railways of Great Britain: North West* (Newton Abbott, 1978), p. 23. Eventually the railway companies themselves took over responsibility for running all traffic on their lines (Gourvish, *Mark Huish and the London & North Western Railway,* pp. 31–33.)

7. Simmons, *The Victorian Railway*, pp. 273, 292–3; *Preston Chronicle*, 9 October 1841. There may have been a gap after the early 1840s, as an LSWR report in March 1851 implies that excursions were a new experiment in 1850 (*Hampshire Advertiser*, 1 March 1851).

8. *The Standard*, 9 April 1844, 9 September 1844; *Hampshire Telegraph and Sussex Chronicle*, 29 April 1844.)

9. *Morning Post*, 10 April 1847 (from *Railway Record*).

10. A. and E. Jordan, *Away for the Day: The Railway Excursion in Britain, 1830 to the Present Day*, (Kettering, 1991), p. 103.

11. *Bristol Mercury*, 17 September 1842, 24 September 1842; 7 September 1844; *Morning Post*, 30 September 1842; *The Standard*, 17 August 1844; *Chambers Edinburgh Journal*, 29 October 1853, p. 279.

12. *Bradford Observer*, 9 August 1849.

13. *Yorkshire Gazette*, 23 September 1848.

14. *Yorkshire Gazette,* 7 September 1847.

15. *Manchester Guardian*, 11 August 1856.

16. Barton, *Working Class Organisations and Popular Tourism 1840–1970*, pp. 41–71.

17. Simmons, *The Victorian Railway*, pp. 275–277.

18. *Morning Post*, 4 July 1853.

19. *Sheffield & Rotherham Independent*, 9 August 1851; Charles H. Grinling, *The History of the Great Northern Railway 1845–1895* (London, 1898), pp. 103–104.

20. *Morning Chronicle*, 26 February 1852.

21. *Yorkshire Gazette*, 26 July 1851.

22. *Charles H. Grinling, The History of the Great Northern Railway 1845–1895 (London, 1898), p. 103.*

23. It is also clouded by the competitive and diversionary effects of Great Exhibition excursion traffic in 1851.

24. *Morning Post*, 30 January 1850.

25. *The Observer*, 25 January 1852 (obviously affected by the Great Exhibition).

26. *The Builder*, 14 September 1850.

27. *The Builder*, 21 August 1852.

28. Douglas Knoop, *Outlines of Railway Economics* (London, 1913), pp. 71, 81, 167–8, 230.

29. *Morning Chronicle*, 13 September 1850.

30. *Morning Post*, 15 August 1851.

31. *Daily News*, 15 August 1851.

32. *Daily News*, 13 February 1852.

33. *Railway Times*, 29 May 1852.

34. *Blackburn Standard*, 10 February 1858 (from *Liverpool Daily Post*); *Cheshire Observer*, 6 February 1858.

35. *Cheshire Observer*, 5 June 1858.

36. *Sheffield & Rotherham Independent*, 4 September 1852. Demonstration here meant an orderly meeting rather than its modern use as a campaigning event.

37. *Blackburn Standard*, 22 April 1857.

38. The Lancashire manufacturing districts were reported to be better off in 1849 and thus able to participate in excursions (*Morning Chronicle*, 21 June 1849, 5 November 1849.); J.F.C. Harrison, *Early Victorian Britain 1832–51* (London, 1988), p. 169.

39. *Manchester Times*, 17 August 1850 (from *Liverpool Times*).

40. *Railway Times*, 14 June 1851 (from *Liverpool Standard*).

41. *The Observer*, 2 February 1852 (from *Railway Times*).

42. *Bristol Mercury*, 26 August 1854; *Morning Chronicle*, 21 August 1854; *York Herald*, 25 June 1864, 30 September 1865, 6 November 1869, 28 April 1874, 30 May 1874; *Evening Gazette*, 18 June 1870; *Northern Echo*, 13 March 1873; *Birmingham Daily Post*, 12 November 1866; *Manchester Guardian*, 2 January 1886; *Preston Chronicle*, 22 April 1871.

43. Simmons and Biddle, *The Oxford Companion to British Railway History from 1603 to the 1990s*, pp. 412–13.

44. P. S. Bagwell, *The Railway Clearing House in the British Economy* (London, 1968), pp. 56–61.

45. The National Archives, London, RAIL 1080/99, *Railway Clearing House Superintendents' Meetings Minutes*, 20 February 1851.

46. Bagwell, *The Railway Clearing House in the British Economy*, pp. 56–57; Simmons, *The Victorian Railway*, p. 275; *Blackburn Standard*, 28 May 1851 (from *Herapath's Journal*).

47. Paxton and the Duke of Devonshire encouraged thousands of pleasure seekers to visit Chatsworth (see page 149), and his Crystal Palace at Sydenham was known as the 'People's Palace' (Jan Piggott, *Palace of the People: The Crystal Palace at Sydenham 1854–1936* (London, 2004)). See also letter from Paxton to *Hampshire Advertiser*, 25 January 1851.

48. *Blackburn Standard*, 28 May 1851; *Royal Cornwall Gazette*, 30 May 1851.

49. *Yorkshire Gazette*, 26 July 1851.

50. The National Archives, London, RAIL 1080/99, *Railway Clearing House Superintendents' Meetings Minutes*, 23 September 1852, 21 October 1852, 2 December 1852. The group consisted of Blackmore from the

Lancashire & Yorkshire, Hargreaves (Manchester, Sheffield & Lincolnshire) and two representatives from the York & North Midland. There appears to be no record in later minutes of decisions made by the whole group and detailed statements are missing.

51. The National Archives, London, RAIL 1080/114, *Railway Clearing House Superintendents' Meetings Minutes,* 7 April 1857.

52. Bagwell, *The Railway Clearing House in the British Economy*, p. 60.

53. *Preston Chronicle*, 31 August 1850.

54. *Household Words*, III 1851, pp. 355–356. Anon. but probably Ossian MacPherson according to A. Lohrli, *Household Words: A Weekly Journal 1850–1859* (Toronto, 1973), p. 352.

55. *York Herald*, 29 June 1844; *Hampshire Advertiser*, 14 September 1844; *The Standard*, 9 September 1844; *Manchester Times*, 26 July 1845 (also syndicated to the *Morning Post*, 29 July 1845); *Nottinghamshire Guardian*, 25 July 1850; *Bradford Observer*, 19 September 1850 (taken from *The Builder*). In 1850 the *Standard* and other papers attempted to summarise the impact of the excursion train on the profits of various railway companies (*The Standard*, 17 September 1850).

56. It was very complex, see Simmons and Biddle, *The Oxford Companion to British Railway History*, pp. 114–116; Knoop, *Outlines of Railway Economics*, pp. 71, 81, 167–8, 230.

57. *The Standard*, 9 September 1844 (from *Railway Chronicle*).

58. *Hampshire Advertiser*, 22 February 1851, 1 March 1851.

59. For example 1846 (687) *Second Report from the Select Committee on Railway Acts Enactments*, p. 235; 1867 (3844) *Royal Commission on Railways*, pp. 509, 588–89, 614, 863.

60. Simmons and Biddle, *The Oxford Companion to British Railway History from 1603 to the 1990s*, p. 322; *Leicester Chronicle*, 26 October 1844. St. Pancras was not opened until 1868.

61. The dangerous size of excursion trains eventually led to a Board of Trade report with safety recommendations (1846 (698) (752) *Report of the Officers of the Railway Department to the Lords of the Committee of Privy Council for Trade: with appendices I. & II. for the years 1844–45).*

62. *Chambers Edinburgh Journal*, 21 September 1844 (excerpts from this appeared in the *Manchester Times* of the same date); *Bradford Observer*, 18 October 1849.

63. S. Major, 'The Million Go Forth: Early Railway Excursion Crowds 1840–1860' (PhD dissertation, University of York, 2012); *Liverpool Mercury*, 8 May 1846 – 2 October 1846; *Manchester Times*, 30 May 1846 – 25 July 1846; *Manchester Guardian*, 16 May 1846 – 5 August 1846; *Preston Chronicle*, 4 April 1846 – 12 September 1846; D.A. Reid, 'The 'Iron Roads' and 'the Happiness of the Working Classes': the Early Development and Social Significance of the Railway Excursion', *Journal of Transport History,* 17 (1996), 57–73; John R. Kellett, *Railways and Victorian Cities* (London, 1979), p. 18; Simmons and Biddle, *The Oxford Companion to British Railway History*, p. 308.

64. Simmons, *The Railway in Town and Country 1830–1914*, pp. 110–112, Simmons and Biddle, *The Oxford Companion to British Railway History*, pp. 308–311, 396–397.

65. *Manchester Times*, 30 May 1846 – 25 July 1846; *Manchester Guardian*, 16 May 1846 - 5 August 1846.

66. *Manchester Guardian* 3 June 1846.

67. This line had opened up from Derby to Nottingham in June 1839, with a link to Leicester in May 1840 and on to Rugby in July 1840 (C.E. Stretton, *The History of the Midland Railway* (London, 1901), pp. 38–40.)

68. *The Midland Counties' Railway Companion: With Topographical Descriptions of the Country Through Which the Line Passes and Time, Fare and Distance Tables Corrected to the 24th August. Also, Complete Guides to the London and Birmingham, and Birmingham and Derby Junction Railways* (Nottingham, 1840). The Liverpool & Manchester Railway had generated guide books as soon as it opened, for example *A Guide to the Liverpool & Manchester Railway* (Liverpool, 1830).

69. Stretton, *The History of the Midland Railway*, p. 42.

70. A similar return trip ran a week later on 27 July. In order to reduce the amount of passenger duty payable, the fares were only charged one way (Susan Barton, 'The Mechanics Institutes: Pioneers of Leisure and

Excursion Travel', *Transactions of the Leicestershire Archaeological and Historical Society,* 67 (1993), 47–58). Recognising the economic benefits of these two trips, the Midland Counties Railway itself organised two further trips in August, for example from Leicester to Nottingham at 2s. return third-class (Stretton, *The History of the Midland Railway*, pp. 42–44.)

71. *Chambers Edinburgh Journal*, 1853, p. 279.

72. Samuel Salt, *Railway and Commercial Information* (London, 1850), p. 27.

73. T.L. Alborn, *Conceiving Companies: Joint-stock Politics in Victorian England* (London, 1998), pp. 1–2.

74. James Taylor, *Creating Capitalism: Joint Stock Enterprise in British Politics and Culture* (Woodbridge, 2006), p. 145.

75. D. Brooke, 'The Opposition to Sunday Rail Services in North Eastern England, 1834–1914', *Journal of Transport History,* 6 (1963), pp. 96–97; Simmons and Biddle, *The Oxford Companion to British Railway History from 1603 to the 1990s*, p. 478.

76. Geoffrey Channon, *Railways in Britain and the United States, 1830–1940: Studies in Economic and Business History* (Aldershot, 2001), pp. 41–42.

77. T.R. Gourvish, 'A British Business Elite: The Chief Executive Managers of the Railway Industry, 1850–1922', *Business History Review,* 47 (1973), 289–316.

78. D. Joy, *Regional History of the Railways of Great Britain: Vol VIII South and West Yorkshire (the Industrial West Riding)* (Newton Abbot, 1975), pp. 38–9; *Derby Mercury*, 24 May 1843.

79. Brooke, 'The Opposition to Sunday Rail Services in North Eastern England, 1834-1914', p. 96.

80. 1844 (318) *Fifth Report of the Select Committee on Railways*, paras. 4214, 4278–4280, 4298, 4343, 4347, 4381.

81. 1846 (687) *Second Report from the Select Committee on Railway Acts Enactments,* paras. 3319, 3328.

82. *The Standard*, 26 June 1845, 1 July 1845.

83. Simmons and Biddle, *The Oxford Companion to British Railway History from 1603 to the 1990s*, pp. 150, 248.

84. *Morning Post*, 26 July 1850. Laing reported that in 1852 the company had generated £17,750 from excursion traffic in 1851, of which around £15,000 related to the Great Exhibition; *Morning Post*, 24 January 1852.

85. See Major, 'The Million Go Forth: Early Railway Excursion Crowds 1840–1860' for a further example, Mark Huish at LNWR.

86. John K. Walton, *Lancashire: a Social History 1558–1939* (Manchester, 1987), p. 116.

87. *Manchester Guardian*, 21 July 1849.

88. Simmons, *The Railway in Town and Country 1830–1914*, pp. 201–2; John K. Walton, *The English Seaside Resort: A Social History, 1750–1914* (Leicester, 1983), p. 26. The Lancashire & Yorkshire took over the Preston & Wyre jointly with the London & North Western (LNWR) in 1849.

89. Walton suggests that this was not as a result of Sabbatarian pressure but more an economic move (John K. Walton, *The Blackpool Landlady: A Social History* (Manchester, 1978), pp. 18–19.)

90. *Manchester Guardian*, 21 July 1849.

91. T. Normington, *The Lancashire and Yorkshire Railway* (London, 1898), pp. 49, 53.

92. G.P. Neele, *Railway Reminiscences* (London, 1904), p. 59; J. Marshall, *The Lancashire & Yorkshire Railway: Volume Two* (Newton Abbott, 1970), p. 250. Blackmore retired in 1875.

93. *Manchester Times*, 12 September 1849.

94. *Manchester Times*, 21 April 1855. The East Lancashire Railway offered a free copy of a guide to attractions along the line as an incentive.

95. *Manchester Guardian*, 30 May 1855; *Manchester Times*, 2 June 1855.

96. *Manchester Times*, 2 October 1858.

97. *Liverpool Mercury*, 1 July 1857; 1857 Session 2 (2288) *Reports of the Inspecting Officers of the Railway Department upon certain Accidents which have occurred on Railways during the months of March, April, May, June, and July, 1857. (Part third.)*, pp. 32–34. The railway company's liability to its passengers extended as far as a duty to use

care and diligence, and avoid neglect (R.W. Kostal, *Law and English Railway Capitalism 1825–187* (Oxford, 1994), pp. 279–313.

98. Simmons, *The Railway in Town and Country 1830–1914*, p. 248.

99. *Manchester Times*, 30 June 1849.

100. It was also reported that until 1872 at each Whitsuntide, 150–200 cattle wagons were 'fitted up' for use on their excursion trains. Simmons, *The Railway in Town and Country 1830-1914*, p. 248; J. Marshall, *The Lancashire & Yorkshire Railway: Volume One* (Newton Abbott, 1969), p. 258.

101. 1852–3 (246) *Third Report from the Select Committee on Railway and Canal Bills, Appendix No 10*.

102. Marshall, *The Lancashire & Yorkshire Railway: Volume Two*, p. 250; Normington, *The Lancashire and Yorkshire Railway*, pp. 67–68.

103. D. Joy, *Regional History of the Railways of Great Britain: Vol VIII South and West Yorkshire (the Industrial West Riding)* (Newton Abbot, 1975), p. 108.

104. *Preston Chronicle*, 14 January 1860.

105. 1867 (3844) *Royal Commission on Railways*, paras.13,187–13,194.

106. Ibid., paras.12, 998–13,001.

107. Walton, 'The Demand for Working Class Seaside Holidays in Victorian England', p. 253; Marshall, *The Lancashire & Yorkshire Railway:Volume Two*, p. 250.

108. Normington, *The Lancashire and Yorkshire Railway*, pp. 53, 62, 65, 70,138, 148.

Chapter Three

1. *Lloyds Weekly Newspaper*, 18 August 1844.

2. *Manchester Guardian*, 27 July 1844.

3. For examples see Preston Working Men's Committee Free Library Fund (*Preston Chronicle,* 19 July 1856), Peel Park Committee (*Bradford Observer*, 4 September 1856), LNWR Literary Institution (*Royal Cornwall Gazette*, 16 July 1858).

4. Reid, 'Playing and Praying', p. 797; Asa Briggs, *Victorian Cities* (Harmondsworth, 1968), p. 63.

5. E. Baines, *The Social, Educational, and Religious State of the Manufacturing Districts; with Statistical Returns of the Means of Education and Religious Instruction in the Manufacturing Districts of Yorkshire, Lancashire, and Cheshire* (London, 1843), pp. 22–26, 71.

6. K.D.M. Snell, 'The Sunday-School Movement in England and Wales: Child Labour, Denominational Control and Working-Class Culture', *Past & Present,* 164 (1999), p. 163.

7. Simmons, *The Victorian Railway*, p. 272.

8. P. Bailey, *Leisure and Class in Victorian England: Rational Recreation and the Contest for Control*, p. 46.

9. *Manchester Times*, 6 June 1846.

10. *Manchester Times*, 6 June 1846.

11. *Leeds Mercury*, 26 August 1848, 9 September 1848.

12. *Leeds Mercury,* 12 September 1846.

13. Cook, *Britain in the Nineteenth Century 1815–1914*, p. 119.

14. *Manchester Guardian*, 25 August 1858, *York Herald*, 9 October 1858.

15. For example a Sunday school trip from Hull to Beverley in July 1849 (*Yorkshire Gazette,* 28 July 1849); R.J. Morris, *Class, Sect and Party: the Making of the British Middle Class, Leeds 1820–1850* (Manchester, 1990), p. 197.

16. *Fraser's Magazine*, June 1856 Vol LIII pp. 639–647.

17. See also Jordan, *Away for the Day,* p. 15. An early use of the railway as a moral theme appeared in Nathaniel Hawthorne's short story *The Celestial Railroad*, published in 1843, and based on Bunyan's *Pilgrim's Progress.* This theme was then used in many American poems and songs in the nineteenth century. Usually only the upline stanzas appear in print – the downline stanzas about hell appear rather less often, as a parody

(Norm Cohen and David Cohen (eds.), *Long Steel Rail: the Railroad in American Folksong* (2nd edn., Urbana, 2000.) p. 607.)

18. *Leeds Mercury,* 22 August 1846.

19. *Bradford Observer*, 9 July 1857.

20. *York Herald*, 31 March 1888, *Sheffield & Rotherham Independent*, 3 April 1888.

21. Morris, *Class, Sect and Party*, p. 197.

22. Mabel Tylecote, *Mechanics Institutes of Lancashire and Yorkshire Before 1851 (Manchester, 1957)*, pp. 121–122, 274.

23. M. Tylecote, *Mechanics Institutes of Lancashire and Yorkshire Before 1851*, p. 122. Presumably distributing knowledge refers to the shared learning of useful subjects and access to newspapers.

24. R.J. Morris, 'Voluntary Societies and British Urban Elites, 1780–1850: an Analysis', *Historical Journal,* 26 (1983), 95–118.

25. J. R. Lowerson, 'Baines, Sir Edward (1800–1890)', *Oxford Dictionary of National Biography,* (Oxford, 2004) [www.oxforddnb.com/view/article/1090, accessed 8 Dec 2014].

26. *Blackburn Standard*, 12 August 1846.

27. See page 44.

28. *Hull Packet*, 22 May 1846 – 25 September 1846.

29. Victor Bailey, *'This Rash Act': Suicide Across the Life Cycle in the Victorian City* (Stanford, 1998), pp. 105–115.

30. *Morning Chronicle*, 10 March 1851.

31. Ibid.

32. *Leeds Mercury*, 15 September 1846; Walton, *The English Seaside Resort*, p. 28.

33. *Lloyds Weekly Newspaper*, 18 August 1844.

34. E. Royle, 'Mechanics Institutes and the Working Classes, 1840–1860', *Historical Journal*, 14 (1971) pp. 307–308.

35. Tylecote, *Mechanics Institutes of Lancashire and Yorkshire before 1851*, pp. 68–69.

36. Ibid., pp. 74–5.

37. E. Royle, 'Mechanics Institutes and the Working Classes, 1840–1860', p. 305.

38. J. M. Ludlow and L. Jones, *Progress of the Working Class, 1832–1867* (1867, reprint, Clifton, 1973), pp. 169–170; Barnett Blake, 'The Mechanics Institutes of Yorkshire', *Transactions of the National Association for the Promotion of Social Science*, (1859), 335-340; John V. Godwin, 'The Bradford Mechanics Institute', *Transactions of the National Association for the Promotion of Social Science*, (1859), 340–345.

39. Leicester Mechanics Institute passed a motion in 1841 'if any opponent of Mechanics Institutes…charges them with being hot beds of political discussion, and schools for Socialism … would take the trouble to attend a few of the meetings at the Leicester Mechanics Institute … we believe his mouth would be for ever stopped in this strain.' (*Leicester Chronicle*, 22 May 1841).

40. Tylecote, *Mechanics Institutes of Lancashire and Yorkshire before 1851*, p. 274.

41. *Leeds Mercury*, 27 June 1840.

42. Tylecote, *Mechanics Institutes of Lancashire and Yorkshire before 1851*, p. 173.

43. Ibid., pp. 120–1, 173–174.

44. It is not clear whether this was at a special reduced rate.

45. *York Herald*, 16 June 1838.

46. Tylecote, *Mechanics Institutes of Lancashire and Yorkshire before 1851*, p. 274.

47. *Yorkshire Gazette*, 9 June 1849.

48. *Yorkshire Gazette,* 9 June 1849.

49. *The Yorkshireman*, 29 August 1840.

50. Simmons, *The Victorian Railway*, p. 272.

51. *Leeds Mercury*, 20 July 1850, Tylecote, *The Mechanics Institutes of Lancashire and Yorkshire before 1851*, pp. 78, 220–1, 237, 275.

52. *Yorkshire Gazette,* 2 June 1849.

53. *Leeds Mercury*, 18 July 1846.

54. Tylecote, *The Mechanics Institutes of Lancashire and Yorkshire before 1851,* p. 275.

55. *Leeds Mercury*, 27 June 1846, 4 July 1846, 18 July 1846; *Northern Star*, 25 July 1846; *Bradford Observer*, 16 July 1846.

56. *Leeds Mercury*, 8 August 1846.

57. *Leeds Mercury,* 18 July 1846.

58. See for example *York Herald*, 16 June 1838; *Leeds Mercury*, 27 June 1840.

59. *Bradford Observer*, 25 May 1848, 1 June 1848, 8 June 1848; *Leeds Mercury*, 10 June 1848.

60. *Bradford Observer*, 8 June 1848. The MI did not mention the name of the railway company involved, but this appears to be a frequent practice in such advertisements.

61. See for example the Leeds MI trip to the Lakes, *Leeds Mercury*, 20 July 1850.

62. *Manchester Times,* 12 September 1849.

63. *The Temperance Movement: its Rise, Progress and Results* (London, 1854).

64. F.M.L. Thompson, *The Rise of Respectable Society: A Social History of Victorian Britain 1830–1900* (London, 1988), p. 310; Edward Royle, *Modern Britain: A Social History, 1750–1997* (2nd ed., London, 1997), p. 46.

65. M. Hewitt, *The Emergence of Stability in the Industrial City: Manchester, 1832–67* (Aldershot, 1996), pp. 173–177.

66. Morris, 'Voluntary Societies and British Urban Elites, 1780–1850', pp. 102–3.

67. *Derby Mercury*, 4 August 1841.

68. *Yorkshire Gazette*, 13 July 1850.

69. *Preston Chronicle*, 17 August 1844, 14 June 1845, 25 October 1845; James Weston, *Joseph Livesey: The Story of his Life, 1794–1884* (London, 1884), pp. 93–94. Joseph Dearden was one of the committee behind it.

70. *Preston Chronicle,* 28 July 1849.

71. *Leeds Mercury,* 15 August 1846, 22 August 1846, 29 August 1846.

72. West Yorkshire Archive Service (WYAS): Bradford. DB16 C25, *The sixth annual report of the Bradford Long-Pledged Teetotal Association, 1849; Bradford Observer,* 8 April 1858.

73. *The Leader*, 27 July 1850.

74. *The Leader*, 27 July 1850; *Lloyds Weekly Newspaper*, 20 July 1851, 22 July 1860; *Morning Post*, 23 June 1852, 30 September 1857; *John Bull*, 7 July 1855, 2 July 1859, 17 August 1867; *The Lady's Newspaper*, 7 July 1855; *Daily News*, 28 June 1859, 11 July 1861, 15 August 1867; *Pall Mall Gazette*, 11 July 1865; *Illustrated London News*, 3 July 1852.

75. *The Leader*, 27 July 1850.

76. *Illustrated London News,* 3 July 1852.

Chapter Four

1. *North Wales Chronicle*, 31 December 1853 (reprinted from *Liverpool Chronicle*).

2. Simmons and Biddle, *The Oxford Companion to British Railway History from 1603 to the 1990s*, p. 150.

3. John K. Walton, 'Thomas Cook: Image and Reality', in Richard Butler and Roslyn Russell, *Giants of Tourism* (Cambridge, Ma., 2010), p. 87. For examples of agent advertisements and comments see *York Herald*, 24 September 1853; *Berrow's Worcester Journal*, 3 June 1854, 12 July 1856; *Wrexham and Denbigh Weekly Advertiser*, 15 July 1854. A Mr. Jones was organising cheap trips from Liverpool in 1857 (*Liverpool Mercury*, 5 June 1857). See also page 52.

4. *Leeds Mercury*, 18 April 1846 -10 October 1846; *York Herald*, 24 October 1846; *Bradford Observer*, 30 July 1846; *Hull Packet*, 22 May 1846 – 25 September 1846; *Liverpool Mercury*, 8 May 1846 – 2 October 1846; *Manchester Times*, 30 May 1846 – 25 July 1846; *Manchester Guardian*, 16 May 1846 – 5 August 1846; *Preston Chronicle*, 4 April 1846 – 12 September 1846; Reid, 'Iron Roads', pp. 57–73.

5. *Bradford Observer*, 16 July 1846.

6. *Chambers Edinburgh Journal*, (1853) p. 279.

7. J. Denton (ed.), *The Thirlway Journal: A Record of Life in Early Victorian Ripon* (Ripon, [1997]), p. 44.

8. See for example the Midland Railway three day excursion from Leicester to Scarborough at 7s second-class return fare in 1845 (*Leicester Chronicle*, 30 August 1845).

9. Jack Simmons, 'Thomas Cook of Leicester', *Transactions of the Leicestershire Archaeological and Historical Society*, 47 (1973), pp. 22–26; *Leeds Mercury*, 18 April 1846; *Bradford Observer*, 16 April 1846.

10. *Derby Mercury*, 26 August 1840; Simmons, *The Victorian Railway*, pp. 295–6; *Freeman's Journal*, 27 April 1844; *Liverpool Mercury*, 11 July 1845. However his advertisements for cheap trips from Preston to London in 1844 appeared to be aimed at the middle-classes, and it was certainly Simmons' view that this was the case (*Preston Chronicle*, 4 May 1844; Simmons, *The Railway in Town and Country, 1830–1914*, p. 134; *Liverpool Mercury*, 19 May 1843; *Preston Chronicle*, 27 May 1843.)

11. John K. Walton, 'British Tourism between Industrialisation and Globalisation', in H. Berghoff and others (eds.), *The Making of Modern Tourism: the Cultural History of the British Experience 1600–2000* (New York, 2002), p. 113–115.

12. *Liverpool Mercury*, 23 March 1869, 24 March 1869.

13. 'Henry Marcus', *1841 Census*, Liverpool, Lancashire, HO107, piece 561, folio 18/18, page 28; *1851 Census*, Liverpool, Lancashire, HO107, piece 2183, folio 560, p. 13; *Cheshire Marriage Licence Bonds and Allegations, 1606–1905*, 22 August 1843.

14. *Leeds Mercury*, 18 May 1850, *Preston Chronicle*, 11 May 1850.

15. Neele, *Railway Reminiscences*, p. 30.

16. *North Wales Chronicle*, 24 April 1849. Although at 34s third-class return between London and Paris these were not particularly cheap.

17. *Liverpool Mercury*, 27 August 1852, Terry Gourvish, *Mark Huish and the London & North Western Railway: a study of Management*, p. 123; *Morning Chronicle*, 17 June 1850, 9 September 1850.

18. *Manchester Times*, 24 December 1853.

19. *The Era*, 29 September 1850.

20. *North Wales Chronicle*, 21 December 1850; *Liverpool Mercury*, 21 November 1851.

21. *Bradford Observer*, 5 December 1850.

22. *Liverpool Mercury*, 10 March 1854.

23. *Chambers Edinburgh Journal* (1853), p. 280.

24. *Preston Chronicle*, 29 May 1852.

25. *Liverpool Mercury*, 2 August 1864

26. *Liverpool Mercury*, 2 August 1864; *North Wales Chronicle*, 21 December 1850.

27. For examples see item in *Liverpool Mercury*, 11 May 1847 (the original letter cannot be traced in this paper), *Preston Chronicle*, 11 October 1851, 22 November 1851; *Liverpool Mercury*, 21 November 1851, 9 June 1859, 9 November 1859; *Birmingham Daily Post*, 22 September 1858; *North Wales Chronicle*, 31 May 1862.

28. *Liverpool Mercury*, 23 March 1869, 24 March 1869.

29. *Liverpool Mercury*, 23 March 1869; The National Archives, London, RAIL 1080/99, *Railway Clearing House Superintendents' Meetings Minutes*, 20 February 1851.

30. 'Henry Marcus', *1861 Census*, Strand, London, RG09, piece 179, folio 77, p. 25.

31. G.P. Neele, *Railway Reminiscences*, pp. 140–141; *Manchester Times*, 11 December 1875.

32. He lived at 40 Falkner Street at that time. The brief record of his Will indicates that he left somewhere between £1,000 – £8,000 when he died, to his daughter, Julia. (England and Wales, National Probate Calendar (Index of Wills and Administrations), 1858–1966.)

33. *Huddersfield Chronicle*, 25 June 1853.

34. *Weekly Standard*, 24 March 1894. In addition to Thomas Cook, excursion agents included for example Mr Bower with the Midland Railway in the 1870s (*Birmingham Daily Post*, 12 April 1870, 28 June 1870), Mr

Caygill with the Great Northern Railway in the 1870s and 1880s, eventually declared bankrupt (*Leeds Mercury*, 12 April 1879; *Leicester Chronicle*, 12 May 1883; *The Standard*, 6 November 1884), Mr Coles with the Great Western Railway in the 1870s (*Leeds Mercury*, 27 May 1872).

35. Normington, *The Lancashire and Yorkshire Railway*, p. 67.

Chapter Five

1. E.P. Rowsell, 'Crushed on a Sunday', *New Monthly Magazine,* 110 (1857), p. 447.
2. Reid, 'Playing and Praying', p. 752; Royle, *Modern Britain: A Social History 1750–199*, p. 244. Brooke, 'The Opposition to Sunday Rail Services in North Eastern England, 1834-1914', pp. 95,108.
3. *Preston Chronicle*, 2 August 1845.
4. *Derby Mercury*, 7 November 1860.
5. B.S. Trinder, 'Joseph Parker, Sabbatarianism and the Parson's Street Infidels', *Cake and Cockhorse,* 1 (1960), pp. 25, 27.
6. Tomlinson, *The North Eastern Railway: its Rise and Development*, pp. 373–374.
7. *The Standard*, 24 July 1857.
8. *Preston Chronicle*, 2 August 1845; *Sheffield & Rotherham Independent*, 23 August 1856.
9. *Hampshire Advertiser*, 19 November 1859, 26 November 1859, 17 December 1859; Simmons, *The Railway in Town and Country 1830–1914*, p. 156, *Hampshire Advertiser*, 16 June 1860, *Hampshire Advertiser*, 30 June 1860.
10. *Preston Chronicle*, 2 August 1845.
11. E.P. Rowsell, 'Crushed on a Sunday', pp. 446–451.
12. Brooke, 'The Opposition to Sunday Rail Services in North Eastern England, 1834–1914', p. 104.
13. J. Wigley, *The Rise and Fall of the Victorian Sunday* (Manchester, 1980), p. 85.
14. Railway Clauses Consolidation Bill, *Hansard,* HC Deb., 13 March 1845, vol.78, cols. 776–83.
15. *Northern Star*, 29 March 1845 (taken from *Punch*).
16. Walvin, *Beside the Seaside*, p. 42.
17. Newcastle Railway – Sunday Travelling, *Hansard,* HL Deb., 11 June 1835, vol. 28, cols. 646–54.
18. Western Railway – Travelling on Sundays, *Hansard,* HC Deb., 26 May 1835, vol. 28, cols. 150–61.
19. Railway Clauses Consolidation Bill, *Hansard,* HC Deb., 13 March 1845, vol.78, cols. 776–83; *Derby Mercury*, 18 April 1861.
20. *The Examiner*, 20 November 1841.
21. Wigley, *The Rise and Fall of the Victorian Sunday*, p. 56.
22. *Northern Star*, 10 August 1844; Railways Bill, *Hansard,* HL Deb., 5 August 1844, vol. 76, cols.1720–5; *Punch*, 24 August 1844. Wigley, *The Rise and Fall of the Victorian Sunday*, pp. 54–57.
23. *Preston Chronicle,* 24 August 1844.
24. Wigley, *The Rise and Fall of the Victorian Sunday*, p. 120; Simmons, *The Victorian Railway*, pp. 285, 287.
25. The Richmond Steamboat Company ran a Sunday boat to Margate. 1831–32 (697) *Report from Select Committee on the Observance of the Sabbath Day,* pp. 205–210.
26. 1831–32 (697) *Report from Select Committee on the Observance of the Sabbath Day,* pp. 91–95, Armstrong and Williams, *The Steamboat and Popular Tourism*, p. 72.
27. Wigley, *The Rise and Fall of the Victorian Sunday*, p. 54; Simmons, *The Victorian Railway*, p. 282; 1847 (167) *Railways. Copy of all Regulations of every Railway Company on the subject of Travelling on Sunday.*
28. *Sheffield & Rotherham Independent*, 23 August 1856, Brooke, 'The Opposition to Sunday Rail Services in North Eastern England, 1834–1914', p. 96.
29. Brooke, 'The Opposition to Sunday Rail Services in North Eastern England, 1834–1914', pp. 95–6; Hull and Selby Railway, *Hansard,* HC Deb., 30 March 1836, vol. 322, cols. 843–6; *Manchester Guardian*, 21 July 1849.
30. Brooke, 'The Opposition to Sunday Rail Services in North Eastern England, 1834–1914', p. 96.
31. *Manchester Guardian*, 21 July 1849.

32. *Manchester Times*, 1 August 1849. Although by 1850 it appears that their excursions were running from Saturday to Monday again (*Manchester Guardian*, 3 August 1850).

33. Brooke, 'The Opposition to Sunday Rail Services in North Eastern England, 1834–1914', p. 102.

34. *Manchester Guardian*, 11 August 1849.

35. *Manchester Guardian*, 23 July 1845.

36. Brooke, 'The Opposition to Sunday Rail Services in North Eastern England, 1834–1914', p. 97; *Hull Packet*, 16 October 1835. When the Grand Junction Railway under Mark Huish extended third-class travel to Sundays in 1844, it was only at very inconvenient hours (Gourvish, *Mark Huish and the London & North Western Railway*, p. 69.)

37. *Berrow's Worcester Journal*, 22 April 1854.

38. Wigley, *The Rise and Fall of the Victorian Sunday*, p. 54.

39. Jordan, *Away for the Day: The Railway Excursion in Britain, 1830 to the Present Day*, p. 29.

40. Marshall, *The Lancashire & Yorkshire Railway: Volume One*, p. 49–52.

41. Brooke, 'The Opposition to Sunday Rail Services in North Eastern England, 1834–1914', p. 96.

42. Ibid., p. 108.

43. Ibid., p. 99; Wigley, *The Rise and Fall of the Victorian Sunday*, p. 54.

44. *Leeds Mercury*, 29 August 1840.

45. *Leeds Mercury*, 5 September 1840.

46. *Morning Chronicle*, 10 October 1850.

47. *Essex Standard*, 16 May 1851; *The Times*, 14 May 1851.

48. J. Wrottesley, *The Great Northern Railway: Vol 1 Origins and Development* (London, 1979), p. 96; Wigley, *The Rise and Fall of the Victorian Sunday*, p. 85; *The Standard*, 26 October 1850.

49. D.A. Reid, 'The 'Iron Roads' and 'the Happiness of the Working Classes': the Early Development and Social Significance of the Railway Excursion', *Journal of Transport History*, 17 (1996), 57–73. Reid does not explore the policies of the companies involved around Birmingham – the Grand Junction and the London & Birmingham (later LNWR), the Midland and the Great Western Railway.

50. Major, 'The Million Go Forth: Early Railway Excursion Crowds 1840–1860'; *Leeds Mercury*, 18 April 1846 – 10 October 1846; *York Herald*, 24 October 1846; *Bradford Observer*, 30 July 1846; *Hull Packet*, 22 May 1846 – 25 September 1846; *Liverpool Mercury*, 8 May 1846 – 2 October 1846; *Manchester Times*, 30 May 1846 – 25 July 1846; *Manchester Guardian*, 16 May 1846 – 5 August 1846; *Preston Chronicle*, 4 April 1846 – 12 September 1846. Reid, 'Iron Roads', pp. 57–73.

51. Walton, *Lancashire: a Social History, 1558–1939*, p. 184.

52. *Preston Chronicle*, 2 May 1846.

53. John K. Walton, 'The Social Development of Blackpool, 1788–1914' (Unpublished PhD thesis, University of Lancaster, 1974), p. 383; John K. Walton, *Blackpool* (Edinburgh, 1998), pp. 24–29.

54. Royle, *Modern Britain: A Social History 1750–1997*, p. 329; Walton, *Lancashire: a Social History, 1558–1939*, p. 184.

55. Jack Simmons, *The Express Train and other Railway Studies* (Nairn, 1994), p. 182.

56. *Leeds Mercury*, 29 August 1840.

57. *Leeds Mercury*, 6 June 1846.

58. Granville, *Spas of England and Principal Sea-Bathing Places*, pp. 411, 415.

59. In 1856 the Chairman of the Midland Railway, John Ellis, confirmed that they never ran Sunday excursion trains, although they did run some other types of train on that day (*Sheffield & Rotherham Independent*, 23 August 1856).

60. 1844 (318) *Fifth Report from the Select Committee on Railways*, para. 4343.

61. *Hull Packet*, 9 October 1846.

62. *The Standard*, 26 June 1845; *Hampshire Advertiser*, 22 May 1852.

63. Brooke, 'The Opposition to Sunday Rail Services in North Eastern England, 1834–1914', p. 95.

64. L. Faucher, *Manchester in 1844* (1844, reprint, London, 1969), p. 24.

65. Brooke, 'The Opposition to Sunday Rail Services in North Eastern England, 1834–1914', p. 104. There was also evidence in 1845 that Sunday travel was more expensive than other days (*Manchester Guardian*, 23 July 1845).

66. *Leisure Hour*, 1857, p. 334.

67. A.J. Kidd, 'The Middle Class in Nineteenth Century Manchester' in Alan J. Kidd (ed.) *City, Class and Culture: Studies of Social Policy and Cultural Production in Victorian Manchester* (Manchester, 1985), p. 10; *Cheshire Observer*, 25 June 1859; Wigley, *The Rise and Fall of the Victorian Sunday*, pp. 101, 131.

68. Simmons, *The Victorian Railway*, p. 284.

69. Catholicism in Preston was extremely strong, with support from around 35 per cent of Preston people, dominated by a rural elite and few Irish, whereas Liverpool Catholics were mostly working-class Irish (Walton, *Lancashire: A Social History, 1558–1939*, pp. 184–185; Michael Savage, *The Dynamics of Working Class Politics: The Labour Movement in Preston, 1880–1940* (Cambridge, 1987), pp. 110–11.

70. Jack Simmons, *The Victorian Railway* (London, 1991), pp. 285–286.

Chapter Six

1. Re-used in *Manchester Times*, 17 August 1850.

2. Mark Harrison, 'The Ordering of the Urban Environment: Time, Work and the Occurrence of Crowds 1790–1835', *Past & Present*, 110 (1987) p. 140.

3. T. Wright, *Some Habits and Customs of the Working Classes by a Journeyman Engineer* (London, 1867), pp. 115–116.

4. D.A. Reid, 'The Decline of Saint Monday 1766–1876', *Past and Present,* 71 (1976), 76-101; Wright, *Some Habits and Customs of the Working Classes by a Journeyman Engineer,* pp. 115–116; *Morning Chronicle*, 7 October 1850.

5. J. Burnett, *Useful Toil: Autobiographies of Working People from the 1820s to the 1920s* (Harmondsworth, 1974), p. 302.

6. *Morning Post*, 1 November 1849.

7. Walton, *The Blackpool Landlady: A Social History*, pp. 34–35.

8. *Preston Chronicle,* 2 October 1841.

9. *Manchester Times*, 17 August 1850.

10. Robert Poole, *Popular Leisure and the Music Hall in Nineteenth-Century Bolton* (Lancaster, 1982), p. 52; *Bury & Norwich Post*, 10 September 1856.

11. Alastair J. Reid, 'Wright, Thomas (1839–1909)', *Oxford Dictionary of National Biography* (Oxford, 2006) [www.oxforddnb.com/view/article/47426, accessed 8 Dec 2014].

12. Wright, *Some habits and customs of the working-classes by a Journeyman Engineer*, pp. 115–130.

13. Royle, *Modern Britain: A Social History, 1750–1997*, pp. 58–59.

14. K. Morgan, *The Birth of Industrial Britain: Social Change, 1750–1850* (Harlow, 2004), p. 10.

15. John K. Walton, 'The North-West' in F.M.L. Thompson, *The Cambridge Social History of Britain 1750–1950, Vol.1* (Cambridge, 1990), p. 362.

16. Baines, *The Social, Educational, and Religious State of the Manufacturing Districts*, p. 55.

17. Harrison, *Early Victorian Britain 1832–51*, p. 39.

18. C.H. Feinstein, 'Pessimism Perpetuated: Real Wages and the Standard of Living in Britain during and after the Industrial Revolution', *Journal of Economic History* 58 (1998), pp. 625–658.

19. John Burnett, *Idle Hands: The Experience of Unemployment, 1790–1990* (London, 1994), p. 93.

20. Walton, *Lancashire: A Social History, 1558–1939*, p. 167.

21. R.D. Baxter, 'National Income: The United Kingdom', paper read before the Statistical Society of London, 21 January 1868 (London, 1868).

22. Reid, 'Playing and Praying', p. 747.

23. Royle, *Modern Britain: a Social History 1750–199*, p. 271.

24. Reid, 'Playing and Praying', p. 751; *Morning Chronicle*, 27 October 1852; Walvin, *Beside the Seaside*, p. 54; Reid, 'The Decline of Saint Monday 1766–1876', p. 86.

25. Baines, *The Social, Educational, and Religious State of the Manufacturing Districts*, p. 55.

26. *Leisure Hour*, 6 April 1854.

27. *Manchester Guardian*, 19 June 1844.

28. *Manchester Times*, 8 October 1870; *Essex Standard*, 6 August 1856.

29. Tomlinson, *The North Eastern Railway: its Rise and Development*, p. 372; Simmons, *The Victorian Railway*, pp. 303–304.

30. *Preston Chronicle,* 4 September 1858.

31. *Preston Chronicle,* 24 Aug 1844.

32. *Preston Chronicle,* 11 August 1849.

33. *Aberdeen Journal,* 28 January 1852, 16 August 1854.

34. Best, *Mid-Victorian Britain 1851–75*, p. 134.

35. *Aberdeen Journal,* 4 April 1860, 4 July 1860.

36. *Leeds Mercury*, 18 April 1846 – 10 October 1846; *York Herald*, 24 October 1846; *Bradford Observer*, 30 July 1846; *Hull Packet*, 22 May 1846 – 25 September 1846; *Liverpool Mercury*, 8 May 1846 – 2 October 1846; *Manchester Times*, 30 May 1846 – 25 July 1846; *Manchester Guardian*,16 May 1846 – 5 August 1846; *Preston Chronicle*, 4 April 1846 – 12 September 1846.

37. Reid, 'The 'Iron Roads'', 57–73.

38. Walton, *The Blackpool Landlady*, p. 34; Reid, 'The 'Iron Roads', p. 84.

39. *Manchester Times*, 27 March 1850.

40. Bailey, *'This Rash Act'*, pp. 106–109.

41. Douglas Reid, 'Weddings, Weekdays, Work and Leisure in Urban England 1791–1911: The Decline of Saint Monday revisited', *Past and Present*, 153 (1996), pp. 135–163.

42. *Leeds Mercury,* 6 June 1846.

43. *Manchester Guardian,* 3 June 1846.

44. *Manchester Guardian*, 10 June 1840.

45. *Manchester Times*, 6 June 1846.

46. Dunham Park was a country estate near Altrincham, 10 miles south of Manchester. *Manchester Guardian,* 6 June 1846; *Manchester Times*, 5 June 1846, 12 June 1846. Swift packets were drawn along the canal by trotting horses (David E. Owen, *Canals to Manchester* (Manchester, 1977), p. 15.)

47. Simmons and Biddle, *The Oxford Companion to British Railway History*, p. 308.

48. L. Faucher, *Manchester in 1844* (1844, reprint, London, 1969), p. 15; B.R. Mitchell, *British Historical Statistics* (Cambridge, 1988), pp. 24–26.

49. *Manchester Guardian,* 10 June 1846.

50. *York Herald*, 9 February 1856.

51. Baines, *The Social, Educational, and Religious State of the Manufacturing Districts*; *Leeds Mercury*, 29 August 1840.

52. See for example *Bradford Observer*, 12 August 1858.

53. Elizabeth J. Stewart, 'Melly, George (1830–1894)', *Oxford Dictionary of National Biography* (Oxford, May 2012) [www.oxforddnb.com/view/article/55914, accessed 8 Dec 2014]; Philip Hoare, 'Melly, (Alan) George Heywood (1926–2007)', *Oxford Dictionary of National Biography* (Oxford, 2011) [www.oxforddnb.com/view/article/98953, accessed 8 Dec 2014].

54. Charles P. Melly, *A Paper on Drinking Fountains, read in the Health Department of the National Association for the Promotion of Social Sciences* (Liverpool, 1858).

55. *Newcastle Courant*, August 22, 1856, *Leeds Mercury*, 2 July 1857.

56. *The Standard*, 14 April 1859.

57. *Derby Mercury*, 29 August 1860.

58. *Liverpool Mercury*, 4 January 1864.

59. *The Standard*, 14 April 1859.

60. *The Standard*, 12 January 1858; *Liverpool Mercury*, 26 October 1864.

61. *Daily News*, 3 June 1858.

62. *Liverpool Mercury*, 24 June 1858.

63. *Liverpool Mercury*, 3 December 1863.

64. *Cheshire Observer*, 8 May 1858; *Morning Chronicle*, 8 November 1861.

65. *Aberdeen Weekly Journal*, 7 July 1879.

66. *Liverpool Mercury*, 19 April 1880.

67. *Huddersfield Chronicle*, 24 April 1880.

68. *Liverpool Mercury*, 12 November 1888.

69. Melly, *A Paper on Drinking Fountains.*

70. *The Standard*, 14 April 1859.

71. *Lloyds Weekly Newspaper*, 17 July 1859.

72. Briggs, *Victorian Cities*, p. 124.

73. R.J. Morris, 'Structure, Culture and Society in British Towns', in M.J. Daunton (ed.), *The Cambridge Urban History of Britain Vol. 3, 1840–1950* (Cambridge, 2000), pp. 400–401.

74. Briggs, *Victorian Cities,* pp. 89–94, 101.

75. Hewitt, *The Emergence of Stability in the Industrial City: Manchester, 1832–67,* pp. 43–44.

76. Walvin, *Beside the Seaside,* p. 41.

77. *Manchester Guardian*, 15 June 1844, 19 June 1844.

78. Reid, 'Playing and Praying', pp. 758, 762–3; David Hodgkins, *The Second Railway King: the life and times of Sir Edward Watkin, 1819–1901* (Cardiff, 2002); David Hodgkins, *Writing the Biography of Edward Watkin* (York, 1999), IRS Working Paper, www.york.ac.uk/inst/irs/irshome/papers/watkin.htm [accessed 7 December 2010]; C.W. Sutton, *Watkin, Sir Edward William, first baronet (1819–1901)*, rev. Philip S. Bagwell, *Oxford Dictionary of National Biography* (Oxford, 2004) [www.oxforddnb.com/view/article/36762, accessed 8 Dec 2014]; Hewitt, *The Emergence of Stability in the Industrial City: Manchester, 1832–67,* pp. 162–3. Briggs, *Victorian Cities,* p. 135; Kidd, *Manchester,* p. 46.

79. Simmons and Biddle, *The Oxford Companion to British Railway History from 1603 to the 1990s,* p. 558.

80. See for example Reid, 'Playing and Praying', pp. 788–790; James Obelkevich, 'Religion' in F.M.L. Thompson (ed.), *Cambridge Social History of Britain 1750–1950 Vol. 3: Social Agencies and Institutions* (Cambridge,1990), pp. 337–340.

81. B.E. Maidment, 'Class and Cultural Production in the Industrial City' in A.J. Kidd (ed.), *City, Class and Culture,* p. 157.

82. *Northern Star*, 17 June 1843, 8 June 1844.

83. *Northern Star*, 19 July 1845, 9 August 1845, 23 August 1845.

84. See the *Northern Star,* 20 August 1842, 17 June 1843, 29 July 1843, 12 August 1843, 26 August 1843, 2 September 1843, 8 June 1844, 22 June 1844, 31 May 1845, 19 July 1845, 9 August 1845, 23 August 1845, 30 August 1845, 11 July 1846, 29 May 1847, 14 August 1847, 9 September 1848, 5 May 1849, 26 May 1849, 28 July 1849, 20 April 1850, 27 April 1850, 25 May 1850, 13 July 1850, 27 July 1850,14 June 1851, 19 July 1851.

85. *Northern Star*, 26 August 1843, 19 July 1845.

86. Malcolm Chase offers no information about the collective use of the railway for excursions to events or other cultural/social activity by Chartist crowds (see Malcolm Chase, *Chartism: A New History* (Manchester 2007), pp. 38, 214).

87. See for example the Camp Meeting at Oldham Edge in 1848 *(Manchester Times,* 25 March 1848). On the occasion of the London demonstration in April 1848, the report in the *Sheffield & Rotherham Independent,*

11 April 1848, indicates that several railway companies brought up 'an immense quantity of persons', but the *Liverpool Mercury* of the same date reported railway companies as, 'very properly refusing to furnish any facilities for such a purpose.'

88. Jack Simmons, *The Victorian Railway* (London, 1991), p. 365.

89. John Saville, *1848: The British State and the Chartist Movement* (Cambridge, 1987), pp. 109, 115–7, 143.

90. Morris, *Structure, Culture and Society in British Towns*, p. 407, 423.

91. *Liverpool Mercury*, 29 May 1855.

92. *Leeds Mercury*, 22 August 1846; *Bradshaw's Monthly Railway and Steam Navigation Guide*, 1 March 1846.

93. *Leeds Mercury,* 22 August 1846.

94. Tylecote, *Mechanics Institutes of Lancashire and Yorkshire before 1851*, pp. 58, 61.

95. Donald Read, *Press and People 1790–1850: Opinion in three English Cities* (Westport, 1975), p. 89.

96. *Morning Post*, 12 August 1853.

97. *The Economist*, 1 February 1851.

98. *Dundee Courier*, 24 June 1857.

99. *Leicester Chronicle*, 29 August 1840; *The Standard*, 13 August 1844. The 'monster quadrille' was made famous by the French conductor Louis Julien in his 'monster' concerts in the 1840s (John Rosselli, 'Jullien, Louis (1812–1860)', *Oxford Dictionary of National Biography* (Oxford, 2004) [www.oxforddnb.com/view/article/15164, accessed 8 Dec 2014]).

100. *Living Age*, 5 October 1844.

101. *Bradford Observer*, 10 October 1844.

102. *Leicester Chronicle*, 5 October 1844.

103. *Chambers' Edinburgh Journal*, 21 September 1844 (excerpts from this appeared in the *Manchester Times* of the same date).

104. *The Standard*, 26 December 1857.

105. *Manchester Times*, 22 August 1849.

106. *Manchester Times*, 25 May 1850.

107. *Dundee Courier*, 4 September 1850; *Manchester Times*, 25 May 1850.

108. For example *North Wales Chronicle*, 28 May 1852 (reprinted from the *Liverpool Mail*), *Northern Star*, 29 September 1849. The writer was described as GAF.

109. *Manchester Times*, 25 May 1850.

110. For example *Manchester Times*, 25 May 1850, *North Wales Chronicle*, 28 May 1852 (reprinted from the *Liverpool Mail*).

111. See for example *Manchester Times*, 25 May 1850, *Living Age*, 26 October 1844 (reprinted from the *Athenaeum*).

112. *Manchester Times*, 27 August 1853.

113. For example *Morning Post*, 13 April 1860, *Manchester Times*, 25 May 1850.

114. *Manchester Guardian*, 2 June 1841.

115. For example Lord Brougham in the debate on the Railway Bill in 1844, in talking about Sunday excursionists (*Morning Chronicle*, 3 August 1844.)

116. *Sheffield & Rotherham Independent*, 17 September 1853 (reprinted from the *Liverpool Journal*).

117. *Knight's Excursion Companion: Excursions from London 1851* (London, 1851), p. iv; *Morning Chronicle*, 31 October 1851.

118. For example *Illustrated London News*, 21 September 1850, *Manchester Times*, 25 May 1850.

119. For example *Bradford Observer*, 27 September 1849, *The Observer*, 16 August 1857.

120. *The Standard*, 17 September 1850; *Illustrated London News*, 21 September 1850.

121. *Manchester Times*, 11 May 1850; A.J.A. Morris, 'Edwards, John Passmore (1823–1911)', *Oxford Dictionary of National Biography* (Oxford, 2009), www.oxforddnb.com.libproxy.york.ac.uk/view/article/32981 [accessed 8 December 2014].

122. *Daily News*, 20 April 1849. (A Simoom is a hot, dry, dusty desert wind.) A subsequent report (*Daily News*, 30 April 1849) noted that a police presence on this train discouraged the pickpockets from travelling to Norwich.

123. *The Times*, 16 June 1859; 1859 Session 1 (2498) *Report to the Lords of the Committee of Privy Council for Trade upon the accidents which have occurred on railways during the year 1858*, pp. 15–16.

124. *Leisure Hour*, 1857, p. 334.

125. *Morning Chronicle*, 9 October 1850, 10 October 1850; *The Standard*, 10 October 1850; *Lloyds Weekly Newspaper*, 13 October 1850.

126. Jack Simmons, *The Railway in England and Wales, 1830–1914: the System and its Working* (Leicester, 1978), p. 37.

127. Herbert Spencer, *Railway Morals and Railway Policy* (London, 1855), p. 23; Geoffrey Alderman, *The Railway Interest* (Leicester, 1973).

128. Tomlinson, *The North Eastern Railway: its Rise and Development*, p. 373.

129. Simmons, *The Victorian Railway*, p. 274; 1840 (474) *Fifth Report from the Select Committee on Railway Communication*, p. 242.

130. C.E. Lee, *Passenger Class Distinctions* (London, 1946), pp. 8–9, 18.

131. Jordan, *Away for the Day*, p. 222; *Northern Star*, 7 June 1851.

132. Henry Parris, *Government and the Railways in Nineteenth-Century Britain* (London, 1965), pp. 97–98, 141, 144.

133. 1851 (1332) *Report of the Commissioners of Railways for the year 1850. Appendix No. 78: Cheap Excursion Trains*; *Morning Post*, 17 October 1850. It is not clear why only 24 hours notice was unavoidable in some cases.

134. *Morning Post*, 17 October, 1850. This exemption did not include first-class carriages within excursion trains. It is not clear why companies such as the LNWR were excluded.

135. *Household Words*, 111 (1851) 355–6, anon but probably Ossian MacPherson according to Lohrli, *Household Words: A Weekly Journal 1850–1859*, p. 80; see also *Household Words*, 19 July 1851.

136. *Morning Chronicle*, 15 September 1851; *The Standard*, 30 September 1851, 13 October 1851; *Daily News*, 12 August 1852; *Morning Post*, 27 January 1853.

137. 1856 (2114) *Report to the Lords of the Committee of Privy Council for Trade and Foreign Plantations of the Proceedings of the Department relating to Railways, for the year 1855*, pp. xvii–xviii.

138. P.S. Bagwell, *The Transport Revolution from 1770* (London, 1974), p. 176.

139. *The Standard*, 23 October 1844; 1846 (698) (752) *Report of the Officers of Railway Dept 1844–45*, pp. xxvi–xxvii.

140. 1846 (698) (752) *Report of the Officers of the Railway Department to the Lords of the Committee of Privy Council for Trade: with appendices I. & II. for the years 1844–45*, pp. 489–490; Simmons, *The Victorian Railway*, p. 274; *Manchester Times*, 11 December 1846.

141. Parris, *Government and the Railways in Nineteenth-Century Britain*, p. 145.

142. This does not include deaths and injuries of railway workers, of which there were a considerable number.

143. 1856 (2114) *Report to the Lords of the Committee of Privy Council for Trade and Foreign Plantations of the Proceedings of the Department relating to Railways, for the year 1855*, pp. xvii-xviii. This figure excluded ordinary cheap third-class and Parliamentary trains.

144. It has proved impossible to find collected data on accidents relating to steamer excursions. The 1839 (273) *Report on Steam-vessel Accidents* attempted to aggregate steamship accidents generally, identifying accidents to 92 vessels over the previous ten years, with 634 deaths (seamen and passengers combined) (p.1). These generally resulted from boiler explosions, collisions, fires and shipwrecks.

145. Gourvish, *Mark Huish and the London & North Western Railway: a Study of Management*, p. 38.

146. Lee, *Passenger Class Distinctions* (London, 1946), pp. 21–2, 33–5; 1845 (419) *Railway Carriages. Lithographed Plans of Carriages sanctioned by the Railway Department of the Board of Trade, for the Conveyance of Third Class Passengers; with Returns relative to Railway Carriages*.

147. Simmons, *The Victorian Railway*, p. 77.

Chapter Seven

1. *Manchester Times,* 21 July 1860; C.W. Sutton, *Brierley, Benjamin (1825–1896),* Rev. John D. Haigh, *Oxford Dictionary of National Biography* (Oxford, 2008), [www.oxforddnb.com/view/article/3405, accessed 8 Dec 2014].

2. *Punch*, 21 August 1852.

3. Jack Simmons (ed.), *The Railway Traveller's Handy Book of Hints, Suggestions and Advice before the Journey, on the Journey and After the Journey* (1862, reprint, Bath, 1971), p. 44.

4. Walton, *British Tourism between Industrialisation and Globalisation*, pp. 113–115.

5. *Daily News,* 20 October 1855 (from *Household Words). The Daily News* was noted for its occasional use of satirical pieces (C. Mitchell, *Newspaper Press Directory* (London, 1847), p. 65).

6. The anonymous writer was identified by Lohrli as playwright, journalist and poet Robert Barnabas Brough (Lohrli, *Household Words:A Weekly Journal 1850–1859*, pp. 145, 214); Cynthia Dereli, *Brough, Robert Barnabas (1828–1860), Oxford Dictionary of National Biography* (Oxford, 2004) [www.oxforddnb.com/view/article/3577, accessed 8 Dec 2014].

7. See for example *Bury & Norwich* Post, 24 September 1856, Simmons and Biddle (eds.), *The Oxford Companion to British Railway History*, pp. 454–455, Matthew Hilton, *Smoking in English Popular Culture* (Manchester, 2006), p. 48.

8. *Preston Chronicle,* 1 August 1857.

9. See also page 53 about Mr Marcus's excursions.

10. Henry Mayhew, *London Labour and the London Poor: a Cyclopaedia* (London, 1851).

11. *Daily News,* 7 September 1857.

12. A commonly used name for the London & South Western Railway.

13. *Manchester Times,* 21 July 1860.

14. C.W. Sutton, *Brierley, Benjamin (1825–1896),* Rev. John D. Haigh, *Oxford Dictionary of National Biography* (Oxford, 2008) [www.oxforddnb.com/view/article/3405, accessed 8 Dec 2014].

15. Resonating with the approach of modern tourism development techniques which adopted literary and mythical figures as a theme around which to build marketing campaigns.

16. James Walvin, *Leisure and Society, 1830–1950* (London, 1978), pp. 97–112.

17. Newcastle Railway – Sunday Travelling, *Hansard*, HL Deb., 11 June 1835, vol. 28, cols. 646–54.

18. H. Berghoff and B. Korte, 'Britain and the Making of Modern Tourism: an Interdisciplinary Approach', in H. Berghoff and others (eds.), *The Making of Modern Tourism: the Cultural History of the British Experience 1600–2000* (New York, 2002), p. 11.

19. Chancellor (ed.), *Master and Artisan in Victorian England*, p. 142.

20. H. Hibbs (ed.), *Victorian Ouseburn: George Whitehead's Journal* (Ouseburn, 1990), p. 52.

21. *Manchester Times,* 31 August 1850 (from *Leicester Mercury*).

22. Schivelbusch, *The Railway Journey: The Industrialization of Time and Space in the 19th Century* (Berkeley, Ca., 1986), pp. 60, 75–6.

23. *A Guide to the Liverpool & Manchester Railway* (Liverpool, 1830); *Hull Packet,* 17 July 1835.

24. *Preston Chronicle,* 18 July 1846, 25 July 1846.

25. Victoria Cooper and Dave Russell, 'Publishing for Leisure', in David McKitterick (ed.), *The Cambridge History of the Book in Britain 1830–1914* (Cambridge, 2009), 475–499; *The Bookseller,* 3 August 1871.

26. P. Joyce, *Democratic Subjects: the Self and the Social in Nineteenth Century England* (Cambridge, 1994), p. 63.

27. Paul J. Zak and Jorge A. Barraza, *Empathy and Collective Action,* (2009), http://ssm.com/abstract=1375059 [accessed 18 July 2012].

28. *Manchester Times,* 23 November 1850.

29. See, for example, the account of a mechanics institute trip in *Leeds Mercury,* 27 June 1840.

30. *Preston Chronicle,* 23 July 1842.

31. *Bell's Life in London & Sporting Chronicle,* 21 Sep 1828. This trip unfortunately ended with a series of mishaps.

32. A.R. Schoyen, *The Chartist Challenge* (London, 1958), p. 105.

33. *Preston Chronicle,* 27 July 1850.

34. *Leeds Mercury,* 28 August 1852.

35. *Jackson's Oxford Journal,* 21 September 1850.

36. *Northern Star*, 3 August 1844.

37. *Manchester Times,* 21 July 1860.

38. A. Delgado, *The Annual Outing and other Excursions* (London, 1977), pp. 53–54; for background on Walker see *The Era,* 7 March 1847, *Leeds Mercury,* 7 June 1879.

39. A middle-class outing, as only second and first-class tickets were sold (P. Brendon, *Thomas Cook: 150 Years of Popular Tourism* (London, 1991), pp. 36–7; *Leicester Chronicle* 5 July 1845, 2 August 1845).

40. *Bell's Life in London and Sporting Chronicle,* 26 Sep 1858 (from the *Preston Chronicle*).

41. *Daily News,* 13 October 1853.

42. *Preston Chronicle,* 20 July 1844. Some of those who travelled as far as Dublin on this excursion took the opportunity to visit the political leader Daniel O'Connell in prison there.

43. *Preston Chronicle, 23 July 1842.*

44. Simmons, *The Victorian Railway*, pp. 86, 259.

45. *Daily News,* 1 June 1849.

46. *Bradford Observer*, 17 May 1855; *York Herald*, 27 September 1856. See also the representation of South Eastern Railway open carriages on the cover.

47. *Morning Chronicle,* 3 August 1852.

48. *Preston Chronicle,* 2 June 1849.

49. *Daily News,* 20 October 1855.

50. *Newcastle Courant,* 27 July 1849.

51. See page 89.

52. *Leeds Mercury*, 5 October 1844.

53. *Leeds Mercury*, 7 September 1844, *Morning Chronicle*, 7 September 1844.

54. *Hull Packet* 13 Sep 1844; *Manchester Times* 14 Sep 1844.

55. *Hull Packet,* 9 August 1850.

56. *Morning Chronicle,* 3 August 1852.

57. *Bradford Observer*, 1 August 1850.

58. *The Times,* 26 August 1852.

59. *The Standard,* 6 November 1860.

60. *Morning Post*, 19 August 1854.

61. *Hull Packet,* 4 September 1857; *Leeds Mercury*, 8 September 1857.

62. *Hull Packet,* 12 September 1851.

63. *Leeds Mercury*, 2 September 1848.

64. *Manchester Guardian,* 16 November 1850.

65. *Liverpool Mercury,* 21 August 1846.

66. She was born in 1833 and died in 1909 (see Derek Hudson, *Munby: Man of Two Worlds: The Life and Diaries of Arthur J. Munby, 1828–1910* (London, 1972); Liz Stanley (ed.) *The Diaries of Hannah Cullwick, Victorian Maidservant* (London, 1984), pp. 45, 53, 79, 128, 139).

67. *Derby Mercury*, 13 August 1851.

68. *Preston Chronicle,* 2 June 1849.

69. *Preston Chronicle,* 19 June 1858.

70. *Bradford Observer*, 28 July 1859.

71. *Reynolds' Newspaper,* 14 September 1851.

72. *Bristol Mercury,* 27 September 1851.

73. *Daily News*, 18 August 1852.

74. *Preston Chronicle,* 28 August 1852.

75. *Manchester Times,* 9 July 1853

76. Vivienne Richmond, *Clothing the Poor in Nineteenth-Century England* (Cambridge, 2013), p. 39.

77. *Manchester Times,* 16 September 1854.

78. *Liverpool Mercury,* 26 April 1856.

79. *Fraser's Magazine*, June 1856 Vol LIII pp. 639–647.

Chapter Eight

1. 1857 Session 2 (2288) *Reports of the Inspecting Officers of the Railway Department to the Lords of the Committee of Privy Council for Trade, upon certain Accidents which have occurred on Railways during the months of March, April, May, June, and July, 1857. (Part third.),* p. 27.

2. *Liverpool Mercury*, 3 June 1857.

3. *Liverpool Mercury*, 3 June 1847.

4. *Sheffield & Rotherham Independent*, 14 July 1849.

5. *Daily News,* 20 October 1855 (from *Household Words);* Schivelbusch, *The Railway Journey: The Industrialization of Time and Space in the 19th Century*, p. 72. See for example *Daily News,* 20 October 1855, 7 September 1857, *Bradford Observer,* 17 May 1855, *York Herald,* 27 September 1856, *Leicester Chronicle,* 9 June 1860. See also C. Hamilton Ellis, *Railway Carriages in the British Isles: from 1830 to 1914* (London, 1865), p. 40.

6. *Leicester Chronicle*, 9 June 1860.

7. 1876 (312) *Report from the Select Committee on Railway Passenger Duty*, p. 11; Henry Parris, *Government and the Railways in Nineteenth-Century Britain* (London, 1965), pp. 141, 144.

8. 1846 (681) *Reports of the Inspectors of Factories to Her Majesty's Principal Secretary of State for the Home Department, for the half-year ending 31st October, 1845*, p. 12.

9. 1859 Session 1 (2498) *Report to the Lords of the Committee of Privy Council for Trade upon the Accidents which have occurred on Railways during the year 1858*, p. 110.

10. *Morning Chronicle,* 13 July 1857; *Preston Chronicle,* 1 August 1857; *Bradford Observer,* 9 July 1857 (from *Preston Guardian*).

11. See for example *The Times of India*: http://articles.timesofindia.indiatimes.com/2011-10-23/delhi/30313088_1_passenger-trains-express-ghaziabad-station [accessed 10 June 2012].

12. 1857–58 (2405) *Reports of the Inspecting Officers of the Railway Department, upon certain Accidents which have occurred on Railways during the month of May, 1858. (Part third.)* pp. 41–2. NB: the term 'break' rather than 'brake' was used throughout the nineteenth century. See also 1860 (2600) *Reports of the Inspecting Officers of the Railway upon certain Accidents which have occurred on Railways during the months of July, August, September, October, and November, 1859. (Part fifth.)* pp. 65–66 for a further example.

13. Lee, *Passenger Class Distinctions*, pp. 24–31.

14. Peter Lecount, *A Practical Treatise on Railways* (Edinburgh, 1839), p. 141.

15. For examples of roof travel on excursions see *Yorkshire Gazette,* 2 September 1848, *Preston Chronicle,* 25 May 1849, *Leicester Chronicle,* 6 June 1857.

16. Jordan, *Away for the Day*, p. 17.

17. *Sheffield & Rotherham Independent*, 7 September 1844; *Morning Chronicle,* 7 September 1844 (from the *Sheffield Iris*).

18. The capacity of the carriages was forty.

19. Gareth Rees, *Early Railway Prints: a Social History of the Railways from 1825 to 1850* (Oxford, 1980), p. 62. Lecount describes the placing of two double seats on top of a first carriage in his recommended design in 1839 (Peter Lecount, *A Practical Treatise on Railways* (Edinburgh, 1839), p. 124).

20. Lee, *Passenger Class Distinctions*, p. 13.

21. *Sheffield & Rotherham Independent*, 7 September 1844; *Morning Chronicle*, 7 September 1844 (from the *Sheffield Iris*).

22. *York Herald*, 29 June 1844.

23. Hugh Cunningham, *Leisure in the Industrial Revolution: c1780 – c1880* (New York, 1980), p. 129.

24. Amy G. Richter, *Home on the Rails: Women, the Railroad, and the Rise of Public Domesticity* (London, 2005), p. 88.

25. Barbara Y. Welke, *Recasting American Liberty: Gender, Race, Law, and the Railroad Revolution* (Cambridge, 2001), p. 254.

26. Simmons, *The Victorian Railway*, p. 334; Simmons and Biddle (eds.), *The Oxford Companion to British Railway History*, p. 566, *Railway Chronicle*, 22 November 1845; *The Observer*, 11 November 1861; *The Spectator*, 16 July 1864; *Saturday Review*, 23 July 1864.

27. *Railway Chronicle*, 22 November 1845.

28. *Manchester Guardian*, 17 June 1846.

29. *Manchester Times*, 1 September 1855.

30. *Lloyds Weekly Newspaper*, 14 September 1851. (The case was adjourned after contradictory evidence from a number of people.)

31. See also Cunningham, *Leisure in the Industrial Revolution: c1780 – c1880*, pp. 130–1; Peter Bailey, 'Adventures in Space: Victorian Railway Erotics, or Taking Alienation for a Ride', *Journal of Victorian Culture*, 9 (2004), pp. 9–17.

32. *Manchester Guardian*, 10 July 1850.

33. *Bristol Mercury*, 6 October 1855.

34. *Morning Chronicle*, 27 April 1859.

35. *Huddersfield Chronicle*, 1 October 1859.

36. *Hull Packet*, 17 July 1846.

37. *Morning Chronicle*, 3 September 1856.

38. *Huddersfield Chronicle*, 14 June 1851.

39. *Manchester Times*, 10 August 1853.

40. *Wrexham and Denbighshire Weekly Advertiser*, 18 September 1858.

41. *Household Words* 24 April 1858 pp. 433–436; *Morning Chronicle* 12 March 1858, 16 March 1858.

42. *Preston Chronicle*, 28 July 1855, 15 September 1855; *Morning Chronicle*, 31 July 1855; *Blackburn Standard*, 29 August 1855, 12 September 1855. The court case was heard at Darwen and later at Blackburn.

43. *Manchester Guardian*, 16 September 1843.

44. Redfern discussed the lack of a consumer movement generally in the early twentieth century (Percy Redfern, *The Consumer's Place in Society* (Manchester, 1920)). See also John K. Walton, 'Towns and Consumerism', in Martin Daunton (ed.) *The Cambridge Urban History of Britain Volume 3 1840–1950* (Cambridge, 2000), 715–744, and Matthew Hilton, *Prosperity for All: Consumer Activism in an Era of Globalisation* (New York, 2009), p. 5. There is some evidence of a Railway Passengers Association existing in 1852, relating to commercial travellers, and again in the 1870s, mainly opposing passenger duty, on behalf of commercial travellers (*The Standard*, 28 December 1852; *The Observer*, 5 March 1876; *Manchester Guardian*, 23 December 1876; *Morning Post*, 26 December 1876; *Sheffield and Rotherham Independent*, 20 April, 1882).

45. Brian Harrison, *Drink and the Victorians* (London, 1971), p. 62; Thompson, *The Rise of Respectable Society*, pp. 310–311; Cunningham, *Leisure in the Industrial Revolution: c1780 – c1880*, p. 73; Walvin, *Leisure and Society 1830–1950*, pp. 37–38.

46. *Saturday Review*, 29 October 1859.

47. *Leeds Mercury*, 16 September 1856.

48. Normington, *The Lancashire and Yorkshire Railway*, p. 61. In 1846 there were press complaints about levels of drunkenness on Bradford Temperance trips (*Bradford & Wakefield Observer*, 27 August 1846).

49. *Morning Chronicle*, 26 June 1858.

50. *The Standard*, 4 September 1847 (reprinted from *Perthshire Courier*).

51. For a discussion of crowd characteristics see Elias Canetti, *Crowds and Power* (London, 1962).

52. *Sheffield & Rotherham Independent*, 17 May 1845.

53. *Preston Chronicle*, 9 Aug 1845

54. *Hampshire Advertiser*, 2 June 1838, 9 June 1838.

55. See for example Jordan, *Away for the Day*, p. 80.

56. *Daily News*, 9 September 1851.

57. Schivelbusch, *The Railway Journey: The Industrialization of Time and Space in the 19th Century*, pp. 174–177.

58. *Manchester Guardian*, 6 June 1846.

59. *Wrexham and Denbighshire Advertiser*, 30 July 1859.

60. *The Observer*, 30 October 1854.

61. W. Collins, *The Works of Wilkie Collins: Vol 12: No Name* (London, 1862), p. 268.

62. *Wrexham and Denbighshire Weekly Advertiser*, 18 September 1858.

63. *Reynolds's Newspaper*, 13 September 1857.

64. *Manchester Times*, 6 June 1846.

65. *Sheffield & Rotherham Independent*, 7 September 1844.

66. *Preston Chronicle*, 20 July 1850; *Blackburn Standard*, 17 July 1850; *Morning Chronicle*, 25 July 1850.

67. *Lloyds Weekly Newspaper*, 18 Aug 1844.

68. *Morning Chronicle*, 27 January 1854.

69. *Morning Chronicle*, 27 January 1854, 25 August 1858.

70. Walvin, *Leisure and Society, 1830–1950*, pp. 41–44; *Hampshire Advertiser*, 22 September 1860; W.W. Sanger, *History of Prostitution: its Extent, Causes, and Effects throughout the World* (New York, 1858), p. 313; Walvin, *Victorian Values*, p. 130.

71. *Hampshire Advertiser*, 26 July 1851; *Leicester Chronicle*, 26 June 1852; *Morning Post*, 18 August 1852, 29 June 1858; *Morning Post*, 12 April 1859, *The Standard*, 31 July 1858.

72. *The Standard*, 15 September 1858.

73. *Bury and Norwich Post*, 29 September 1891.

Chapter Nine

1. *Morning Chronicle*, 19 August 1851.

2. *Daily News*, 12 February 1856.

3. *Manchester Guardian*, 23 April 1851.

4. *Manchester Times*, 23 April 1851.

5. *The Era*, 27 April 1851; *Bell's Life in London and Sporting Chronicle*, 27 April 1851.

6. *Liverpool Mercury*, 22 February 1856; *Manchester Guardian*, 10 May 1864, 24 November 1903, 11 March 1904, 16 March 1904; National Archive RAIL 532/16 North Staffordshire Railway Traffic Committee Minutes 1860. The Chairman of NSR, John Lewis Ricardo, had also been a chairman of the Trent and Mersey Canal and was a director of the LNWR (H. Pollins, 'The Jews' Role in the Early British Railways', *Jewish Social Studies*, 15 (1953), 53–62.)

7. Neil MacMaster, 'The Battle for Mousehold Heath 1857–1884: 'Popular Politics and the Victorian Public Park', *Past & Present*, 127 (1990), pp. 117–154; Peter Gurney, 'The Politics of Public Space in Manchester, 1896–1919', *Manchester Regional History Review* (1997), 12–23.

8. Walton, 'The Social Development of Blackpool, 1788–1914', pp. 243–244, 269, 379–388; Walton, *Blackpool*, pp. 23–43.

9. *Yorkshire Gazette*, 27 March 1852.

10. *The Observer*, 12 October 1851.

11. There were numerous excursion trip crowds to Hull from West Yorkshire and Lancashire, described in the *Hull Packet*, 30 August 1844.

12. For example: John Grundy, *The Stranger's Guide to Hampton Court Palace and Gardens* (London, 1847), *The Stranger's Guide through Gloucester* (Gloucester, 1848).

13. *Hull Packet*, 14 August 1840.

14. *Yorkshire Gazette*, 12 August 1848.

15. *York Herald*, 2 June 1855.

16. *Belfast Newsletter,* 23 April 1851.

17. *The Observer*, 12 October 1851.

18. Others suggested there were in fact only around 6,000 teetotallers (*Lloyds Weekly Newspaper*, 10 August 1851).

19. *Ipswich Journal*, 9 August 1851, *Northern Star*, 9 August 1851, *Lloyds Weekly Newspaper*, 10 August 1851.

20. *Nottinghamshire Guardian*, 15 August 1850; *Morning Post*, 5 August 1850; *OED*.

21. *Hull Packet,* 22 May 1846, 29 May 1846.

22. *Nottinghamshire Guardian*, 2 December 1858.

23. *Hull Packet*, 30 August 1844.

24. *Preston Chronicle,* 26 October 1844.

25. *Blackburn Standard*, 13 August 1851.

26. *Liverpool Mercury*, 5 June 1857.

27. *Preston Chronicle,* 29 September 1849.

28. *Preston Chronicle,* 21 July 1849.

29. *John Bull*, 4 August 1849.

30. *Manchester Times,* 21 March 1857.

31. *Caledonian Mercury*, 6 July 1846.

32. *Sheffield & Rotherham Independent*, 28 July 1849.

33. *Hull Packet*, 5 August 1859.

34. R.J. Morris, *Cholera 1832:The Social Response to an Epidemic* (London, 1976), pp. 95–96, 172–183, 201–202; Virginia Berridge, 'Health and medicine', in F.M.L.Thompson (ed.) *Cambridge Social History of Britain 1750–1950:Vol 3 Social Agencies and Institutions* (Cambridge, 1990), pp. 171–242.

35. *Manchester Guardian*, 21 July 1849.

36. Reinhard S. Speck, 'Cholera', in Kenneth F. Kiple (ed.), *The Cambridge World History of Human Disease* (Cambridge, 1993), pp. 643–649; William E.C. Nourse, *A Short and Plain History of Cholera: its Causes and Prevention* (London, 1857), pp. 12–16. See, for example, reports on cholera deaths in the *Daily News*, 2 August 1854, which emphasise sewerage arrangements. A report in the *Sheffield & Rotherham Independent*, 17 September 1853, about cholera in Newcastle, suggests that medical officers attributed impure water supplies as a cause.

37. *Sheffield & Rotherham Independent*, 2 September 1854.

38. *Lancaster Gazette*, 9 September 1854, 16 September 1854, 23 September 1854. Poulton-le-Sands was later absorbed into Morecambe.

39. Stephen Ward, *Selling Places:The Marketing and Promotion of Towns and Cities 1850-2000* (London, 1998), p. 31.

40. *Manchester Times,* 28 July 1849.

41. *Ipswich Journal*, 16 August 1851.

42. *Wrexham & Denbighshire Advertiser*, 28 August 1858.

43. *Nottinghamshire Guardian*, 6 September 1849; *Derby Mercury*, 24 September 1851.

44. *Essex Standard*, 1 September 1854, 24 August 1855, 29 August 1856,

45. *Sale of Beer, &c Act,* 17 & 18 Vict. Cap.79, also known as the Wilson-Patten Act; Brian Harrison, *Drink and the Victorians* (London, 1971), pp. 328–329.

46. 'Bona fide' meant 'genuine' (OED).

47. *Morning Post*, 13 July 1855, 20 July 1855; *The Standard*, 20 July 1855; 1854–55 (407) *First Report from the Select Committee on Sale of Beer, &c. Act,* para.1535, p. 113.

48. *Morning Post*, 14 August 1854, 9 October 1854; *Sheffield & Rotherham Independent*,16 December 1854; *Morning Post*, 11 July 1855; Brian Harrison, 'The Sunday Trading Riots of 1855', *Historical Journal* 8 (1965) 219–245; *Huddersfield Chronicle*, 2 September 1854; *Essex Standard*, 26 July 1854; Joseph Livesey, *A letter to J.Wilson Patten, Esq., MP on the Drinking System, the late Sunday Bill, and the Maine Law* (Preston, 1855); *Morning Post*, 13 July 1855.

49. 1854–55 (407) *First Report from the Select Committee on Sale of Beer, &c. Act*; 1854–55 (427).

50. *Huddersfield Chronicle*, 2 September 1854.

51. Brian Harrison, 'The Sunday Trading Riots of 1855', p. 220.

52. Ibid., pp. 220, 235.

53. 1854–55 (407) *First Report from the Select Committee on Sale of Beer, &c. Act;* 1854–55 (427) (427–I) *Second Report from the Select Committee on Sale of Beer, &c. Act.*

54. Sale of Beer, &c., Act, *Hansard,* HC Deb., 26 June 1855, vol.139, cols.182–206; Charles Kent, 'Berkeley, (Francis) Henry Fitzhardinge (1794–1870)', rev. Matthew Lee, *Oxford Dictionary of National Biography* (Oxford, 2004) [www.oxforddnb.com/view/article/2207, accessed 8 Dec 2014].

55. *Sale of Beer Act, 1855*, 18 & 19 Vict. c18; *Manchester Guardian*, 30 July 1855, *The Standard*, 15 August 1855.

56. Brian Harrison, 'The Sunday Trading Riots of 1855', pp. 235-236.

57. Walvin, *Victorian Values*, pp. 108–111; Briggs, *Victorian Cities*, p. 85.

58. *Yorkshire Gazette*, 26 August 1848, p. 5.

59. Walvin, *Victorian Values*, p. 109.

60. *Wrexham Advertiser*, 11 July 1857. This description appears to differentiate between those working in coal mines and those in other types of mining, such as lead.

61. *Bradford Observer*, 12 August 1858.

62. *Sheffield & Rotherham Independent*, 13 September 1845, 5 September 1846.

63. Briggs, *Victorian Cities*, p. 36; Walvin, *Victorian Values*, p. 12.

64. Briggs, *Victorian Cities*, pp. 148–149,153.

65. *Ibbetson's General and Classified Directory, Street List and History of Bradford* (Bradford, 1850), p. vii.

66. *Bradford Observer*, 22 August 1850.

67. *Nottinghamshire Guardian*, 22 January 1857.

68. *The Yorkshireman*, 10 October 1840.

69. *Yorkshire Gazette*, 17 August 1850.

70. Walton, 'British Tourism between Industrialisation and Globalisation', pp. 113–115.

71. *Yorkshire Gazette*, 5 June 1852. The population of York at that time was only around 41,000 (C.H. Feinstein, *York 1831–1981: 150 Years of Scientific Endeavour and Social Change* (York, 1981)), p. 113.

72. John Ashton, *Modern Street Ballads* (London, 1888), p. 80 refers to its use in *Drakard's Paper*, 3 October 1813.

73. *Eliza Cook's Journal*, 19 July 1851. The term 'cheap trip' was used in the press at least as early as 1828, with a reference to a cheap trip to France (*Bell's Life in London & Sporting Chronicle*, 21 September 1828). A letter to the *Bradford Observer*, 12 September 1850, is signed 'an unfortunate cheap tripper'. The term was also used in a report in the *Lancaster Gazette,* 16 August 1851.

74. John Travis, 'Continuity and Change in English Sea-Bathing, 1730–1900: A Case of Swimming against the tide', in Stephen Fisher (ed.), *Recreation and the Sea* (Exeter, 1997), pp. 14–19.

75. Walton, *The English Seaside Resort*, p. 11; Walton, *Blackpool*, pp. 22–24.

76. Walton, *The English Seaside Resort*, pp. 195–196.

77. *Bristol Mercury*, 7 June 1856 (taken from the *Weston-super-Mare Gazette*). It has not proved possible to find further evidence about this incident, the report of which is surprising as it features a very negative view

of Bristolians in their own newspaper. It may reflect underlying Sabbatarian motives from Weston-super-Mare.

78. Data from www.visionofbritain.org.uk [accessed 5 December 2014].

79. *The Times*, 18 May 1849. This trip was not particularly cheap: Marcus offered third-class carriages at Whitsun, Manchester to Paris return, for £2.15s (*Manchester Guardian*, 23 May 1849).

80. *Morning Chronicle* 15 December 1860, 7 May 1861, 27 May 1861; *The Standard*, 18 May 1861; *Reynolds's Newspaper*, 2 June 1861.

81. *Ipswich Journal*, 10 November 1860.

82. Peter Mandler, *The Rise and Fall of the Stately Home* (New Haven and London, 1997), pp. 71–106.

83. Adrian Tinniswood, *The Polite Tourist: Four Centuries of Country House Visiting* (London, 1998), pp. 91–92, 99.

84. Although it later opened throughout. See discussion in Mandler, *The Rise and Fall of the Stately Home*, pp.73–85, about the era of mass visiting.

85. *The Gardener's Magazine,* August 1831; Deborah V.F. Devonshire, *The House: a Portrait of Chatsworth* (London, 1982), p. 86.

86. *Derby Mercury*, 27 June 1849; *Sheffield & Rotherham Independent*, 16 June 1849. The Duchess also refers to an account in a scrapbook in the library at Chatsworth (Devonshire, *The House: a Portrait of Chatsworth*, pp. 86–88.)

87. *Derby Mercury*, 4 July 1849.

88. Mandler, *The Rise and Fall of the Stately Home,* p. 82.

89. Tinniswood, *The Polite Tourist: Four Centuries of Country House Visiting*, p. 153; 1854 (367) *Report from the Select Committee on Public Houses,* para. 3110.

90. *Leeds Mercury*, 12 June 1847.

91. Susan H. Oldfield, *Some Records of the Later Life of Harriet, Countess Granville* (London, 1901), p. 161.

92. *Preston Chronicle*, 22 June 1850, 10 August 1850; *Liverpool Mercury*, 22 August 1851; *Preston Chronicle*, 5 June 1852.

93. *Bradford Observer*, 31 May 1849.

94. *Yorkshire Gazette*, 6 November 1852; Alan Bell, 'Denison, Albert, first Baron Londesborough (1805–1860)', *Oxford Dictionary of National Biography* (Oxford, 2004) [www.oxforddnb.com/view/article/7485, accessed 8 Dec 2014].

95. *Sheffield & Rotherham Independent*, 23 June 1849, 11 August 1849, 10 August 1850.

96. *Berrow's Worcester Journal*, 19 April 1856.

97. *Manchester Guardian*, 28 September 1850.

98. M.J.S. Stanley, *Ladies of Alderley: being the letters between Maria Josepha, Lady Stanley of Alderley and her daughter-in-law Henrietta Maria Stanley during the years 1841–1850* (London, 1938), pp. 62–3, 72–4.

99. *Manchester Times,* 14 Sep 1844; *Manchester Guardian*, 4 September 1844.

100. F. David Roberts, 'Still More Early Victorian Newspaper Editors', *Victorian Periodicals Newsletter*, 5 (1972), pp. 21–23.

101. G.A. Cranfield, *The Press and Society: from Caxton to Northcliffe* (London, 1978), pp. 190-1.

102. *Morning Post*, 26 August 1850 (taken from *Wolmer's (Exeter) Gazette*); *Trewman's Exeter Flying Post,* 29 August 1850 (all Conservative); *Manchester Times*, 28 August 1850 (taken from *Western Times*) (Liberal).

103. *Bristol Temperance Herald*, 1851 p. 156 (from *Kelso Mail*). The name of the works was misspelt Stevenson in the press report.

104. R.V.J. Butt, *The Directory of Railway Stations: details every Public and Private Passenger Station, Halt, Platform and Stopping Place, Past and Present* (Sparkford, 1995), pp. 113, 134; E.P.A. Law, *The History of Hampton Court Palace: Volume 3* (London, 1891), p. 362; William Howitt, *Visits to Remarkable Places* (London, 1840), pp. 235–239.

105. Tinniswood, *The Polite Tourist: Four Centuries of Country House Visiting*, p. 139; William Howitt, *Visits to Remarkable Places* (London, 1840), pp. 235–236.

106. *Gentleman's Magazine,* May 1840, p. 455.

107. *The Times,* 30 October 1852, 2 November 1852, 5 November 1852, 20 November 1852, 22 November 1852.

108. E.P.A. Law, *The History of Hampton Court Palace: Volume 3* (London, 1891), p. 365. It appears that the Sabbatarians could not claim that the Palace staff did not enjoy a day's rest, as it was closed on Fridays, nor that people could not attend church, as the Palace did not open until the afternoon on Sundays.

109. David Brooke, 'Brassey, Thomas (1805–1870)', *Oxford Dictionary of National Biography* (Oxford, 2006) [www.oxforddnb.com/view/article/3289, accessed 8 Dec 2014].

110. *North Wales Chronicle,* 16 September 1854; *Liverpool Mercury*, 12 September 1854.

111. *North Wales Chronicle,* 16 September 1854.

112. Ibid.

113. *North Wales Chronicle,* 30 September 1854.

114. John K. Walton, *The British Seaside: Holidays and Resorts in the Twentieth Century* (Manchester, 2000), p. 20.

115. *Morning Post*, 11 December 1844.

116. *Morning Post*, 20 December 1844.

117. *Preston Chronicle*, 12 Aug 1848.

118. *Preston Chronicle*, 19 Aug 1848.

119. *The Times,* 22 August 1848, *Preston Chronicle,* 26 August 1848.

120. *Preston Chronicle*, 26 May 1849, 25 August 1849.

121. *Morning Post*, 28 August 1856.

122. J.D. Marshall and John K. Walton, *The Lake Counties from 1830 to the Mid-Twentieth Century: a Study in Regional Change* (Manchester, 1981), pp. 205–206.

123. *Lancaster Gazette*, 2 May 1857.

124. *Hull Packet*, 18 September 1857.

125. See for example *Daily News*, 20 August 1857, *Morning Post*, 28 May 1857, *Morning Chronicle*, 12 October 1857.

126. *Leicester Chronicle*, 22 August 1857; *Glasgow Herald*, 11 September 1857, 21 September 1857.

127. *Manchester Guardian*, 10 September 1857.

128. 1 January 1859; *Exhibition of Art Treasures of the United Kingdom held in Manchester in 1857: Report of the Executive Committee* (Manchester, 1859), p. 42.

129. *Leicester Chronicle*, 22 August 1857.

130. *Liverpool Mercury*, 19 August 1857.

131. George Scharf, 'On the Manchester Art Treasures Exhibition, 1857, *Transactions of the Historic Society of Lancashire and Cheshire,* Vol 10 1857–8, pp. 313–314.

132. E.T. Bellhouse, *What to See and Where to See it: Or, an Operative's Guide to the Art Treasures Exhibition, Manchester, 1857* (Manchester, 1857).

133. *Household Words,* 10 October 1857, pp. 349–350.

134. *Sheffield & Rotherham Independent*, 28 January 1854, 10 June 1854.

136. David J. Eveleigh, 'Jennings, (Josiah) George (1810–1882)', *Oxford Dictionary of National Biography* (Oxford, 2014) [www.oxforddnb.com/view/article/56370, accessed 8 Dec 2014]; Blair, M. *Ceramic water closets* (Princes Risborough, 2000). p. 15.

136. *Nottinghamshire Guardian*, 25 September 1851.

137. *Royal Cornwall Gazette*, 31 December 1852.

138. *Morning Post*, 21 January, 1853.

A Different View

1. *Huddersfield Chronicle*, 14 June 1851.

Index